DECORATING EDEN

DECORATING EDEN

A Comprehensive Sourcebook of Classic Garden Details

Edited by Elizabeth Wilkinson and Marjorie Henderson

Chronicle Books   San Francisco

Printed in Japan

LIBRARY OF CONGRESS CATALOGING-IN-PUBLICATION DATA

House of boughs.
Decorating Eden : a comprehensive sourcebook of classic garden
details / edited by Elizabeth Wilkinson and Marjorie Henderson.
p.   cm.
Previously published as: House of boughs.
Includes bibliographical references.
ISBN 0-8118-0124-1 (hard). — ISBN 0-8118-0118-7 (pbk.)
1. Gardens—Design—Encyclopedias.   2. Garden structures—
Encyclopedias.   3. Garden ornaments and furniture—Encyclopedias.
I. Wilkinson, Elizabeth, 1926–   II. Henderson, Marjorie.
III. Title.
SB469.25.H67   1992   91-878
712—dc20   CIP
Cover photograph by Saxon Holt © 1991
Distributed in Canada by Raincoast Books,
112 East Third Avenue, Vancouver, B.C. V5T IC8

10 9 8 7 6 5 4 3 2 1

CHRONICLE BOOKS
275 Fifth Street
San Francisco, CA 94103

Acknowledgments

THE EDITORS gratefully acknowledge the people whose help was instrumental in the compilation of this book: Mr. Arthur B. Waugh and Mr. James R. Burch of the Environmental Design Library, and Maryly Snow of the Architectural Slide Library at the University of California, Berkeley; Mr. and Mrs. George R. Mortimer for their help in researching copyrights; Grethe Brady and William Teas of Aero Photographers, Inc., for their patience and skill in getting the best out of our negatives and old photographs; Mrs. Ernest Bridgewater, Mr. and Mrs. William Grier, Ms. Carolyn Jarin, Mr. Thomas Kyle, the Lee Hysan Family, Mr. Ron Lutsko, Jr., Mr. and Mrs. Alfred Gray Parmelee, and Mr. and Mrs. J. Liddon Pennock, Jr., for their kind permission to photograph their gardens.

Acknowledgment is given to the following for permission to reprint photographs: Asian Arts Museum of San Francisco, The Avery Brundage Collection: p. 28 top, p. 45 top, p. 51 top, p. 60, p. 85 top; British Tourist Authority: p. 5 bottom right, p. 200, p. 204 bottom, p. 206 center left, p. 210 top left; California Historical Society: p. 24 center and bottom right, p. 79, p. 112 top left; California Redwood Association: p. 37, p. 48, p. 52 bottom right, p. 123, p. 160 right, p. 161 bottom, p. 191 top right; Thomas Church: p. 151 bottom left; Freer Gallery of Art, Washington, D.C.: p. 181 right; French Government Tourist Office: p. 4 top left, p. 20 bottom right, p. 168 bottom right; General Electric Company: p. 106 top right; Mr. Connie Howard: p. 127 top left, p. 205 top right; Phebe W. Humphrey, *The Practical Book of Garden Architecture*, Lippincott: p. 182 bottom right; Lynn Hunton: p. 21 bottom; Italian State Tourist Office: p. 167 bottom left, p. 168 left, p. 201 bottom left; Japan National Tourist Organization: p. 17 bottom right, p. 29 bottom left, p. 46 bottom left, p. 107 bottom right, p. 162, p. 163 center left, bottom right, p. 207 top center, bottom left, p. 208 bottom left; Peter Palmquist: p. 7, p. 12 bottom left, p. 18, p. 59 center right, p. 64 center left, p. 65 bottom, p. 108 bottom, p. 133, p. 136 top, p. 141 left, p. 206 bottom; Preservation Society of Newport County, Newport, Rhode Island: p. 172, p. 176 bottom; Spanish National Tourist Office: p. 70, p. 72 bottom right; University of California, Berkeley, Documents Collection of the College of Environmental Design: p. 25 bottom (a Gertrude Jekyll photograph), p. 69 bottom (Gertrude Jekyll), p. 153 bottom left (Gertrude Jekyll), p. 171 bottom left (a Beatrice Ferrand photograph).

Preface

"GARDENING HAS BEEN the inclination of kings and the choice of philosophers." So wrote Sir William Temple, the 17th-century English statesman. Although Sir William didn't say so, common folk have found no less pleasure in the planning and planting of gardens than have their more exalted brethren. The satisfaction derived from building gardens, whether cottage plots or princely estates, goes far beyond the obvious rewards of harvest or prestige, for the practice seems to fill some basic spiritual need as well. It cannot be mere chance that the garden figures in myth and legend as the ideal abode of mankind and is the image of heaven in most of the world's religions.

The many forms that gardens have assumed over the centuries result not only from the obvious influences of climate, topography, and water supply, but also from those of social conditions, religious beliefs, economics, and political systems. A garden style developed out of the specific conditions of one culture was often introduced elsewhere by conquest or trade, and in the process subtly modified to satisfy new conditions. Gardens have been built to express the pride of monarchy and the love of God; they have offered escape from reality and release from cares; they have stimulated healthful labor and delight in all the senses.

Because gardens are by nature ephemeral, we are fortunate that gardeners have so often been writers and artists as well. They have left behind a legacy of literature and images. We have representations of gardens in Assyrian bas-reliefs, Egyptian tomb paintings, and Roman frescoes. Chinese scroll paintings lay their ancient gardens before our eyes. Precious illuminated manuscripts show medieval cloister and castle gardens in radiant color. From the Renaissance on, there is no aspect of the gardener's art that need be left to the imagination.

The story of the origin and evolution of the garden has been told many times. There are literally hundreds of books on the subject. It is not our intention to add to that number. Instead, this book isolates and collects the designs and structures that people have built to complement, organize, protect, and embellish their gardens for as long as gardens have existed. The fences, arbors, walls, fountains, pavings, buildings, and scores of other inventions are what concern us here. Our search took us back to the gardens of ancient Persia, to rare books from the 17th, 18th, and 19th centuries, and across the landscape itself with camera in hand. We have not, except peripherally, dealt with the botanical side of garden making. Plant material is discussed only in the context of its use as an architectural component, such as in hedges, alleys, pleached structures, and topiary ornament. We have not attempted to be either historically or geographically complete. We have sometimes omitted the most famous or typical in favor of the more obscure and, we hope, more provocative examples.

As in an encyclopedia, the content of this book is organized topically and in alphabetical order. The material within each category is often, but not always, presented chronologically. The advantage of this organization is that in separating the individual artifacts from the larger picture, viewing them out of their traditional context, we see them in a fresh light, with an eye to new applications.

This is not to suggest that we advocate assembling a garden from a jumble of unrelated and diverse elements. Garden designs, like plants, seldom thrive if simply transplanted. They spread by adaptation and evolution and are generally the result of considerable imagination and a sensitive understanding of local conditions. If this sourcebook is useful in giving gardeners a better understanding of the long tradition of which they are a part and a glimpse of the play of human invention in shaping the garden, we will consider it a success.

Introduction:
A Brief History of Garden Design

WHILE THIS BOOK is in no sense meant to be a history, any discussion of garden artifacts must inevitably include some historical background. Since a chronological narrative is impossible within the main body of the book, we have included this brief outline of the major trends in the development of garden design. For those who wish to go deeper into the subject, there are many fine general histories. The most complete and scholarly is probably Marie Luise Gothein's classic, *A History of Garden Art*, 1928. Less exhaustive and livelier books of more recent publication are Julia S. Berrall's *The Garden*, 1966; Christopher Thacker's *The History of Gardens*, 1979; and Ronald King's *The Quest for Paradise*, 1979. Books on specific types of gardens are listed in the bibliography.

In essence there are only two basic approaches to garden design: the formal, wherein all of the elements are arranged subject to a balanced and controlled plan; and the naturalistic, wherein topography and plant materials are arranged much as they would be found in nature or in such a way as to suggest natural scenery.

The formal garden is by far the oldest of the two designs. It originated some time in the prehistoric past along the river valleys of the Tigris and the Euphrates and the Nile. By 3000 B.C. the Sumerians and Egyptians had developed garden systems involving sophisticated irrigation methods. Sumerian culture produced two distinct garden styles, the enclosed domestic garden and the ziggurat. The ziggurat was primarily a religious edifice and only secondarily a garden. It consisted of a stepped pyramid of from three to seven terraces. Each of these was planted with trees and vines. A temple was built at the top. The gods were believed to inhabit such high places.

The enclosed domestic garden was the more common Sumerian type. It was virtually an outdoor room. The ideal form was a square or rectangular plot, walled against animals and the desert wind. In the center was a storage tank for water. Eventually this form took on religious connotations with the addition of four canals fed from the central tank, symbolizing the four rivers of heaven said in the Old Testament to flow from Eden. These "paradise" gardens contained trees and shrubs and probably, though the evidence is sketchy, flowers. Grapevines were trained on arbors along the walls.

After the Assyrians overran the Sumerian Empire, around 1275 B.C., a third form of formal garden emerged. With the domestication of the horse at about this time, it became the fashion to build hunting parks. These were huge tracts of land walled around, planted with trees in orderly rows, and stocked with wild animals that were to be hunted from horseback. Hunting parks, particularly the ones built later by the Persians, were often provided with garden houses where the sportsmen could refresh themselves after the hunt.

Thanks to the ancient Egyptian belief that you *could* take it with you, we have a vivid picture of the kinds of gardens that flourished in Pharaonic Egypt. Tomb paintings show that, as in Mesopotamia, the house and garden were treated as an architectural unit, rectangular in shape and walled. Sycamores, date palms, and fig trees were planted in rows along the walls to provide both shade and fruit. Low walls separated one area from another within the garden. Small pavilions and grape arbors served as shelters from the sun. Flowers figured prominently in these gardens; they were planted in blocks of vibrant colors and were used to make the bouquets and chaplets that were worn for festivals and social occasions. Sir Thomas Browne, the 17th-century English physician and writer, paints a fanciful picture of these wreathed revelers. He writes that at banquets the garlands they wore "had little birds upon them to peck their heads and brows, and so keep them from sleeping at their festal compotations." Garden pools were T-shaped or rectangular, planted with lotus and reeds, and stocked with fish and waterfowl. Some gardens had canals leading from the Nile to private boat landings within the walls.

The remains of another sort of Egyptian garden can be found in the mountains west of Thebes at the tomb of Queen Hatshepsut, circa 1500 B.C. It is a formal geometric garden on three terraces that climb a steep hillside. The terraces, joined by a magnificent central stairway, were decorated with colonnades, pools, flower beds, and trees. On the highest tier was the queen's mortuary temple, which overlooked the gardens and the valley below.

The impact of one ancient garden tradition on another can be traced in the wake of invasion and conquest. When the Persians conquered Assyria in 540 B.C. and Egypt in 525 B.C., they were exposed to the early garden prototypes described above, which were to become the basis for their own great garden traditions and, subsequently, that of their Moslem conquerors. Like the plant species that were gradually disseminated throughout the world, so fashions in garden design were spread to thrive in countries far from their point of origin and in ways never imagined by their originators. The paradise garden, which germinated in Sumeria, was in turn sown in Greece and Rome and ultimately throughout Europe. The idea was carried to India by the Mongols and to Spain by the Moors and from there, many centuries later, to the Americas by Spanish explorers and clergy.

Although ancient Greece was the birthplace for many of the arts of the Western world, she made few contributions to ornamental horticulture. The Greeks were never enthusiastic pleasure gardeners. Except for orchards and kitchen gardens, the only early Greek garden form is the nymphaeum. The nymphaeum was a sacred grove planted next to a stream or spring that was embellished with a basin of stone or marble to catch the water. There was often a natural or artificial grotto and an altar where offerings could be made to the nymphs.

Public gardens made their appearance in Greece around 400 B.C. when the Agora in Athens was planted with trees. Soon cities throughout the Hellenic world were planting public squares with grass and trees, to be used for outdoor assemblies and teaching academies. The Greeks were primarily city dwellers. Their form of government tended to limit the accumulation of personal wealth so that home gardens were modest. Most were confined to a few trees and potted ornamentals in the peristyle or a cottage garden of mixed vegetables and flowers.

The first Roman gardens were copies of the Greek academy parks. They were grassy enclosures planted with trees and often decorated with a portico and statues. By the middle of the Republican period, the hills outside Rome were dotted with great country houses. The gardens that surrounded these villas were beyond anything ever dreamed of by the Greeks. They contained fountains and pools, arbors for grapes and roses, marble statuary and furniture, small temples to the gods and grottoes for cool retreats, tree houses and banqueting halls, indeed, all the comforts and indulgences that great wealth and slave labor could provide.

The Roman city gardens, such as those excavated at Pompeii and Herculaneum, were quite different. There the houses were built directly on the street behind windowless walls, the rooms facing on interior courtyards. These enclosed gardens were open to the sky and surrounded by roofed and colonnaded walkways. They were decorated with small pools or canals, geometric flower beds edged with herbs, ivy or clipped boxwood, statues and fountains. Outdoor dining was popular, so the gardens were often furnished with marble tables and couches set under a grape-covered pergola.

With the decline of the Roman Empire and the ensuing invasions from the north, the center of learning and culture moved back across the Mediterranean, first to Byzantium and subsequently to the Islamic capital at Baghdad. There the teaching of Greek classics, science, mathematics, and medicine flourished. The Arabs adopted the ancient paradise garden form of the Persians. By the tenth century, travelers visiting the courts of the Caliphs reported the wonders of their gardens. They told of marble pavilions hung with silks and furnished with seats of gold, of artificial trees with branches and leaves of silver and gold and fruits of precious gems, and mechanical birds that sang when the wind blew.

When the Arabs conquered northern Africa and moved into Spain, they took their garden styles with them. In Spain they rebuilt the aqueducts that had fallen into ruin after the Romans had abandoned their Iberian colonies. The Moorish palaces in Spain were built on steep hillsides. The patios enclosed behind high walls were redolent of orange blossoms. Paths with colorful insets of glazed tile divided sunken beds planted with cypress, myrtle, or bright flowers. Water that murmured in tiled runnels leading from one level to the next, filling and emptying pools; water that sparkled and leapt in slender fountain jets; water that plashed from overflowing basins brought pleasant relief from the heat of the Andalusian sun. When the Spanish finally regained control of the country in the late 15th century, they retained many of these Moorish features, and it was this garden form that was carried to the Americas.

The Arabs in Persia were conquered by Mongolian invaders in the 13th century. After the manner of invaders before them, the Mongols adopted Islam and much of the culture that went with it. When they moved into India in 1483 and established the Mogul Empire, six generations of emperors made gardens in the Persian style. In Agra, their capital, they built tombs and palaces surrounded by beautiful gardens. The most famous of these garden mausoleums is the Taj Mahal, built in the 17th century by Shah Jahan for his favorite wife. The garden facing the building is in the true paradise form, a square quartered by canals.

Every summer, to escape the heat of the lowlands, the entire Mogul court, some fifty thousand people, moved in procession to the Vale of Kashmir. There the emperors built pleasure gardens of unparalleled beauty. Shalimar-Bagh, one of the two still in existence, is built on four terraces on a gentle rise above Lake Dal; in the background loom the snow-capped Himalayas. Icy water rushing down from the mountains is directed into a central canal and forms pools and cascades on all four levels. Marble pavilions, or throne platforms, sit in the middle of every pool, and hundreds of fountain jets throw water into the air around them. Behind each cascade are little niches where candles can be set to light the falling water. Shade trees, orchards, and beds of brilliant flowers complete the picture. An inscription at Shalimar expresses the Mogul prince's deep attachment to the gardens. "If there be a Paradise on Earth, it is here, it is here."

As the Roman Empire disintegrated in the fifth century and

Europe entered its long period of upheaval, the great villas were sacked and burned or left to crumble. Their beautiful gardens reverted to wilderness. European gardeners, monks, for the most part, withdrew behind cloister walls. The gardens they planted were simple versions of the Roman peristyle, square or rectangular areas surrounded by colonnaded walks, geometric beds divided by paths, and a fountain, wellhead, or water tank in the center.

In the 12th century, after the last of the barbarian invasions, European nobles once more started to build pleasure gardens. At first they were small, enclosed within the protective walls of the castle and fenced against horses and dogs. These little plots, usually the province of the women, were given over to the cultivation of herbs for medicinal use and seasonings and a few flowers. Gradually, larger gardens were built outside the castle fortifications, although still enclosed by high hedges, walls, or fences. One part of such gardens might contain a checkerboard of raised beds sparsely planted with herbs and flowers; another part might be reserved for games and dancing. Seating was provided on built-in benches with sides of stone, wood, or wattle filled with earth and covered with turf. For shelter there were arbored walks, nooks cut into deep hedges, or brightly colored tents. There was, of course, water, either flowing from an ornate fountain or from a simple spring box, conducted in narrow channels throughout the garden.

By the early 15th century, conditions in Italy were settled enough to encourage gardeners to look again beyond their walls. The Crusades had opened up trade routes with the East. This trade spawned a wealthy merchant class with interests in science and philosophy. The writings of classical Greece and Rome were studied, and excavations brought to light the art and architecture that had lain hidden for so long. The early Renaissance villas built in the hills outside Florence were based almost entirely on Roman models as described by Pliny. The gardens were symmetrical, enclosed by clipped hedges, and adorned with statues. Topiary work and intricate geometric parterres were displayed on terraces overlooking the Arno and the hills of Tuscany. The hot, dry summers of Italy precluded the use of flowers as a major feature. The beauty of the gardens depended instead on greenery, views, architectural elements, and the imaginative use of water. By the 16th century even more luxurious villas were being built near Rome. The gardens there included extensive plantations of trees, grassy areas for games and tourneys, theaters and amphitheaters, and always, somewhere near the house, a *giardino segreto*, or private garden, reserved for the use of the family.

Toward the end of the century, the flamboyant designs of the Baroque style overcame classical restraints. Water was employed lavishly in curtains, fountains, and cascades; it ran down balustrades and spilled into elaborate basins, pools, and canals. Water was used to run automatons, to play organs and bird whistles, and to wet strollers with hidden jets. Magnificent flights of stairs led visitors from one terrace to the next. Grottoes adorned with statues of nymphs and satyrs and grotesque animals lured them into their cool shade.

The extravagances of these gardens did not go unnoticed by the rest of Europe. In 1495 Charles VIII of France invaded Italy. When he returned home, he took with him twenty-two Italian artists and gardeners to remodel his gardens in the Renaissance style. The results, however, were quite different; French chateaus were situated in country unlike that of their Italian counterparts. They were most often at the bend of a river, on flat or only gently sloped land. Water usually had to be pumped into reservoirs or moats. Without the help of gravity and abundant water sources, the lively water effects of the Italian gardens were difficult to achieve. Instead, the French used water in large, still sheets in reflecting pools and broad canals.

Instead of the expansive views so essential to the Italian garden, the French relied more on surface decoration to create interest. The designs of the parterres became increasingly intricate, the patterns outlined in low clipped boxwood, the centers colored with sand, brick dust, and iron filings rather than with flowers. These beds became so elaborate and so much resembled the embroidered designs applied to the clothing of the period that they were called *parterres de broderie*. Under Louis XIV the French garden style reached its zenith. Versailles, with its great canals and reflecting pools, its avenues of trees, and its hundreds of fountains all dedicated to the glorification of the king, was the ultimate expression of a monarchy and a society that believed that man's reason could conquer nature.

Versailles was easily imitated because the rules that governed the making of such a garden could be, and were, set out with great precision. Most of the princes of Europe proceeded to build gardens in the French manner. In Holland, however, the style underwent a good deal of modification.

The Dutch were an anomaly in Europe. Since the 13th century they had been a nation of traders with a larger and more prosperous middle class and a more democratic government than any other country in Europe. An egalitarian society and a scarcity of available land combined to make the idea of gardens on the scale of Versailles unthinkable. What land there was, often no more than a thin layer of topsoil virtually floating on the sea, was unsuitable for growing great avenues of trees; hedges were used instead. A great many effects were fitted into very little space, and as a result, everything was miniaturized. The Dutch were flower fanciers and were unwilling to give them up, no matter how passé they were considered elsewhere.

These departures from the French model earned Dutch gardens a reputation for busyness. If one credits the description given by the Italian essayist Edmondo De Amicis of gardens he saw in Broek in 1874, they well deserved the impeachment. "They seem made for dwarfs. The paths are scarcely wide enough for the feet, the arbours can contain two very small persons standing close together, the box borders would not reach the knee of a child of four years old. Between the arbours and the tiny flower beds there are little canals, apparently made for toy boats, which are spanned here and there by superfluous bridges with little painted railings and columns; basins about as large as an ordinary sitz-bath contain a Lilliputian boat tied by a red cord to a sky-blue post."

The English were slow to adopt either Italian or French garden styles. It was not until the reign of Henry VII (1457 to 1509) that conditions were stable enough to lure Englishmen out of their strongholds and start them building country houses with gardens. These gardens were medieval in character, walled and hedged outdoor rooms with rose-covered arbors, shaded walks, and turf benches. The simple geometric flower beds gradually became more complex until mazes and knot gardens, some employing colorful inert material (such as were found in French parterres), came into common use.

Henry VIII built a mount at Hampton Court. It was constructed of 250,000 bricks, which were covered with earth and planted with hawthorns. A winding path led to a pavilion at the top. The flower beds were bordered with low railings painted in bright primary colors. Carved heraldic beasts perched on poles throughout the garden. There was little evidence of Italian Renaissance influence at this period. What there was appeared in minor decorative features and in the fascination with water surprises.

Gardens of this type were the rule in England through the Elizabethan era. The first instance of a strong European influence occurred when Charles II returned from exile in 1660 and started to remodel the gardens at Hampton Court after the manner of Versailles. This work continued during the reign of William and Mary though it was always held within strict limits by Parliament's control of the pursestrings. The influence of Dutch garden styles was felt during this period as well. Gardens planted with fanciful topiary specimens became popular. Bright flowers, particularly tulips, temporarily banished from the garden scene by the influence of French designs, reappeared.

French and Dutch garden styles continued to influence English gardeners until early in the 18th century when a whole new and uniquely English concept of garden design revolutionized the art. This new concept was, of course, new only to the Western world. Before pursuing its history there, we will make an extended detour to the Orient, where this approach to garden design had been the rule from the beginning.

In China gardens had always been thought of as an interpretation of natural scenery. Taoism, Confucianism, and Buddhism, the three major religious and philosophical influences, stressed the basic unity and harmony of nature and taught that man, by meditation and the calm, receptive contemplation of nature, could become part of that harmony. Chinese landscape painting and, in turn, the gardens inspired by these paintings reflected this philosophy.

Since gardens were meant to represent nature, in an idealized form, in all of its richness and variety, the Chinese never made strict rules of design. There were, however, two elements always present: mountains and water, which were regarded as the skeleton and arteries of the earth. The soil dug out to make ponds was piled up to create hills. More rugged mountain scenery was suggested by construction of grotesque water-eroded rocks. These artificial mountains were often laced with tunnels and caves to provide cool hideaways in the heat of summer. The ponds were convoluted with many inlets, peninsulas, and islands.

A Chinese garden can never be encompassed in one glance. Instead, the visitor must follow winding pathways from one vantage point to the next because the features of the garden unfold slowly. Each stopping place—the crest of a hillock, a seat at the highest point of a bridge, a small island gazebo, a wider place where a covered walkway overhangs water—is an invitation to enjoy one more facet of the garden's beauty. Some of these places are designed for use at special times of day or night or in specific seasons of the year. An entire courtyard may be reserved for the enjoyment of chrysanthemums or peonies and never used except when they are in bloom.

Garden features are usually given names. Some are simply descriptive; others are designed to heighten the enjoyment of the spot by some mythical or literary reference. Plaques inscribed with poetry are used in much the same way.

Chinese garden styles reached Japan sometime before the eighth century, for by the Heian period (710 to 1150) the Japanese were building pleasure gardens incorporating hills and large ponds with islands representing the mystical mountains and islands of Chinese myth. These gardens gradually evolved until they became entirely Japanese in spirit. Geoffrey and Susan Jellicoe, in *The Landscape of Man*, 1975, put forth an interesting theory on why these modifications occurred. "Because of the enormous land mass, the Chinese outlook on landscape was extrovert and in breadth. In Japan, because of the tight and hostile sea boundary, it was introvert and in depth. . . . This sense of enclosure forced attention upon the inward minutiae of nature and the discovery and enjoyment of worlds not normally reached by the senses." The introduction of Zen Buddhism in the 13th century intensified these differences. Zen teachings emphasized restraint and austerity. The elimination of all extraneous details produced gardens of extreme subtlety and distinction.

Two different forms of Zen-inspired gardens emerged in Japan at this time. The first, the dry garden, was primarily for contemplation and meditation, designed to be viewed from a particular vantage point. Some of these gardens clearly represent landscapes where the presence of water is suggested by "seas" of raked sand and "mountains" of carefully placed rocks. Others, particularly the garden of the Ryoan-ji with its fifteen stones arranged in a walled rectangle of raked sand, seem to be purely abstract—open to whichever interpretation one chooses.

The second Zen-inspired garden form grew up around the tea house. Ceremonial tea drinking was first practiced by Zen monks to help them stay awake during meditation. Gradually it became imbued with the Zen ideals of simplicity and detachment. The approach to the tea house is through a garden, or *roji* (dewy path). This path is deliberately kept rural and woodsy in character, for the path is symbolic of the transition from the outer world and the concerns of the marketplace to the world of the mind and its purity and aesthetic receptiveness.

The studied simplicity of these gardens carried over into the design of all Japanese gardens and has become part of their national character. The essence of these gardens is best expressed as *yugen*. The term is hard to define; it implies the presence of a mysterious atmosphere, a thing that cannot be stated, only felt, that produces a sense of tranquillity and spiritual kinship with all of nature.

When English gardeners in the first years of the 18th century abandoned the traditions of the formal garden, they embraced more naturalistic forms and evolved what is now commonly referred to as the landscape school of garden design. As it turned out, this departure was not just a reaction to the excesses of previous practitioners but marked the start of a new tradition in the West and, in tandem with garden styles from the Orient, has had profound influence on gardening, particularly in Europe and the United States.

It would be logical to assume that early reports of the fabulous gardens of China inspired English landscape gardeners, but, in fact, they seem to have had only minimal influence. The exotic Chinese gardens did excite interest when the first reports and pictures were circulated in Europe in the 17th century. But attempts to emulate them were superficial and generally confined to inaccurate copies of some of the more obvious architectural features. Pagodas, garden houses with upswept eaves and moon bridges became popular additions to Western gardens at this time. But the underlying principles of Chinese garden design were ignored or dismissed as impractical.

The English landscape revolution seems to have been an entirely homegrown affair. English gardeners, in any case, had never been quick to adopt foreign styles. When they did, the results were usually subject to a great deal of ridicule from their more nationalistic and conservative citizens.

The extreme formality of French and the artificiality and busyness of Dutch gardens were ultimately self-defeating and finally produced a revulsion from all formality in the garden. The initial inspiration for the English landscape garden came from painters and writers. In 1712 Joseph Addison wrote an essay for *The Spectator* suggesting that English gardens had become too regimented and that "there is generally in Nature something more Grand and August, than what we meet with in the Curiosities of Art. When, therefore, we see this imitated in any measure, it gives us a nobler and more exalted kind of Pleasure than we can receive from the nicer and more accurate Productions of Art." Others quickly joined in the general outcry against artificiality and regularity.

Influenced by such thinking and inspired by the romantic landscapes of the French artists Claude Lorrain and Nicolas Poussin, English landscape architects broke away from the whole vernacular of Western garden design. In their hands the English countryside itself, rearranged and idealized, became the garden. The use of the ha-ha, or sunken fence, allowed them to do away with enclosing walls and to make lawn appear to flow into meadow. Serpentine rivers and still lakes reflected hills planted with carefully placed clumps of trees and shrubs. In keeping with the passionate classicism of the day, these picturesque parklands were dotted with Roman bridges, triumphal arches, and temples. Predictably, the landscape enthusiasts did not all agree on what constituted beauty. Several highly vocal groups proceeded to abuse each other over the question.

One such group, led by Capability Brown, favored landscapes of a gentle and peaceful nature with wide vistas of green lawns, browsing cattle, and serene rivers. Another group emulated the dramatic landscapes of the Neapolitan painter Salvitor Rosa by creating "awful" chasms and setting out blasted oaks. They strove for gloomy effects by building counterfeit ruins and tombs. Their efforts provoked Walpole to protest, "It is almost comic to set aside a quarter of one's garden to be melancholy in." An unsuccessful and short-lived attempt was made by another group to utilize the principles of landscape design for practical purposes. The *ferme ornée*, or ornamental farm, was an attempt to fashion a silk purse from a sow's ear by disguising a working farm behind the facade of a Gothic ruin or a Chinese temple. Farm fields were bordered with winding paths, hedgerows planted with flowering vines, and flowers set out in odd corners unsuitable for crops; all the while ducks and geese paddled about in miniature, serpentine rivers.

Most of the large estates in England fell into the hands of the landscape school "improvers," so that by the end of the 18th century few old formal gardens remained. The landscape style soon became popular and "English" gardens were added to many of the formal gardens of Europe. The French were as eager as any to embrace the innovation. The way had been prepared by the writings of Rousseau. His immensely popular book, *La Nouvelle Héloïse*, was set in a garden so wild that it showed no signs of man's interference. In practice, of course, the new English gardens of Europe were never so wild; the temptation to embellish them with a full complement of exotic buildings and ornaments was irresistible. Gothein describes one of the more preposterous collections in the garden of a German count. "Everything was heaped up there that people had thought of for hundreds of years. Beside a Chinese garden and temple there was the Holy Grave; after Christian hermitages came Indian pagodas; here a picturesque hill, there a little town for dwarfs with a royal palace. And from want of dwarfs, the count for a time had children to live there. Next came Druid caves, with altars; then an antique mausoleum, to which sacrifices for the dead were brought."

The dramatic social changes of the early 19th century affected the development of English garden design. Industrialization was spreading the wealth of the country over a broader base and creating a new middle class. Factories were drawing labor from the farms and massing people in city slums. In an attempt to ease urban crowding, huge tracts of land were given over to public parks. These were generally laid out in the landscape style and provided with classic temples and rustic shelters. Around the edges of industrial towns, middle class homes were set either in their own garden plots or provided with common gardens to be shared. In either case these gardens were usually designed as modified parks with informal plantings of trees and shrubs. The lawns were here and there interrupted by flower beds densely planted with flowers. The flowers used in these beds were not the old hearty English types, but exotics, many hothouse grown, that were flooding into England from her colonies throughout the world. Horticultural information was being disseminated as never before through public arboretums and garden publications. Improved propagation methods made the new plant material inexpensive and easily available. As a result, garden building, once the exclusive province of the aristocracy, was on its way to becoming a national pastime.

It is not surprising that the 19th century does not stand out as a high point in the history of garden design. It was marked by misdirected enthusiasm for the new and different and lack of direction. Romantic landscape parks were dotted with flower beds in the shapes of kidneys and tadpoles; French parterres were bedded out with fuchsias, lobelias, heliotrope, and pelargoniums. There was a tentative return to some of the formal elements of the past. Fountains and pools and topiary specimens reappeared but were often placed in awkward juxtaposition with landscape features.

Toward the end of the century some order began to be visible. In England the architect Reginald Blomfield published *The Formal Garden in England*, 1892. In it he raised a basic question: "Is the garden to be considered in relation to the house, and as an integral part of a design which depends for its success on the combined effect of house and garden; or is the house to be ignored in dealing with the garden?" His answer was that they should be treated as an architectural whole and that, since no building, barring a mud hut covered with grass, could be made to look like anything in nature, one should "so control and modify the grounds as to bring nature into harmony with the house. . . . The harmony arrived at is not any trick of imitation, but an affair of a dominant idea which stamps its impress on house and grounds alike."

Blomfield's final assessment was that the most delightful and appropriate gardens ever built in England were those of the Tudor period when "the primary purpose of a garden as a place of retirement and seclusion, a place for quiet thought and leisurely enjoyment, was kept steadily in view. The grass and the yew-trees were trimmed close to gain their full beauty from the sunlight. Sweet kindly flowers filled the knots and borders. Peacocks and pigeons brightened the terraces and lawns. The paths were

straight and ample, the garden-house solidly built and comfortable; everything was reasonable and unaffected." He advocated a return to the old-fashioned flowers and fruit trees "such as English men and women loved three hundred years ago." This was to be done, "not for archaeology, not for ostentation, but because they gave real pleasure and delight."

Blomfield's influence did not entirely overthrow the hold of the landscape school, but it did bring about a more balanced view of how formal and landscape elements might be brought into harmony. Blomfield's plea for a return to the old, winter-resistant English flowers and the integration of design between house and garden was taken up by others. One of the most influential was Gertrude Jekyll.

Jekyll had originally been a disciple of William Robinson, a fine botanist, an advocate of natural, indeed, wild, gardens and a fierce adversary of Blomfield. She later modified her views and entered into collaboration with the architect Sir Edward Lutyns. Together they designed gardens that achieved an effective blending of formal structure with a sensitive use of plant materials. Jekyll wrote books on garden design that are as readable and applicable today as they were more than half a century ago.

It is most difficult to make a general statement as to the characteristics of 20th-century garden design in the Western world. No single trend or style is discernible, unless it is an eclectic one. The availability of information and the great number of gardens in every style and of every period that are accessible to the general public have resulted in more professional and amateur gardeners that are better educated than ever before.

The wide choice of direction is nowhere more evident than in the United States, for we have never been confined to one dominant influence in garden design. Early pleasure gardens in this country were based on different traditions in different areas, depending upon the origin of the settlers. The dramatic variations of climate and topography further diversified these inherited styles. As a result, there has never been an "American" garden style in the sense that there has been an English, a French, a Spanish, and a Japanese style.

In a world where the communication of ideas has become almost instantaneous, this diversity of input has become the rule. Innovations that in the past would have set people's feet on paths different from their neighbor's are so speedily and generally known that new styles tend to become worldwide rather than national or local. There are, in addition, some universal conditions that cannot help but affect the shape of future gardens.

There is our growing realization that we must not only preserve the wholesomeness and beauty of our environment but revive and renew it where it has been exploited and sullied if we are to survive. In addition, the terrible cost of urban congestion in terms of mental and physical well-being is becoming increasingly evident in crime and health statistics. These facts suggest that our need for gardens is a basic one, that the form they take must not too drastically alter nature, and that somehow on this crowded planet we must find a way to provide every human being with a corner of paradise.

DECORATING EDEN

ALCOVES *See Sheltered Seats.*

ALLEYS AND AVENUES

It is perhaps unfortunate that in alphabetically organizing a book on garden structures the first subject to be approached is that of alleys and avenues, for it may strike the reader that such arrangements of growing plants are not truly structures at all. We have included several other topics to which similar objections might be raised; entries on pleached trees and shrubs, hedges, and topiary. We have included them because we think that in these instances the plants are used architecturally, often as a substitute for true structures, and as a result deserve to be included with man-made constructions.

The terms *alley* and *avenue* are often used interchangeably to describe long walks or drives bordered by rows of evenly spaced trees or by hedges. More modern usage, however, usually makes a distinction based on the width of the passage. *Avenue* is now more often used where the spacing between the rows is quite broad, often accommodating a driveway. The term *alley*, or *allée* if one desires to use the French spelling, usually denotes a narrower, more intimate walkway.

Italian Alleys and Avenues Italian Renaissance gardeners were the first to employ long avenues of trees as a method for unifying the garden and adjoining buildings. Marie Luise Gothein in *A History of Garden Art*, 1928, says of the Villa Montalto garden, built in the late 16th century, "One can imagine nothing more magnificent than the approach to the casino from the side of the Esquiline near the church of S. Maria Maggiore. Through a large gate one steps into a garden where three splendid cypress avenues diverge; and at the point where they end there are two grand lion fountains. . . . The middle avenue leads directly to the entrance loggia with its three arches."

Gothein describes the two cypress avenues behind the casino that roughly quarter the flower garden. Where they reach the outer walls on the north and east they can be seen through wrought iron gates as they continue into the outer park until they terminate at a rise of hills. "Here for the very first time the artist is working in a larger style with perspective. Long avenues are made with definite endings, [such as] architecture or sculpture. The beds must be arranged to suit the form of the avenues; large, open, or semicircular spaces at the beginning of the ..venues increase the grandeur of the outlook." A bird's-eye-view of the Villa Montalto in Rome, as it was then, shows the strong lines formed by the avenues and the perspectives suggested by their extension beyond the enclosing walls. Gothein writes that this garden "of all others, presages those that were to be developed in France in the seventeenth century."

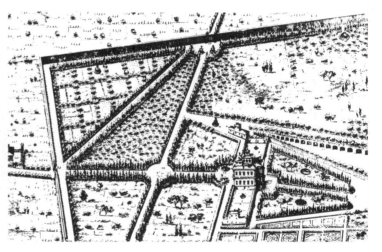

French Alleys The avenues of Italian gardens were soon copied in France where the Italian-born queen, Marie de Médicis, tried to conjure an illusion of her native home in the Luxembourg gardens. But it was not until the reign of Louis XIV that the French alley, *allée*, reached the height of splendor. Those laid out at Versailles by the great garden architect Le Nôtre were often as wide as 48 feet and over half a mile long. They crisscrossed the vast gardens in every direction, and where they intersected were fountains. These great alleys might be planted with two or three rows of elms, oaks, or lime trees to the side. In the photographs stately progressions of trees demonstrate how such alleys suggest great distance. Sometimes the effect was artificially magnified by diminishing the width of the passage and the height of the trees at the far end of the alley. One wonders about the effect of such manipulation, however, when viewed in the "wrong" direction.

Dutch Alleys and Avenues The Dutch adopted the French styles but often used hedges in favor of trees for their alleys because the shallow soil of the Low Countries would not support deep-rooting plants. Where trees would thrive, however, they often used long avenues of them as the main decorative feature of the garden. At Watervliet near Velsen, long avenues of limes radiated out from a large central pool, each one terminating in a small temple or summer house.

English Alleys and Avenues Alleys were popular in English gardens from the Tudor period on. The earliest alleys were small and intimate, sheltered by high hedges or yew, box or privet, or by hornbeam, cypress, or any of various fruit trees. Parkinson, in his *Paradisi in Sole*, 1629, praises the cypress for this use. "For the goodly proportion this tree beareth, as also for his ever grene head, it is and hath beene of great account with all princes, both beyond and on this side of the sea, to plant them in rowes on both sides of some spatious walke, which, by reason of their highe growing, and little spreading, must be planted the thicker together, and so they give a pleasant and sweet shadow." Narrow, sheltered alleys were sanded so that as Thomas Hill says in his *Gardener's Labyrinth*, 1577, "showers of rain falling, may not offend the walkers . . . in them, by the earth cleaving to or clogging their feet." The wider, more open alleys were usually turfed or planted with herbs such as camomile or wild thyme, which gave off sweet fragrances when crushed.

Later, English gardeners followed the example of the French and planted great broad avenues of trees, often two or three rows to a side. Where the avenue terminated at a mansion, the width might equal that of the facade of the building. Others, following the designs of Le Nôtre, were arranged in lines radiating from a central point. This type of planting

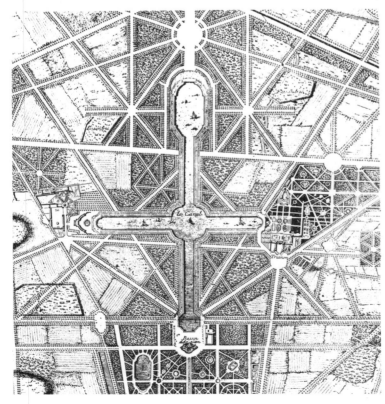

Gezicht aen het inkomen van de groote Laen op de Lustplaets WATERVLIET. / Vue de la grande Allée et avenue du Lieu de Plaisance WATERVLIET.

was known as a *patte-d'oie*, or goose foot. The famous example at Hampton Court, planted in the late 17th century, required 403 lime trees to complete. Many of these magnificent avenues were torn out or partially destroyed in the late 18th century. The advocates of the landscape style considered them a blight on the natural beauty of the countryside.

The use of tree-lined alleys and avenues was revived in the Victorian era. J. C. Louden, in *The Villa Gardener*, 1850, shows a plan for a gentleman's seat laid out with a series of radiating and intersecting avenues reminiscent of the great formal gardens of the 17th century. The central avenue borders a gravel

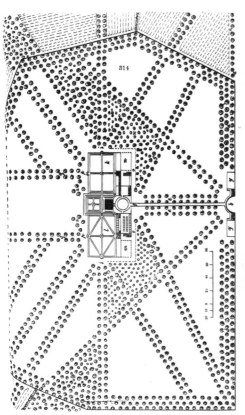

drive, while the side avenues line turf walks. Thomas Mawson, writing some fifty years later, warns against using an avenue as an approach to anything but the most imposing mansion and that it should be "absolutely straight and level from end to end unless there is an even rise throughout its whole length towards the house, and while such a rise, if not too great, is probably even better than an absolutely level course, the reverse, or a drop towards the house, is, of all arrangements, the very worst, giving the house the appearance of being in a hole." He recommends that the trees be planted opposite one another in formal and restrained surroundings and diago-

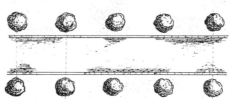

nally in more informal and natural situations. Where avenues are used as walks, he recommends that they "terminate in some architectural feature, such as a sheltered seat or summer-house."

The lime alley at Sissinghurst Castle, planted by Vita Sackville-West, was probably pleached at one time but then allowed to grow unclipped until it reached the stage of semiwildness shown in the photograph.

American Alleys and Avenues English colonists in America followed the traditions of their homeland, and as soon as they were affluent enough to develop large estates, they planted avenues of trees leading to their houses. In the southern states many of these avenues still stand, gnarled, moss-draped, and impressive. At Filoli, in Woodside, California, a formal alley of clipped yews with a turf path planted early in this century has already achieved the appearance of great age.

ANIMAL SHELTERS *See Aviaries, Bird Houses, Utility Buildings.*

APIARIES

An apiary is a place where bees are kept, especially a collection of hives. Bee culture is prominent in the lore, legend, and literature of all cultures. The Egyptians were acquainted with it 4,000 years ago. Barges carrying colonies of bees were floated up and down the Nile to allow the bees to take advantage of different plants as they bloomed.

Aristotle was one of the early students of the habits of bees and recorded his observations in his *Historia Animalium*. Greek beemasters used straw hives, or skeps. Some of them contained wooden bars on which the bees could build their combs. Similar straw skeps were in common use throughout most of Europe until the 19th century.

The utilitarian boxes of modern hives have little of the charm of their earlier counterparts. It is unfortunate from an aesthetic point of view that the old straw skeps are now used only as symbols of beekeeping, or sometimes in garden restorations. The photograph shows them at Williamsburg.

Beehouses of various kinds were incorporated in gardens from an early period. The engraving of a medieval garden shows a row of hives along both sides under roofed shelter.

Eighteenth-century garden designs show beehouses in the form of ornamental pavilions or temples. Glass observation hives were invented early in this century and became fairly common for those who kept bees as a curiosity or for scientific observation.

Aside from their obvious garden utility as pollinators or as producers of honey, bees seem to hold other fascinations. Even the very practical Loudon, in *The Villa Gardener*, 1850, describes the Nutt's patented hive at his own home in Bayswater. It was placed in front of his veranda between pillars where the back doors of the hive could be opened for convenient examination of the bees.

ARBORS

Here, as elsewhere in this book, we come to grips with a tangle of nomenclature that arises from the tendency of gardeners to borrow freely from other times and cultures and apply what they have borrowed to their own devices. When it was time for us to decide precisely what an *arbor* is to be in this book, we were confronted with an array of structural forms, definitions, and competing words, none of which seemed to have been used consistently by others.

In its original form the arbor (and its relatives) was almost certainly used for the purpose of supporting or shaping shrubs or vines—probably grapes. The English word itself is derived from the ancient French and from the Old English *herbere*, which originally meant something quite different—a place for the cultivation of herbs. From early descriptions, it seems, it was apparently nothing more than a small enclosed area set off from the rest of the garden by a low open-work fence. Chaucer uses the word in this old sense when he tells of a "pleasant herbere" . . .

That benched was, and all with turves new
Freshly turved, whereof the greene gras
So small, so thick, so short, so fresh of hew
That most like to greene wool, wot I, it was.

In this book we will use the word *arbor* for a general category of structure that incorporates both earlier meanings: an arbor defines and encloses space and has an open-work roof capable of serving as a support for plants. This definition includes a number of related forms, each of which will be further defined in this section. Below are examples of the three main arbor varieties you will find described: a "true" arbor (in this case sheltering a bench); a pergola (colonnade with a flat roof); and a gallery (tunnellike with an arched roof). The definition excludes several similar forms, which will be found elsewhere. Structures that are built for the *sole* purpose of training or supporting plants will be found under the heading *Trellises*. Structures in which the principal components are formed by living plants will be found under the heading *Pleached Trees and*

Shrubs. Structures that enclose space but have closed roofs will be found under the headings *Garden Houses, Gazebos, Pavilions, Sheltered Seats, Summer Houses, Tea Houses, Temples, and Tree Houses*.

On this page we've collected a group of structures we would classify as arbors. They range from the simplest rustic shelter (almost a trellis, except for the fact you could sit or walk under it) to fairly elaborate structures, which you might need an architect and a big budget to duplicate. In between are a number of much simpler designs. We have included the plans for a small arbor seat, complete with wren house, on page 10.

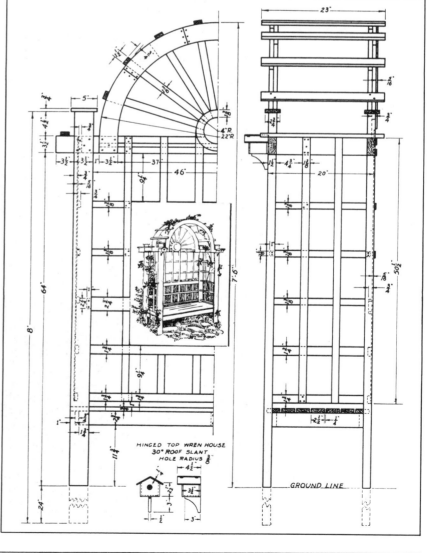

HINGED TOP WREN HOUSE
30° ROOF SLANT
HOLE RADIUS

GROUND LINE

Ancient Arbors It is likely that the earliest representation of an arbor is to be found on the walls of an Egyptian tomb dating from the 12th century B.C. The drawing here shows in the upper left corner an arbor that was probably in the pergola form: a double row of painted columns, which supports a grid of rafters overhead. Vines planted along the rows of columns grow to eventually cover the rafters with a lacy canopy of leaves.

In the drawing of a reconstructed Egyptian villa of about the same period, the arbor may be seen in the center of the garden. It is the dominant feature of the garden and forms a shaded outdoor room. Variations on the arbor were (and still are) popular throughout the hot Mediterranean countries because they provide shade without obstructing views or breezes. The Romans apparently loved such outdoor "rooms." Pliny writes of dining under a canopy of vines supported by marble columns. Many Roman houses had a portion of the garden set aside for dining under arborlike shelters.

By the late 16th century the form had become quite diverse. In this woodcut from a 16th-century English book, the arbor is shown in the corner of a walled garden as a shelter for a bowling court. In a German illustration of the same period, an outdoor revel is taking place under a very graceful arbor pavilion. The scene is apparently in the garden of an inn. The waitress may be seen totting up the bill before her customers get too tipsy to count out their money.

Galleries A close relation of the pergola, the gallery has been known by many names: *berceau*, *charmille*, and *tunnelle* (to give just the French examples). It is essentially an arched tunnel of greenery trained over a light structure of metal or lath.

The earliest picture of a gallery that we could find dates from the end of the 15th century, though references to them are to be found as early as the 13th century. In Boccaccio's *Decameron* the following description gives readers an appealing picture of a garden gallery: "The garden, all walled about, coasted the place. It had about it and athwart the middle, spacious alleys, straight as arrows and embowered with trellises of vines, yielding a rare savor about the garden. The sides of these alleys were walled about with roses, red and white, and with jessamine. While the sun was highest, one might go all about neath odoriferous and delightsome shade."

English and American Galleries Bacon's description of an ideal garden gives a clear picture of the state of elaboration galleries reached even in the relatively conservative gardens of England: "The garden is best to be square, encompassed, on all the four sides, with a stately arched hedge. The arches to be upon pillars, of carpenters' work of some ten feet high, and six feet broad: and the spaces between, of the same dimension, with the breadth of the arch. Over the arches, let there be an entire hedge, of some four feet high, framed upon carpenters' work: and over every arch, upon the upper hedge, a little turret, with a belly enough to receive a cage of birds: and over every space between the arches, some other little figure, with broad plates of round colored glass, gilt for the sun to play upon."

Modest but charming galleries were built in the gardens of colonial America. At Williamsburg and Tryon Palace, and many other places where 18th-century gardens have been lovingly restored, one can see fine examples of these delightful arbor walks.

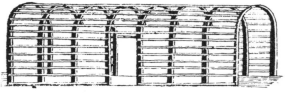

Pergolas Italian garden designers of the early Renaissance had deep admiration for classic Roman culture. They studied the crumbling ruins of ancient villas, pored over the accounts of Roman writers, and tried to reproduce from such evidence the gardens of Imperial Rome. The pergola was usually a primary feature of such gardens. The word comes from the Latin *pergula*, which means projection. We use it in this book to describe a specific form of arbor: a colonnade that supports beams and cross members to form an open roof. Sometimes the structures are free standing; often, especially in Roman gardens, they project from a wall and are supported on the open side by a single row of columns. In the traditional form, plantings—usually vines—occur at each column and are trained up and over the grid. There are many variations, but a consistent characteristic of the classic pergola is its linear form and the flat open-work roof.

Variant Forms Having stated that the classic pergola form is a colonnade with a flat roof, we can introduce variations. In the versions below other roof forms are most apparent.

Here, the line that divides the pergola from the gallery, which has an arched, or vaulted, roof becomes tenuous, and the arbitrariness of categories evident. We have classified these arched variations as pergolas because they are open on at least one side, though elsewhere in these pages you will find versions with slatted sides and at least one in which the columns are supported by a continuous low wall. So much for categories. Like most other forms in this book, variations are limited only by the imagination of the designer.

ARCHES *See Arbors, Pleached Trees and Shrubs, Treillage, Trellises.*

ARMILLARY SPHERES *See Sundials.*

ARTIFICIAL HILLS *See Mounts, Rockwork.*

AVIARIES

An aviary is any large enclosure specifically designed to hold a number of birds in confinement. The first such structures of which there is any record were used by the Romans, who called them *ornithones.*

M. Terrentius Varro, in the first century B.C., described in great detail the aviary at his villa of Casium, here shown in a Renaissance engraving. Square aviaries flanked the entrance, and the double circle of colonnades was enclosed with hemp nets and filled with birds of every species. The domed building in the center was used as a dining hall where guests were seated around a revolving table and could watch and listen to the birds and look through the net to the countryside beyond.

Aviaries came in all shapes and sizes, depending on the rank and wealth of the owner. The construction materials varied with the time and place. Early Chinese aviaries were of bamboo, whole or split. Gothein, in *A History of Garden Art*, describes a "tower . . . in open-work teak" in the garden of the castle of the Tulunids in tenth-century Cairo, "to serve as a bird-cage, painted in many colours, with paved floors, and little streams purling."

Pietro Crescenzi, in the 15th century, wrote of a kind of house for birds "having a roof and walls of copper wire finely netted." Prescott, in *The Conquest of Mexico*, describes the "House of Birds" in the Aztec capital, "an airy and elegant building" of latticework in which "birds of splendid plumage were assembled from all parts of the Empire."

The explorations to far places that began in the 15th century opened new sources for rare and beautiful birds for the avid collectors in western Europe, and by the 16th century the aviary had become a consistent and important

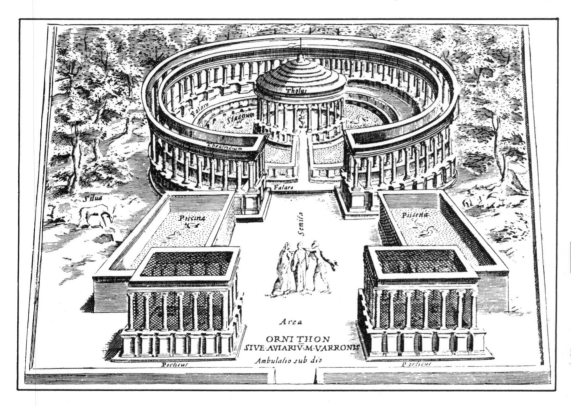

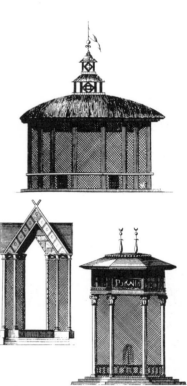

feature of the garden, often built in combination with fountains so that the splashing of water combined with the singing of birds.

Eleanor Von Erdberg Consten, in *Chinese Influences in European Garden Structures*, wrote that "keeping rare and beautiful birds in a gorgeous cage has always been a favorite pastime of the great and mighty. . . . The democratic late eighteenth century extended this privilege to the well-to-do bourgeois class. It was quite natural to build in an exotic style for exotic birds—though on many a small estate the cage was probably more exotic than its inhabitants." The pattern books of the period were filled with confections in many styles:

rustic, Gothic, Hindu-Gothic, chinoiserie, and rococo.

Garden aviaries decreased in popularity in the 19th century; they became only another incident in the landscape, one more difficult to maintain than other features. Later, aviaries were built only by those with a sincere interest in birds.

Simpler in form than those of earlier centuries is the aviary from the late 19th century shown below. It was 5½ feet in diameter with a substantial brick foundation and was approximately 9 feet high. The roof was of 8-inch-thick thatch lined with zinc. Half the aviary was wired, half was of wood boards.

The wired half is visible in the drawing. Nest boxes were attached to the wooden wall where there were also a pipe to supply water and a seed hopper holding several weeks' supply of food.

The photograph shows an empty aviary of similar size and vintage, still standing in a neglected corner of a Hong Kong garden. Built of masonry, it has a handsome domed roof with an unusual finial.

BALUSTRADES *See Paths, Stairs, Terraces.*
BANDSTANDS *See Pavilions.*
BARNS *See Utility Buildings.*

BASINS

Cisterns In the 17th and 18th centuries the English produced many beautiful lead cisterns to collect and store rain water for house and garden use. Some of the smaller ones are intended to be mounted on a wall, while the larger, rectangular and octagonal tanks are placed on the ground or on low pedestals. Wall-hung cisterns or those raised on pedestals are often fitted with taps. The cisterns were usually cast flat and then bent into shape and soldered. In some, the decorative surface patterns were pressed into sand molds and cast with the face of the cistern; in others, the embellishments were added after the cistern was formed. Gilding was often used on panel ribs and ornaments. In the early 20th century the use of lead cisterns for drinking water died out because of the fear of lead poisoning. Many

were destroyed or relegated to garden use only. Both free-standing and wall-hung cisterns have been incorporated into fountains. Smaller ones are often used for planters. Old cisterns can still be found in shops specializing in antique garden ornaments and fountains, and several companies are still manufacturing reproductions and contemporary designs.

Dipping Wells A dipping well is not really a well at all but simply a form of cistern. The dipping well is used to store water, allowing it to reach air temperature before it is used on plants. Such wells were traditionally found in a central position in the kitchen or herb garden. Although occasionally old wellheads were used, generally dipping wells were made in simple designs of brick or local stone. The 18th-century American plantation dipping

well shown in the photograph below was filled by hand. Modern ones are usually fitted with a concealed pipe and tap.

Japanese Water Basins There are two basic types of basins used in Japanese gardens. The *chozubachi*, or tall basin, is usually used in home gardens near the *engawa*, or veranda, of the house. The *tsukubai* is a low basin, originally used outside a shrine and later in tea gardens. The *chozubachi* are made in so many forms that it would be impossible to name them all, but there are certain traditional shapes that are most common and appear in many old garden manuals. One of these is the bridgepost shaped basin, a cylindrical stone pillar 30 to 40 inches high with a shallow basin hollowed out of the top. Partway down the shaft is a rectangular depression. This is meant to represent the mortise where the

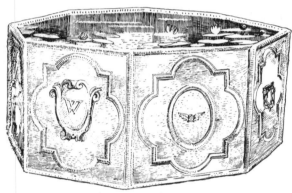

bridge railing would be tenoned into the post. It is believed that sometime long ago some important personage used an old bridgepost for this purpose and started the tradition.

The custom of putting fragments of old buildings, millstones, or parts from old lanterns or pagodas to use in some other capacity is not uncommon in Japan, for it is a way to show reverence for the past. Another shape often used for the *chozubachi* is the lovely jujube shape, so called because it resembles the datelike fruit of the jujube tree. Some *chozubachi* are made of bronze, but more often of stone, which may be finely carved and polished or crudely shaped and rough. Others are made of boulders left in their natural state, with only the basin being shaped by hand. The most highly prized basins are the ones that were formed entirely by nature, where

the basin was carved by the natural action of water.

Tsukubai, or low basins, are used for symbolic purification, the rinsing of mouth and hands before entering a shrine or before participating in the tea ceremony. The basins are deliberately set low so that it is necessary to crouch or kneel to use them. All basins are provided with a ladle, which is laid across the basin. Sometimes a narrow bamboo mat is provided to rest the ladle on. The basin is set in a roughly circular depression called a "sea," which is covered with small pebbles, and often has a concealed drain, which catches the overflow from the basin and prevents the surrounding area from getting muddy. A broad flat stone is placed in front of the basin to stand on, a slightly higher stone to the right is provided as a place to set a container of hot

water in the winter. On the left is a stone where a hand-held lantern or other objects can be placed while washing. However, there is usually a permanent stone lantern placed close to the basin to provide light.

Japanese basins are sometimes simply filled by hand, but more often they are filled from a bamboo pipe or flume. In some the water runs continuously and overflows into the "sea," which may be the source of a little stream; others are connected to a hose or pipe (concealed inside a bamboo casing) that can be turned off.

BATH HOUSES *See Swimming Pools, Bath Houses.*

BED DESIGN

BED DESIGN

Ancient Bed Design Climate and aesthetics have made bedding—growing plants in massed and figured groups—a principal element in garden design. In the ancient world, flower beds were designed to conserve water. Egyptian gardeners bedded plants of a kind together in small, rectangular plots so that each kind got only the water it needed. Early Persian gardens centered on a water tank that fed four channels, dividing the garden into four equal parts, each accessible to the water. More channels and pools were added as gardens expanded. The oasislike quality of the Persian garden, with its gently flowing or still water, is a constant motif in Middle Eastern poetry and art. The Taj Mahal gardens, the Mogul gardens at Kashmir, and the Moorish gardens of Morocco and Spain all follow the basic Persian plan. The Moors added a water-saving innovation: they often sank flower beds

2 or more feet below path level so that rain or wash water also ran into the beds. Ankle-high blossoms of the sunken plants created a carpetlike effect.

What we know about Roman villa gardens comes from written descriptions and a few isolated ruins, but neither gives us much information about bed design on the more palatial estates. However, excavations at Pompeii and Herculaneum reveal much about the smaller urban gardens. These were usually confined within the *peristyle*—the colonnaded interior courtyards of Hellenic houses. Often the planting beds were limited to narrow borders against the enclosing walls and were raised from 12 to 18 inches above the pathways. The walls behind such beds were sometimes painted with garden scenes. Ground-level beds, particularly after the first century A.D., were often laid out with serpentine outlines and edged with box or rosemary.

Though at first consideration the massing of plants into geometric or random forms might be thought of as primarily horticultural, the resulting beds quite often take on architectural importance, thus their inclusion in this book.

Medieval Flower Beds Medieval monastery gardens followed the four-part plan of early Persian gardens, usually centered on a fountain or wellhead and divided by paths. Monks used flowers medicinally and sometimes for altar decoration, but they associated them too closely with paganism to grow flowers for their own sakes.

By the 14th century, returning Crusaders had begun to build gardens in a new way, outside their castle walls. The northern and central European climates did not impose the constraints on water supply that had shaped the Persian garden. At first, the new gardens were often nothing more than grassy enclo-

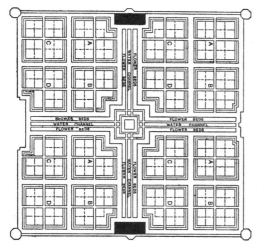

sures dotted with wildflowers, the "flowery medes" of tapestries, paintings, and poetry. Some had rows of rectangular beds, as in a kitchen garden. Medieval gardeners sometimes put beds at ground level, but more often raised them several inches with retaining walls of stone, brick, or wood. They built up some beds as high as 24 inches (either freestanding or against walls), covered them with turf, planted a few flowers here and there, and used them as garden seats.

More elaborate beds evolved gradually in these new gardens. They usually centered around a fountain or a clipped tree. Chessboard arrangements became popular, and somewhat later, round and concave shapes. Plantings were sparse, usually one or two specimens to a bed.

Renaissance Parterres and Knots The *parterre*, or *knot garden* as it was called in England, had its beginning in the early 15th

century when gardeners started to elaborate on the simple geometric flower beds of the Middle Ages. The word *parterre* derives from the Old French *par terre* and the Latin *per terre*, meaning on the ground. In Italy, where the style originated, the garden was divided into a series of square beds separated by grass or gravel paths. Within each bed a pattern was worked out in low-growing herbs or clipped boxwood against a bed of sand. Sometimes the patterns were filled in with flowers. The beds within a single garden area might be identical, or each might be of a different design.

The style soon spread throughout Europe. The restored parterres at Chateau Villandry, shown in the photograph, are accurate examples of the Renaissance style.

English Knot Gardens Medieval gardeners invented the knot garden, with beds planted or otherwise designed in ornamental, knotlike patterns. It remained popular in

many countries until well into the 17th century.

Knot garden beds were almost always square. Often each knot in the garden was of a different design, perhaps a simple geometric pattern, perhaps an intricate figure of heraldic origin, the designs worked out in low-growing herbs or clipped box.

In England, where knot gardens reached a pinnacle, there were two basic types of knot: open knots and closed knots. English gardeners outlined open knots with herbs or boxwood and filled the centers with multicolored "dead materials": clay, sand, or crushed Flanders tile for yellow; chalk, plaster, or lime for white; coal dust or black earth for black; pebbles or coal dust mixed with chalk for blue; brick dust for red. They formed closed knots by outlining the patterns with herbs or box and filling the spaces with dense plantings of flowers. The closed knot in the photograph is

CERTOSA DI PAVIA   *Monks Garden.*

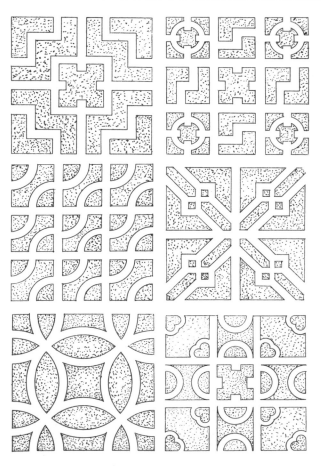

at the Elizabethan Gardens on Roanoke Island.

In *The English Husbandman* Gervase Markham recommended simple patterns for open knots, for example, a double row of tiles outlining the pattern, each thread of which is planted with different colored flowers, so that "if you stand a little remote from the knot and any thing above it, you shall see it appear like a knot made of divers colored ribans, most pleasing and most rare." Such a ribbon design can still be seen in the modern knot gardens at Filoli, where ribbons of marigolds weave through knots made of contrastingly colored herbs.

17th- and 18th-Century Parterres In the early 17th century, French garden design began to break away from Italian models. The Italian garden relied heavily on steep terracing and rushing water for its effects, but these features were not always available in France,

so French gardeners put more emphasis on surface design, on parterres and sheets of still water. They developed intricate, free-flowing designs from the simpler, more geometric, Italian parterres, a broad repertoire of styles that they used to form gardenwide panoramas of varying patterns.

Parterres *en broderie*, with designs resembling the embroidery on clothing, were considered the finest and were set closest to main buildings. Gardeners outlined the embroiderylike tendrils with clipped boxwood and filled the centers with black earth or coal dust. Close-sheared grass plots formed the shell-like figures as well as the heavier scrolls. In the diagram, borders shown with heavy dots are of brick dust, while the lightly dotted area is common sand. The outside border is edged with box, filled with flowers, and punctuated with clipped yews and shrubs.

Parterres de compartiments differed from *par-*

terres en broderie in being symmetrical from end to end and side to side. French gardeners used them in conjunction with *parterres en broderie*, but in subordinate positions. *Parterres de compartiments*, considered a further step down in refinement, were used in beds more remote from the manor or castle. They employed less "embroidery" in box, more grass and "dead materials." *Parterres à la mode Anglais* were plainer still, consisting of large grassy areas separated by sanded paths and bordered by densely planted flower beds. *Parterres de pièces coupées* were also edged with box and filled with flowers, but the sand paths that divided the beds were to be walked upon; in the other styles, they were not.

Colonial Flower Beds The American colonists' gardens reflected their ties with England and Holland. They started making pleasure gardens by the early 18th century, especially in Virginia, where a brisk tobacco

trade and slaves allowed a leisured, plantation society. A constant exchange of plants and information with England kept colonists informed on the latest innovations.

When, in the mid-18th century, the English were busy converting their formal gardens to the new landscape style, this new trend was noted, but only partially adopted by the colonists. Often, as at Mount Vernon, the two styles found their way into the same garden. There the sweeping approaches to the house and the parklike grounds reflect the ideas of the landscape school, while close to the mansion, one finds formality and symmetry.

Executed in box and filled with bulbs and other flowers, the geometric parterres at Gunston Hall and the many precise little gardens at Williamsburg retain a 17th-century, Dutch-English influence. Diamond-shaped parterres of box and periwinkle at the Gover-

nor's Mansion in Williamsburg comprise a formal, evergreen garden of considerable charm.

Carpet Bedding At the height of the mid-18th-century's landscape garden rage, flower beds were relegated to kitchen and cutting gardens. Shortly before that century's end, however, English garden designer Humphrey Repton protested that setting an elegant mansion in a bald meadow left something to be desired, that there was value in formal, architectural gardens close to a house. Similar reactions to the excesses of the landscape school combined with a flood of exotic plants from colonies worldwide to trigger a revival of parterres, rock gardens, and rosaries.

Carpet bedding was made fashionable largely by Prince Puckler, a German advocate of the landscape style who was a flower enthusiast as well. Carpet bedding brought together masses of showy, if not garish, plants,

often hot-house exotics, in fancifully shaped beds and borders distributed about estate lawns. Architect T. James trenchantly protested the excesses of the style in 1839, deploring "scores of unmeaning flower-beds, disfiguring the lawn in shapes of kidneys, and tadpoles and sausages, and leeches, and commas."

Despite ridicule, the carpet bedding vogue lasted well into the 20th century and survives still in some public parks. America adopted the style as enthusiastically as had England, but also produced its own doubters. In *The Art of Beautifying Surburban Home Grounds*, 1873, Frank J. Scott likened carpet beds to "the lace, linen, and ribbon decorations on a lady's dress . . . essential ornaments, and yet to be introduced sparingly. . . . Beware of frequently breaking open stretches of lawn for them. Imagine bits of lace or bows of ribbon stuck promiscuously over the body and skirt

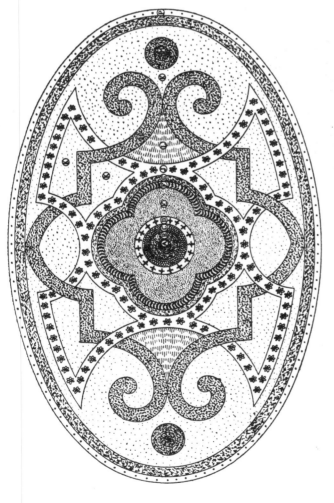

of a lady's dress." In *Gardening for Pleasure*, 1907, Peter Henderson tells the (apocryphal, we suspect) story of an "old Jersey farmer and his wife . . . who, happening to be driving in the grounds [of a John Hoey, who was noted for his carpet bedding] one day when a shower came up, drove up to Mr. Hoey's residence and told the servants to get in the carpets, as they were getting ruined by the rain!"

The Herbaceous Border One of the most influential garden designers of the late 19th century, Gertrude Jekyll, brought a painterly, indeed, impressionistic, eye to the flower bed. Originally influenced by the extreme naturalism of William Robinson, she later modified her ideas in collaboration with architect Edward Lutyns, a collaboration that produced some consummately beautiful gardens. Lutyns stressed strong structural framework and close coordination with adjacent buildings in garden design, maintaining that "every gar-

den scheme should have a backbone, a central idea beautifully phrased. Every wall, path, stone, and flower should have its relationship to the central idea."

Jekyll's use of plant materials was inspired: she rejected stiff carpet bedding, with its masses of tender and exotic plants, for a combination of old winter-resistant English cottage flowers and hardy introductions, arranging the plants in simple, straight beds backed by hedges or walls. Her *Colour in the Flower Garden* stresses the need for structured planning, "the possession of a quantity of plants, however good the plants may be themselves and however ample their number, does not make a garden; it only makes a collection. Having got the plants, the great thing is to use them with careful selection and definite intention. Merely having them, or having them planted unassorted in garden spaces, is only like having a box of paints from the best

colourman, or, to go one step further, it is like having portions of these paints set out upon a palette. This does not constitute a picture."

Gardens of special coloring were a Jekyll trademark, but she never lost sight of aesthetic purposes in planning them. "It is a curious thing that people will sometimes spoil some garden project for the sake of a word. For instance, a blue garden, for beauty's sake, may be hungering for a group of white Lilies, or for something of palest lemon-yellow, but it is not allowed to have it because it is called the blue garden, and there must be no flowers in it but blue flowers. I can see no sense in this, it seems to me like fetters foolishly self-imposed. Surely the business of the blue garden is to be beautiful as well as blue."

BERCEAUX *See Arbors.*

BIRD HOUSES, FEEDERS, AND BATHS

Bird Houses Bird houses, that is, shelters provided to encourage wild birds to nest in the garden, are a fairly recent idea. Three things are required to attract wild birds to a garden: water, food, and a safe place to nest. That these three elements occurred in older gardens was usually coincidence from the birds' viewpoint. Gardens were not planned to attract them. Swans and peafowl were semi-domesticated birds who graced the dinner table as well as the garden and were looked after

accordingly. But, at least through the 18th century, if someone wanted a song bird in the garden, the common practice was to catch and cage one. The caged birds would be concealed in the garden so that visitors could imagine themselves in a natural woodland scene. Sometimes the birds would be blinded, in the belief it would make them sing more sweetly.

It wasn't until late in the 19th century that a more humane attitude toward wild birds began to influence public thought. The Society for the Protection of Birds was founded in England, and in this same period plans for wild

bird houses began to appear. These bird houses were usually rustic in style, incorporating hollowed-out log sections, rough wood or bark, or small kegs, often with thatched roofs. Most of these are still useful designs. Their builders must have studied the habits of wild birds, who generally prefer houses that look like natural objects and are often suspicious of artificial-looking things. Each species has its own requirements, and the shape, size, and placement of the house will determine who will live there.

Bird houses are available that are designed

47

to suit the nesting habits of a variety of birds, particularly wrens and bluebirds, the easiest species to attract to the garden.

Bird Feeders Bird-feeding tables appeared even later than bird houses. In *Practical Book of Garden Architecture*, 1914, by Phebe Humphrey, there is a chapter devoted to "Bird Basins and Feeding Tables: An Interesting Form of Garden Decoration Urged by Audubon Societies and State Grange Committees." As late as 1926, Henslow, in *Garden Architecture*, wrote that "bird feeding tables are more or less of an innovation, but present designs are certain to be improved upon, and to stay." He forecast well; today there are many different and specialized feeders available to supplement the traditional covered tables set on posts.

Bird Baths Bird baths as such were also a late introduction. They serve a dual purpose by furnishing water needed by wild birds and by introducing water as a decorative element in the garden where there is no other fountain or pool. The traditional bird bath, a shallow basin set on a stone or marble column, is the focal point of many small gardens. Many kinds of shallow basins can be adapted as bird baths. Giant clam shells, either real or stylized designs in carved stone or concrete, are sometimes used. An antique baptismal font, carved of pink marble, is set at an intersection of garden paths in the restored 18th-century gardens at Tryon, North Carolina. While intended as a decoration, it also seems to please the birds. *See also Aviaries, Basins.*

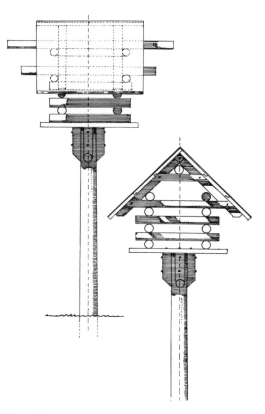

BOAT HOUSES

Wherever there is a body of water large enough in the garden, there is usually a pleasure boat as well. Generally, small rowboats or punts—perhaps only a child's inflatable canoe—will do for the pleasure of being afloat in a garden setting, a pleasure shared by most cultures.

Some of the most imaginative water craft originated in the old "lake and mountain" gardens of China, where dragon- or phoenix-headed boats, in gay colors and with little pavilions or silken canopies, carried passengers to admire the view. In Japan's Heian period, courtiers were rowed about garden lakes in copies of these elegant Chinese boats while they listened to music and composed poetry. The dragon boats appeared again in Europe during the rage for all things Chinese in the 18th century.

The formal canals of the great French gardens, especially at Versailles, were made for boating as well as for their dramatic effect in the landscape. Boats of all sorts enlivened the scene. There were royal barges, Dutch sailboats, and Venetian gondolas. Mock sea battles were staged on special occasions.

Boat houses are used for storage and to protect boats from sun and weather. Some are merely covered sheds over the water; others, more elaborate, are of brick or stone with arched entrances for the boats. Often there are slings inside to hoist the boat out of the water. These buildings often serve as summer houses as well; some were substantial enough to convert into dwellings. Dylan Thomas lived for sixteen years in a pretty white Georgian boat house in Wales.

On tidal waters boat houses are built above the high-water line, with rails or rollers to move the boat inside.

BORDERS *See Edgings.*

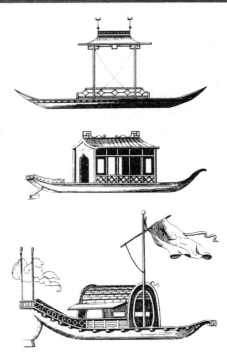

BRIDGES

Chinese Bridges The two ingredients essential to the Chinese garden have always been mountains and water: water in the form of lakes and canals and mountains created by intricate masses of eroded stones, often forming islands. Given these elements, bridges become essential not just in order to get from one point to another, but also to serve as points from which to view the garden. The most characteristic Chinese bridge is the high arched "camel-back" style, which was used most often in important Imperial gardens. These were built of brick or stone, the semicircular opening high enough to accommodate the little pleasure boats that were used on the garden lakes. The balustrades of these

bridges were of marble intricately carved and fitted together. Maggie Keswick says in *The Chinese Garden*, 1978, "In reflection, semicircular bridges complete themselves, producing the ideal round shape—a symbol in China of the moon and of perfection." The small marble bridge in Golden Gate Park, San Francisco, given by the City of Taipei, Taiwan, has the same detailing as the larger ones.

Another characteristic bridge is the zigzag stone bridge. This bird's-eye-view drawing of Chuo Cheng Yuan, or "The Garden of the Stupid Officials," in Soochow shows two such bridges leading to an island with a small gazebo, or *t'ing*. The zigzag form was believed to foil evil spirits who could move only in straight lines. In the background of the pic-

ture is a third bridge, the "Little Flying Rainbow" bridge. This type of bridge is virtually an extension of the roofed walkways, or *langs*, that thread Chinese gardens. Here the decorative latticework of the balustrades and roof lambrequins are made of wood, as is the rest of the bridge.

A favorite style and the one that caught the imagination of Europeans when the first descriptions of Chinese gardens reached them was the arched bridge with a roofed pavilion at the apex. These became almost a symbol of China in the Western world, and many fanciful interpretations of such bridges appeared in English and European landscape gardens in the mid-18th century.

Japanese Bridges Early Japanese

bridges, of the Heian period (710–1150), adhered closely to the Chinese styles. Important gardens had stone "camel-back" bridges with carved stone or marble balustrades that were made to fit together with mortise and tenon joinery. The wooden bridges of the period were arched as well because pleasure boats were used on the lakes in Japan, just as in China. Wooden bridges of this period have decorative latticework balustrades and carved trestles and brackets. They are generally lacquered with vermilion, a bright orange red pigment made by heating mercury with sulphur. The balustrade posts are capped with lotus-shaped bronze finials. Chinese roofed bridges were copied in Japan and often had central pavilions provided with seats where

the courtiers could sit and enjoy the view or observe water festivals. The large covered bridge shown in the photograph below is at the Heian Shrine, Kyoto. It was built in 1894 but duplicates those used a thousand years earlier.

Shorter, less formal bridges are made of slabs of schist or granite and are used where the banks are low. Some are hewn and slightly arched; others are flat and only roughly shaped or left completely natural. For short spans they are simply set from bank to bank and flanked at each end by "bridge-pinching stones" to give a feeling of stability. Longer spans are made with two or more slabs supported by a stone trestle or rough rocks where they join. Some are offset at the joining point

to create a jog in the line of the bridge. Sometimes planks or logs with one side cut flat are used in place of stone for these bridges.

In the 15th century a more rustic style of garden was popularized by the Zen tea masters, and a new type of bridge was introduced, the *dobashi*, or earth bridge. These bridges are made with a single bowed log cut in half lengthwise to form the two sides of the span. The span is supported by a series of graduated trestles. The flooring is made of small logs laid side by side and topped with a layer of bamboo poles and a layer of earth. The center of the bridge is graveled, and the slightly raised sides are planted with grass.

The most distinctive and least common Japanese bridge is the *yatsubashi*, or zigzag

bridge. It is built only a few inches above the water and is used primarily to view flowering water plants in swampy areas. According to Tetsuro Yoshida in *Gardens of Japan*, 1957, "the zig-zag bridge probably expresses the artistic idea that a certain kind of incompleteness is more worth striving for than mere formal completeness. This artistic principle was accepted in Japan from ancient times and as the tea ceremony developed became its basic principle. Real beauty was held to reside in incomplete broken zig-zag lines rather than in perfect straight lines."

European and English Bridges Bridges were not an important element in European gardens until mid-18th century when many formal gardens were "reformed" in the En-glish landscape style. Canals and reflecting pools were eliminated in favor of lakes, streams, and rivers, which often made a bridge a necessity. Others were built as eye-catchers or as stage props to foster the illusion that a small expanse of water was a very large one. Humphrey Repton in his *Art of Landscape Gardening* explains how a bridge could be used spanning the junction of two lakes to create the appearance of a river. "To preserve the idea of a river, nothing is so effectual as a bridge; instead of dividing the water on each side, it always tends to lengthen its continuity by shewing the impossibility of crossing it by any other means, provided the ends [of the lakes] are well concealed."

About the same time there was a vogue for grandiose Palladian bridges, inspired by the designs of the great 16th-century architect Andrea Palladio. An early example of the Palladian style was the massive bridge designed by Sir John Vanbrugh for the Duke of Marl-borough at Blenheim Palace. The bridge, containing thirty-three rooms inside its huge stone span, crossed a small canal connecting two lakes. While the structure was handsome, its pretension called forth some criticism and a good deal of ridicule such as Alexander Pope's satiric verse.

The minnows, as under this vast arch they pass,
Murmur, "How like whales we look, thanks to your
 Grace."

The bridge was later reduced to a more pleasing scale by "Capability" Brown's simple

expedient of damming the outlet of the lower lake, thus flooding the area around the bridge and hiding a good portion of it under water. Smaller editions of the Palladian bridge were constructed at Wilton (see drawing below) and at Stowe and were much admired and freely copied elsewhere.

At this same period there was also a flurry of interest in all things Chinese. Merchants and travelers were returning from the Orient with porcelains, lacquerware, and paintings. Reports of Chinese gardens with their winding streams and lakes seemed to confirm the tenets of the landscape school, and "les jardins Anglo-chinois" became the rage throughout Europe. A number of pattern books showing Chinese-style garden structures were pub-

lished in France and in England. The designs ranged from frivolous but doable to preposterous.

The taste for exotica was not confined to things Chinese. Romantic landscape gardens sported bridges in the "Gothick" and "Moorish" styles—bridges with swings and seesaws—and a whole range of "rustic" bridges. Eighteenth-century rustic bridges were quite intricate, requiring considerable skill to build. Later Victorian examples were less refined and could be made easily by amateurs, which may account for their continued popularity through the 19th century.

A return to structured and formal gardens in the early 20th century produced more restrained bridge designs. Thomas Mawson in

The Art and Craft of Garden Making, 1912, recommends that masonry bridges be built of local stone and be kept very simple for "it is far better to err on the side of plainness than to obtain an ostentatious result. Smaller bridges still should be constructed of oak, but never of the so-called rustic work, which, besides offending the canons of art in its design, invariably looks either brand-new or dilapidated. Where a wooden bridge is necessary, it should be a straight-forward honest piece of good carpentry, with as much quaint construction and strutting as this will allow of." Despite the swing away from the romantic, rustic bridges retained their popularity for park and home use. The two German designs shown in section drawings below date from 1904 and em-

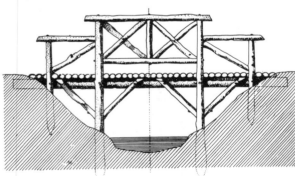

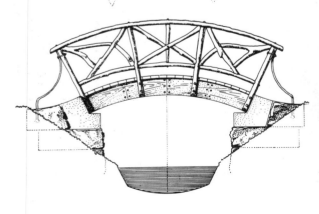

ploy the rustic detail so beloved in the previous century.

American Bridges The 18th-century European fascination with borrowed styles penetrated to the American colonies but didn't reach such a high degree of frivolity. The little Chinese bridge at Williamsburg, Virginia, shows its origins but is sturdy and utilitarian as well. At Middleton Place, near Charleston, South Carolina, there are two unusual bridges, probably dating from the early 19th century. The long arched rustic bridge made of cedar logs is simple and effective. A small wooden bridge with a seat built into one railing provides a cool and shady resting place over a quiet stream. At nearby Magnolia Gardens a romantic mid-Victorian bridge spans the black waters of a cypress lake. A smaller arched footbridge crosses a narrow inlet of the same lake. In rural areas rustic bridges were as popular as they were in Europe until well into the 20th century. More elaborate bridges were built at estates developed in the early 1900s. At Nemours, near Wilmington, Delaware, are two handsome examples: a graceful stone bridge and an elegant wooden one in the Chinese style.

BRODERIES *See Bed Design.*
CABANAS *See Swimming Pools, Bath Houses.*
CANALS *See Water, Formal Uses.*
CARPET BEDDING *See Bed Design.*
CASCADES *See Water, Formal Uses.*
CAVES *See Grottoes.*
CISTERNS *See Basins.*

CISTERNS *See Basins.*
CLAIRVOYÉES *See Walls.*
CLOSED URNS *See Sculpture.*
COLD FRAMES *See Plant Houses.*
COLUMBARIA *See Dovecotes.*
CONSERVATORIES *See Plant Houses.*
CONTAINERS *See Plant Containers, Plant Stands.*
COURTYARDS *See Patios and Courtyards.*
CURBINGS *See Edgings.*

DECKS AND PLATFORMS

Wooden decks in the garden are direct descendants of the wide front porches and verandas of earlier years, particularly the simple wooden porches so characteristic of the Japanese house. Originally a deck was an extended uncovered porch attached to the house, but in recent times the deck has freed itself from this domestic tie and may be found as a separate structure in unexpected parts of the garden. Thus, there is a distinct kinship to those specially sited platforms in the Japanese garden whose purpose is to serve as viewing points for some valued scenic feature.

Japanese Viewing Platforms These platforms took various forms. In the 17th-century Katsura garden a moon-viewing platform juts out from the covered veranda; it is floored with round bamboo poles and has no railing. Here the host and his guests can sit on mats to watch the rising moon, with its twin reflected in the waters of the lake below. Another viewing platform is in the form of an elevated gallery where the fall color of the maple leaves may be seen at eye level. Even the planked zigzag bridges built close to the surface in ponds of water iris seem intended to provide an intimate view of the blossoms rather than a means of getting from one point to another.

Modern Decks In the modern landscape a deck may still serve as an extension of the house. It may provide a bridge between the house and garden or may be detached from and unrelated to the house. Decks and platforms are now built to take the place of what

once would have been a stone terrace, a brick patio, or even a lawn. On steep building sites a deck may itself become the garden—as the only usable space for outdoor living and plant growing.

Decks are being used in hillside gardens, even where more traditional terracing might be desirable. Where there are established trees to be preserved, a deck can be wrapped around them without damaging root systems, as would be the case if cutting and filling were done to level the ground. A tree will continue

growing through the deck so long as space is allowed for it to enlarge and to sway in the wind. In a sloping garden a series of small decks, connected by broad shallow steps, can be a graceful transition from one level to another. These, too, can be sited to take advantage of existing native plants, trees, or rock formations without disturbing them. These smaller decks sometimes reveal views not visible from the house and may be elevated to take in "borrowed" scenery.

Decks are not restricted to hillside gardens,

however. They are used on flat ground to add interest and a change of elevation. In areas where shade, poor soil, or poor drainage prevents successful planting of a lawn or ground cover, a deck may solve a surfacing problem, providing usable space with low maintenance. Wooden decks also have the advantage of draining quickly, so they can be used for play or entertaining even when the ground is wet.
DIPPING WELLS *See Basins.*

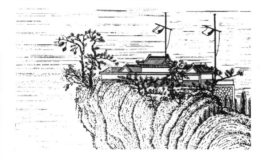

DOVECOTES

A dovecote, or columbarium, is a specialized bird house for keeping doves or pigeons. These birds need no confinement; they are friendly, home-loving creatures. Garden dovecotes seldom house more than a dozen or so birds, for pigeon-keeping is no longer the economic necessity it was when every property from small farm to great estate raised pigeons for the table.

Roman Columbaria Ancient Romans established the basic design for dovecotes that would be followed for fifteen hundred years. Their columbaria, round stone towers with nest holes built into the walls from floor to ceiling, housed as many as five thousand birds. Shelves were built in front of each row of nests, where the birds could alight and strut, as pigeons are wont to do.

French Dovecotes The French learned from the Romans, and they, too, built big round towers, called *columbiers*, for their pigeons. Later these would be highly ornamented with geometric designs in multicolored brick or tile.

An interesting accessory to these dovecotes was a mechanism called a *potence*, a great post set in sockets in floor and ceiling so that it could revolve freely. Horizontal arms attached to it supported a ladder from which all the nests could be reached. Because the whole apparatus rotated, a man could pull himself from nest to nest without climbing up and down the ladder.

English Dovecotes Circular dovecotes were introduced into England in the 11th century by the Normans. They were massive structures with walls more than 3 feet thick.

Historians use wall thickness as one method of dating old dovecotes. Later dovecotes became lighter in scale and more decorative in design. They were often hexagonal in shape but could also be square or rectangular, the latter forms being easiest to build. Windows, in walls or dormers, were added; and usually there was a cupola at the top as well. Often a weather vane was used as a finishing ornament.

Construction was of various types of stone and rubble, and of brick in later years. Many Tudor dovecotes were half-timbered. No two were quite alike, although it was estimated that in the mid-17th century there were twenty-six thousand dovecotes in England alone. Many still exist; some have been converted into garden houses, others preserved as historical buildings.

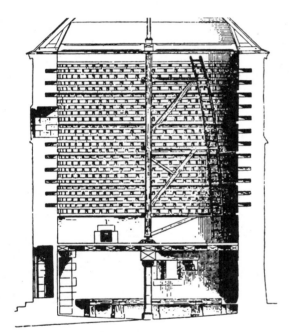

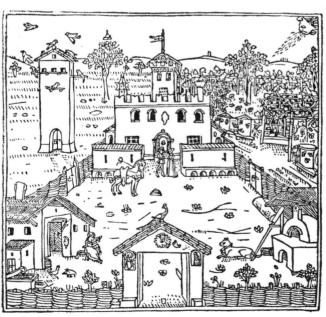

According to A. O. Cooke in *A Book of Dovecotes*, the day of the great dovecotes came to an end in England with the introduction of turnips and swedes (rutabagas) in the early 18th century. According to Mr. Cooke, this is not a paradox; before these fodder crops were available for winter feeding of livestock, all except breeding animals were slaughtered in the late fall. Thus, pigeons, once a principal source of fresh meat during the winter months, were no longer of vital importance. As dependence on them decreased, so did the size of dovecotes. Every country house still built its dovecote, but now only as a small turret or gable attached to another building or atop a garden wall.

Colonial American Dovecotes Several attractive dovecotes may be seen in the restorations of American 18th-century gardens. There is a fine round brick cote at Tryon, North Carolina, with a band of white stucco beneath a conical roof. Another small dovecote at Tryon is built as the top of a brick gatepost. At Williamsburg, Virginia, there is a simple white rectangular dovecote mounted on four posts.

By the 19th century most dovecotes had assumed their now familiar form of a small house set on a single post or column. Some were designed in chinoiserie or other exotic style, but most seem to be scaled-down versions of the large dovecotes of the past. Round or hexagonal, often with a miniature cupola or at least a finial, or squared with gables, these small dovecotes are well suited to take their place in the garden.

EDGINGS

Open Edgings Edgings and curbings are small but important details in the garden. They delineate, contain, and define specific areas where some sort of low barrier, either physical or visual, is needed to divert foot traffic or to separate ground covers or other surfacing. There are two basic types: open-work edgings—really small fences—and solid curbings of masonry or boards.

Some open-work edgings are made of woven wire and come in rolls or in short lengths that can be fastened together as needed. They are seldom more than 12 inches high, sufficient to deter pedestrians and polite dogs. They became popular in the 19th century for outlining flower beds. Sometimes a small circular or oval bed would be encircled with ornate wire edging, then a "handle" would be added on which vines would be trained. This ensemble resembled a basket of flowers and appealed very much to Victorian tastes.

Other edgings were of cast iron with various cut-out designs. They came in heights of 6 to 9 inches with spikes to push into the ground for support. Cast iron was also used to make semicircles in imitation of rustic branches, also with ground spikes. These could be placed end to end or overlapped.

Similar in shape, but totally different in character, are the lengths of split bamboo bent into arcs that are a gentle reminder in Japanese gardens to keep off.

Solid Curbings Curbings have several functions. They are used to outline planting beds to keep the shape crisply defined, to make a neat edge between beds and lawn or other surfacing, and to keep soil from washing away if

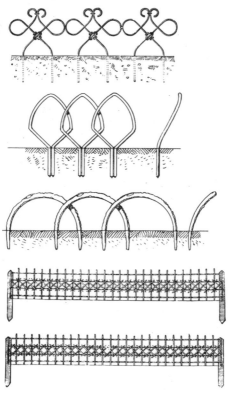

beds are slightly raised. Curbings are used to keep path edges straight and to give a finished appearance. They are important if the path surface is of gravel or loose aggregate to keep those materials from spilling into adjacent areas.

The simplest curb is of boards, usually 2 × 4s or 2 × 6s set on edge into the ground and supported by stakes. These are also referred to as *headers*.

In woodland or wild gardens rough branches may be staked in place to outline paths. A variety of materials are used for curb-ings, the choice depending on the character of the garden. Stone, adobe, tiles, and steel are used. Brick edgings are as popular today as they were in medieval gardens. Bricks may be laid flat, on edge, on end with even tops, or set diagonally to form a saw-toothed edge.

Precast curbings of concrete or terra cotta come in various designs, ranging from simple scalloped tops to more formal rope borders. They are made in manageable lengths, from 9 to 24 inches, and usually have accessory pieces for finishing—for example, corner posts and arcs for making circular-shaped beds.

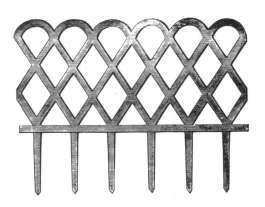

ESPALIERS *See Fruit Walls, Trellises.*

FENCES, BAMBOO

If you were to walk through ancient Japanese towns such as Kamakura or Kyoto, you would find the narrow streets bordered by beautiful bamboo fences. Even in some of the back streets of Tokyo they are still in use. They are made in a variety of styles, almost all of which are of ancient origin. Many have names that are associated with the temple or palace where they were first built. They are built in degrees of refinement to harmonize with the spirit of the gardens they contain. And although many Japanese streets present a virtually unbroken line of these enclosures, the impression they give is never oppressive. That is partly because of the natural materials that are used—usually bamboo or other local plants—and partly

because of the variations of form.

Kennin-ji Fences The kennin-ji fence takes its name from the temple where it first appeared, and it may be the most common bamboo fence in Japan. Kennin-ji fences may be classified into three main groups: common, or rustic; normal; and elaborate, or finished—according to the degree of refinement. Common to all kennin-ji fences is the basic tying of split bamboo uprights to a framework of whole bamboo posts and rails. Heavy wooden posts are used at intervals to provide support. In the common, or rustic, fences of the kennin-ji type, the splits are tied on one side of the rails and are left untrimmed at the top, without a cap. In the intermediate, or normal, grade the splits are also tied to one side only, but they are trimmed evenly at the top

and capped with a larger split. The elaborate versions are two sided; splits are attached on both sides of the rails and staggered, presenting a finished appearance on both sides and permitting a flow of air through the fence but cutting off most of the view. This version is also trimmed and capped. A cord made from the fiber of the sago palm and dyed either black or dark brown is traditionally used for tying. In some versions vines or creepers are used instead.

Kennin-ji fences may be made of heavy or fine bamboo, may be tall or low, sometimes appear in partnership with rock walls or other materials; but despite great variety of form, they remain true to the traditional structural design described above.

Nightingale Fences So called to evoke a picture of the stillness and serenity of the countryside, this ancient fence is made of small, untrimmed bamboo closely packed together and held upright by heavy bamboo posts and rails. In some fences the bamboo is first tied in bundles, then attached to the supporting rails; in other cases it is simply woven through the horizontal members. We have no idea how old the design is, but the print shown is from the 17th century. The design is still in use today, virtually unchanged in detail. Sometimes the nightingale fence is made from lindera twigs (spicebush) or ilex (Japanese holly), instead of bamboo. There are other variations: occasionally the tops will be trimmed to subtly alter the rough character, or the fence will be constructed of two or three tiers of shorter twigs.

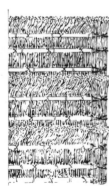
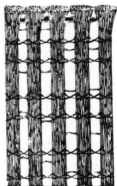

Open Bamboo Fences *Yotsume-gaki* is the Japanese word that describes a group of light and airy fence designs most commonly used within the garden where a change of function or mood occurs. Many of these designs originated in the 15th and 16th centuries at a time when the tea ceremony was an important part of Japanese culture. The object of the ceremony was to induce in participants a mood of serenity and detachment from everyday concerns, preparation for the discussions on the nature of beauty, art, and existence that fol-

lowed. The garden leading to the teahouse is called "the dewy path" and is deliberately made rustic to heighten the sense of isolation. Relatively low, *yotsume-gaki* fences are used to divide the garden and contribute to the woodsy and remote atmosphere of its inner reaches. Generally 3 to 4 feet high, the bamboo poles are staggered along horizontal members and are tied. These verticals and horizontals occur at regular intervals; although sometimes they are irregular. Often they are planted at the base, the fence itself

forming a trellis for vines and small trees. Support for these fences is provided by heavy wooden posts, set at the corners and at intervals in between.

Gates through the *yotsume-gaki* are light and open in the same spirit as the fences; the most common ones are simple bamboo frames with diagonal bamboo braces or a lattice pattern of diagonals. The latch is often nothing more than a loop of bamboo dropped over the fence post.

Roofed Bamboo Fences Japanese bam-

boo fences are sometimes roofed. This treatment is found generally in fences of some refinement and serves the purpose of preserving the life of the fence by protecting it from rainfall. Such roofs are usually made of thin wooden boards, thatch, or bark, depending on the type of fence being sheltered, and are supported by stringers and brackets that are attached to the main fence posts.

Sleeve Fences The Japanese call these fences *sode-gaki* because they resemble the sleeve of a kimono. Very common in Japanese gardens, they are always attached to a building or another fence at one end and extend a short distance, usually no more than 2 or 3 feet into the garden. Their function is to screen some portion of the garden from immediate view and to contain or direct views of the garden as seen from within an adjacent building. Sleeve fences are found in the same designs as regular running fences, as well as a number of more elaborate forms used only for this type of fence. Often these special designs have fanciful names such as "moon entering," "looking through," and "clothes horse." Often these fences do not block the view, but simply introduce an intervening structure to break up or interrupt it.

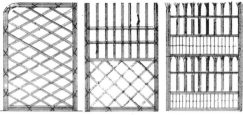

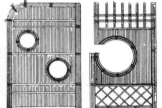

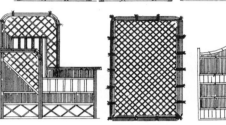

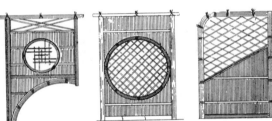

FENCES, CLOSE BOARD

Knowledgeable fencemakers distinguish between close and open board fences. Generally speaking, a close board fence is any wooden structure that divides space in such a way that a more or less solid barrier is formed, breaking the line of sight and restricting the flow of air. The archetypical close board fence consists of heavy posts that are planted in the soil at regular intervals and usually joined by a sill, or a plinth board, at the bottom and one or more rails, or stringers, above that. The intervening spaces are closed by less-thick wooden boards, sometimes called *pales*, which are fastened to the bottom member and stringers, usually in a vertical direction. Pales are often pointed (a detail that may be pleasing but also inhibits rot by shedding water) and, in some

instances, are cut square. As you will see on this and the following pages, within these rather simple limits are enormous possibilities for design variation.

The first close board fence was probably the *palisade*, a barrier formed by setting long poles into the ground, either vertically or obliquely, very close together. It was used for defensive purposes and generally was given pointed tops to discourage climbers. The word *pale* is most often used to describe a single vertical member in a fence, but it once meant the entire structure and also referred to the territory enclosed. The expression "beyond the pale" describes something or someone who is out of bounds. The word probably related to the Greek word *tele*, meaning far off or distant, hence our word *pale*ontology (and

others). *Pale* is also the word from which our words *picket* and *pole* derive.

Some of the earliest images of close board fences are in wood engravings of 15th-century medieval gardens. These early engravings tell us practically nothing about the gardens themselves, but the enclosure is unmistakable. Many of the fences shown during this period are equipped with little roofed gates. Notice the latch in this one. With the Renaissance, board fences seem to have virtually disappeared, to be replaced by masonry walls, iron fences, or trelliswork of the grand houses and palaces. Aside from an appearance in Holland in the mid-18th century, close board fences were not to be seen in significant numbers again until much later. The real revival came in England in the late 19th century.

Japanese Close Board Fences Fourteenth-century Japanese scrolls show close board fences very similar to ones built in medieval Europe. The Japanese versions are used for the outer enclosures for houses and temples, the lighter, open-work fences being reserved for inner divisions. Never painted, they are sometimes rubbed with fine pumice to a satiny finish and allowed to weather to soft silvery grays. Others are scoured by hand with sharp sand so that the hard grain of the wood stands out in relief. They are then rubbed with earth and moistened to promote the growth of moss. Small ferns are encouraged to grow in the cracks between the boards. Weathered lumber from old boats is sometimes used; the holes left by the original dowels provide interest and pattern to the fence. Another decorative method is to char the boards in random patches by burning them with torches.

Japanese close board fences are constructed with heavy wooden posts that are sunk in the ground and connected by a strong top rail and sill, or bottom rail. The sill is generally raised several inches above the ground and supported by stones set at 6- or 8-foot intervals. The boards are nailed flush to the rails, and the cracks are covered with thin strips of halved bamboo, or the boards are nailed alternately on either side of the rails, slightly overlapping, leaving slits for the passage of air. Grilled openings or windows are often let into these fences, allowing the passerby a glimpse of flowering trees or twisted pines inside.

Japanese gardens of any great size always have two outer gates, the main entrance and a smaller back gate, known as a "sweeping opening." The function of the latter is precisely that, a door to use when removing the trash after the garden has been swept. The main entrance is usually quite imposing, often a double gate flanked by a wicket for pedestrian use. Many are roofed. Wood, tile, and thatching are used, depending on the character of the garden. The doors are of solid wood, or, in less formal gardens, of woven bamboo. Latticework openings, or windows, are often introduced in these large doors to relieve the solid surfaces.

English Close Board Fences The revival of the wooden fence in Europe was brought about by the industrial revolution and the sudden emergence of a middle class. First in Holland, and later in England, newly prospering merchants built their homes along the lines of the great palaces of the nobility—only smaller. Since these "estates" were often quite small and in close proximity to the neighbors, the question of privacy was answered often with a wooden fence of the close board variety, partly at least because it was cheaper than building a masonry wall. In England, oak was the preferred material because it resisted rot. Left unpainted, these oak fences weathered to a beautiful soft gray. Less expensive models used oak for the posts and soft woods, such as pine, for the stringers and pales. These fences were usually painted either brown or a dull green.

Though restrained in a typically English manner, these late 19th-century fences look surprisingly modern and can be regarded as the European ancestors of a host of variations popular right up to the present day. (We also borrowed heavily from the Japanese to achieve the present close board fence.) Open work at the top of some of these early fences makes otherwise heavy construction look lighter, but it also allows "borrowed scenery" from outside the fence to add to the view on the inside. Height variations and the addition of finials lend some rhythm and grace to an otherwise monotonous structure. Heavy plinth boards give a good, solid look to the bottom of the fence, as well as protecting the cut ends of the vertical boards from ground moisture.

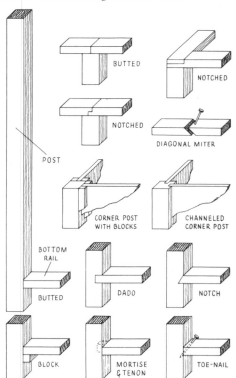

FENCES, LATTICEWORK

One of the oldest types of garden enclosures is the latticework fence. In its simplest form it is made of slender poles or lath laid in a criss-cross pattern and supported by posts. We see fences of this type in Roman wall paintings and in early medieval woodcuts. Over time the techniques became increasingly intricate until by the 17th century latticework was used not only for fences but for towering screen walls, temples, and triumphal arches.

Such latticework is discussed in the section on *Treillage*. In the mid-18th century small-scale latticework fences, often with a suggestion of Gothic influence, were used in romantic landscape gardens. Pattern books of the period included many designs that could be executed by estate carpenters.

Modern Latticework Fences The early 20th-century garden designer, Thomas Mawson, recommended latticework fences for situations where immediate effect was desired at little expense, but advised that the design should be of "very unassertive order, or it will compete with the flowering and foliage plants with which it is adorned." He quotes a Mr. Belcher, who maintained that the chief function of a latticework fence was the "seductive mystery gained by partly concealing and judiciously screening some parts from immediate view. By this means the imagination is tempted to conjecture the presence of hidden delights beyond."

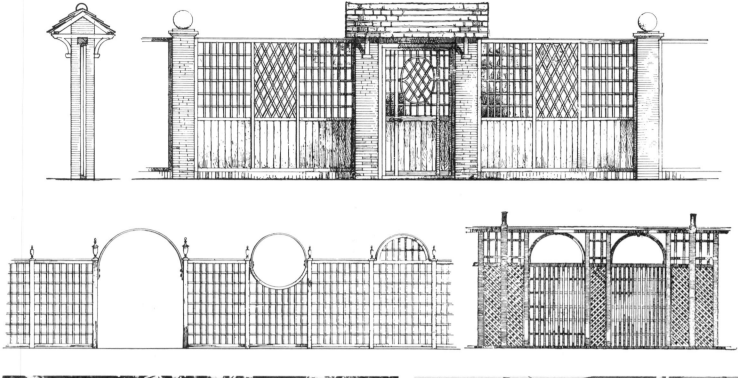

FENCES, METAL
Wrought Iron Fences Iron fencing and gates are made by two methods. The oldest and the one that has enjoyed a revival in the last century is wrought iron. Wrought iron work came into prominence in relation to architecture during the Middle Ages when beautiful screens and railings were forged to protect the sanctuaries and treasures of great cathedrals. In Renaissance Italy, wrought iron gates were sometimes used for important entrances or as clairvoyées to extend the view beyond enclosing walls. But it was not until the 17th century that wrought iron work was used extensively for exterior gates and fences.

The grand garden schemes designed by Le Nôtre for Louis XIV employed miles of such enclosures punctuated by elaborate gateways. The fences were basically composed of iron pickets topped with pointed heads of various shapes set between pillars of dressed stone or brick. This design served the double purpose of providing an effective barrier and at the same time allowing an unlimited view. It was in the gates that the ironworker displayed his inventiveness and talent, for gates were highly decorative and often gilded as befitted the palaces of the Sun King.

The French styles were introduced into England by the ironsmith William Tijou, who designed the magnificent gates and fences at Hampton Court as well as at numerous other places, often working in conjunction with architect Christopher Wren.

Imposing wrought iron work was used throughout the 18th century and into the 19th, though the designs in the 19th century tended to be simpler than those of Tijou and the workmanship less exacting.

With the development of inexpensive cast iron fences in the mid-19th century, the use of wrought iron virtually died out. It was not until the turn of the century that wrought iron craftsmanship was revived under the aegis of the new style called *art nouveau*. The art nouveau movement, led by artists and craftsmen in England and on the continent, rejected the ornate, cast iron styles, advocating a return to hand-crafted, honest workmanship. They drew their inspiration largely from Gothic ironwork, which they felt exploited the true nature of the material rather than disguising it as had the techniques of subsequent periods. Motifs for their gates and fences were often natural forms, stylized interpretations of leaves, flowers, and vines.

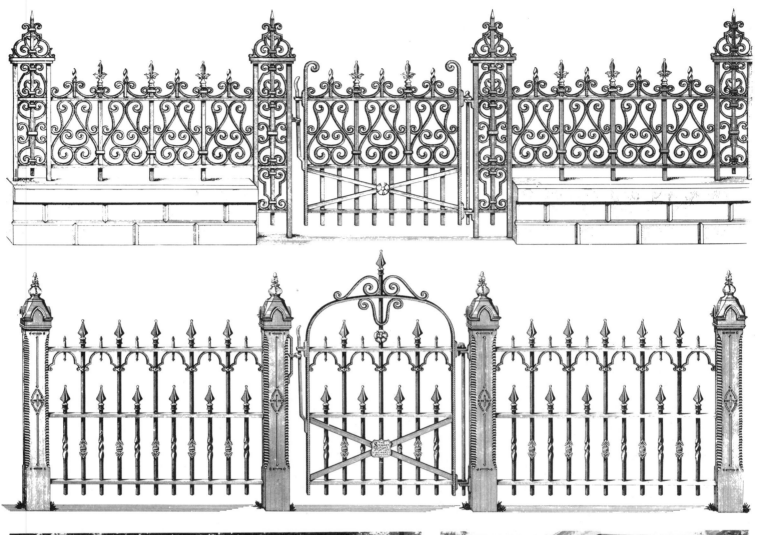

Cast Iron Fences In the 19th century, as industrialization spread and the demand for inexpensive ironwork grew, the manufacture of fencing and gates moved from the forge to the foundry, where they could be cast at a fraction of the cost of wrought iron. By 1850 manufacturers' catalogs and pattern books were widely available and homeowners could choose from a vast array of designs. In some, the components were cast separately and assembled; in others, cast ornaments and posts were combined with wrought iron pickets and scrolls; and still others were cast in large sections. The latter type provided the greatest freedom of design because it allowed for a complete departure from the restrictions imposed by wrought iron techniques.

Modern reproductions of these Victorian fences are often made in aluminum as well as iron, and manufacturers in both the United States and England will cast replacement parts for many existing fences.

Iron Wire Fences Another style of fence occasionally found during the 19th century used bent iron wire. This was neither wrought nor cast but simply bent, woven, then often fastened with cast iron rosettes. This type of fencing was particularly popular in Savannah, Georgia, though it was not unknown in other parts of the country. In one of the photographs below, the entrance gate on an Ohio farm doubles as a piece of playground equipment. It is a homespun gate of wood and wire, probably inspired by a more sophisticated catalog counterpart.

FENCES, OPEN BOARD
European Open Board Fences

Low fences of open design became popular in Europe and England in the mid-18th century. The inspiration for many of them were the balustrades depicted in Chinese paintings and the porcelains flooding into Europe at that time. The discussion of the actual Chinese prototypes appears in the section on *Paths*; here only the Western interpretations are discussed. Below are two patterns from the 16th-century Chinese garden manual, *Yuan Yeh*; an 18th-century French interpretation; and the "Chinese" fence at Williamsburg. The three

are a fascinating progression: a system of design developed over centuries of practice; a wildly romanticized pasticcio; and, finally, a pleasant and functional adaptation.

In the 19th and early 20th centuries a simple style of open board fence was being built in England. These unostentatious oak fences were often left to weather naturally or, if made of less durable wood, were painted dull green or brown.

American Open Board Fences

The earliest open board fences built in the United States were those fashioned from whole trees or sections split from whole trees, generally

described as *split rail* fences. As milled lumber became widely available, the split rail fence was refined and used to enclose gardens and grounds. The earliest ones were usually left unpainted. When cattle were to be excluded, such fences sometimes were given the extra lateral support of crossed poles and riders.

Today board fences are usually whitewashed or painted. They are from three to five rails high. The posts are usually set 8 feet apart, and the 16-foot rails are nailed with the joints on alternate posts. Post tops are cut straight across or at a slight angle and capped

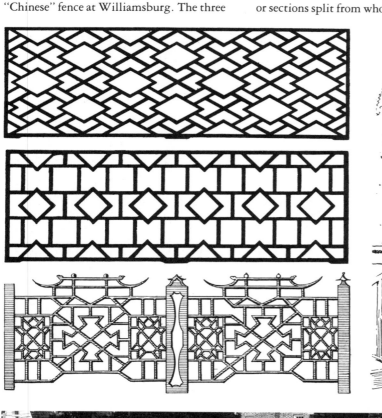

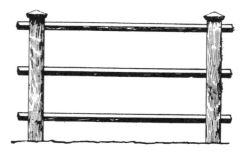

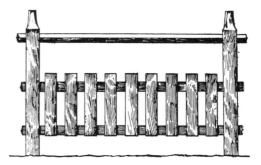

with a square of wood to prevent water from seeping into the cut end. Fences of a more finished quality have a facing board nailed over the posts to conceal the joints where rail boards meet.

Though open board fences are by definition simple, their openings are sometimes anything but. The old Stanyan Street entrance to San Francisco's Golden Gate Park, shown in the photograph below, is a good example of Victorian excess unleashed.

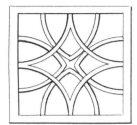
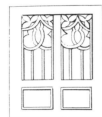
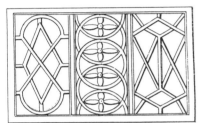
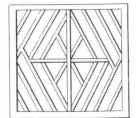
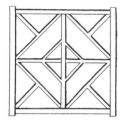
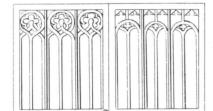

FENCES, PICKET

Oriental Picket Fences Picket fences appear in Chinese garden scenes as early as the eighth century A.D. These fences were made with square-cut palings and, as did most Chinese enclosures, followed the contour of the terrain. In the 17th-century Japanese painting reproduced opposite, a similar fence is shown, but this one is rectilinear and more solid than its Chinese ancestor. Similar styles are still in use in Japan today. The palings of these fences are made of heavy, square stakes, morticed to permit the rails to pass through them. The rails are bolted on alternate sides to the stakes. Such fences sometimes have two rails closely positioned at the top of the stakes and a single bottom rail raised well above the ground. In the low fence shown in the photograph below, the bottom rail is eliminated entirely and each picket is raised above the ground, and supported by a flat stone.

Medieval Picket Fences Picket fences were a common garden enclosure from the mid-14th through the 15th centuries in Europe and seem to have virtually replaced the earlier wattle fence toward the end of this period. The earliest picket fences were of the form still familiar today, palings with pointed or square heads nailed to rails top and bottom.

Colonial American Picket Fences The picket fence came to America on the Mayflower, along with the Brewsters, the Aldens, and the Standishes, and it flourished. The first ones in the New World were built at the Plymouth Colony. They were simple: boards, sharpened at the bottom, were driven into the ground and held together with a single rail along the top. Such fences were highly effective for preventing small animals from getting

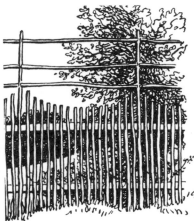

into the gardens, but the pickets soon rotted due to their contact with the soil. Longer-lasting fences were built with top and bottom rails connected to posts; the pickets were turned sharp end up and nailed several inches above ground level.

In 1705, when the colonial town of Williamsburg was being built, the law required that properties along Duke of Gloucester Street be enclosed by walls, pales, or post-and-rail fences within six months after a house was built. Today the restored picket fences alone present a fascinating assemblage of theme and variation.

These fences became the favorites throughout small-town America and the delight of every child who dared shatter the afternoon silence by running a stick along the street-long rows of pickets.

New England Picket Fences Though we have covered the picket fence of colonial America, we believe the New England variety deserves special mention, for there it reached the highest degree of elegance and refinement. The dignity and beauty of these wooden fences lifted them from their simple beginnings at Plymouth to nearly the level of an art form. Designed by the same builders who produced the lovely homes they enclosed, they functioned less as barricades than as frames for the architecture within. Open and inviting, they welcomed those outside to view and enter. The pickets in these fences are often reduced to slender squared or rounded spindles that are painstakingly let through the rails. The upper rails are sometimes straight but often curved, sweeping upward to meet posts topped with cornices and graceful urns. Sometimes these finials are carved pineapples, the ancient symbol of hospitality. Built of durable white pine and painted sparkling white, these lovely fences still line the tree-shaded streets of small towns from Connecticut to Maine.

Victorian Picket Fences The picket fences of the Victorian era and the early years of the present century became, as one might expect, more fanciful and elaborate. Some imposing examples had shaped and fretted pickets and posts resembling Gothic steeples or Italian bell towers. Others relied on lacy gates or decorative arrangements of pickets and rails to provide richness and what seems like endless variety. Country versions often had delightful posts with eaves to match those of the Gothic farmhouses they enclose. Some of these old fences still stand. Their descendants are to be found all over rural and small-town America. Some examples are shown on the following two pages.

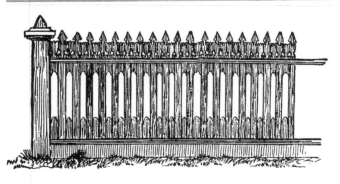

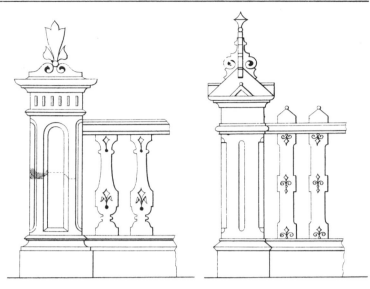

FENCES, POST AND RAIL

Worm Fences One of the most widely used forms of rural fencing in the early days of the American colonies was the Virginia rail fence; variously called a *worm*, a *snake*, or a *zigzag* fence because of its serpentine form. New Englanders, in revolutionary times, had a saying that a staggering drunk was "building a Virginia fence." In the well-wooded southern colonies these fences were the least expensive and most versatile type of barrier that a farmer could build. The 10- or 12-foot rails were split from oak or chestnut logs. A strong and experienced man could split a hundred rails in a day; and, in 1790, he would earn 50 cents for his labor if he could find a rich landowner willing to pay for it.

The rails were laid in alternate courses—one on top of the other—sometimes to the height of twelve rails. The zigzag shape of these fences gave them stability, even on steep slopes, and they required no scarce and expensive hand-wrought nails. Laboriously dug post holes were unnecessary, unless the farmer owned a particularly smart animal that had learned to knock the rails down, one at a time. If so, a more substantial support could be achieved by using two vertical posts at each corner. These might be placed on opposite sides of the fence or placed in the outside angles formed by the rails; the posts were then bound together with wire.

Straight Fences The northern colonists, in New England and Pennsylvania, generally preferred the post-and-rail fence. It could be built in straight lines and was more economical of land and materials than the sprawling Virginia rail fence, but it required more intensive labor and a wider variety of tools—posthole diggers and the augers to bore holes in the heavy posts that carried the rails. Durable, made of hickory and locust, these fences would easily last the lifetime of the builder.

Buck Fences The handsome buck fence, indigenous to the Teton region of Wyoming, is ideal cattle and horse fencing. It adapts easily to rugged terrain and requires no postholes. The supports, or bucks, are mitered where they cross, and the rails are either nailed or bolted to the bucks.

Hurdle Fences The hurdle fence, long in use in England, is one of the most attractive of the post-and-rail types. Each hurdle, or section, is constructed as a unit; the fence is then assembled by setting the post of one hurdle side by side with the post of the next and pegging them together near the top. These fences were, and still are, ideal for sheep pastures: they could be easily moved from place to place as the grass was depleted since only an occasional post was placed in a hole.

FENCES, RUSTIC
18th-Century Rustic Fences In the late 18th century, as a reaction to long years of formality and restraint, European garden planning underwent drastic changes; and landscape architecture, or the art of constructing seemingly "natural" plantings and vistas, was born. With this new concept came a predilection for exotic accessories, and some of the most popular were executed in what is known as the *rustic* style. These constructions were seldom truly countrified but were rather a romanticized interpretation of rural structures. The designs for fences in this style required the use of natural branches, usually with the bark left on them, assembled in intricate patterns, often with a Chinese or Gothic flavor.

Not a simple craft, skill and ingenuity as well as an almost unlimited supply of suitable branches were required to build these fanciful creations.

Victorian Rustic Fences Rustic fences continued to be popular throughout the 19th century. However, the later ones tended to be rather crude in design and workmanship. The materials used for these fences varied to some degree with locality, but for the most part the preferred woods for the supporting members were oak, chestnut, and beech, or, where perfectly straight pieces were desired, larch, fir, or pine. The lighter, bent members were made of hazel (prized for its smooth, decorative bark), split chestnut rods, willow, birch, or alder.

FENCES, WATTLE
Early Wattle Fences The first pictorial evidence of wattle fences is found in medieval manuscripts and paintings. The great numbers of such representations suggest a long and common use of wattlework for this purpose. Osier, or willow, branches were the most frequently used wattle material in Europe. The fenced plots were most often circular, though square enclosures are sometimes shown. The construction was extremely simple. Stakes driven into the ground at regular intervals were woven round with flexible branches in a simple basket pattern, forming a dense, rigid barrier.

The most common gate used with wattle fences was the high, roofed variety, either

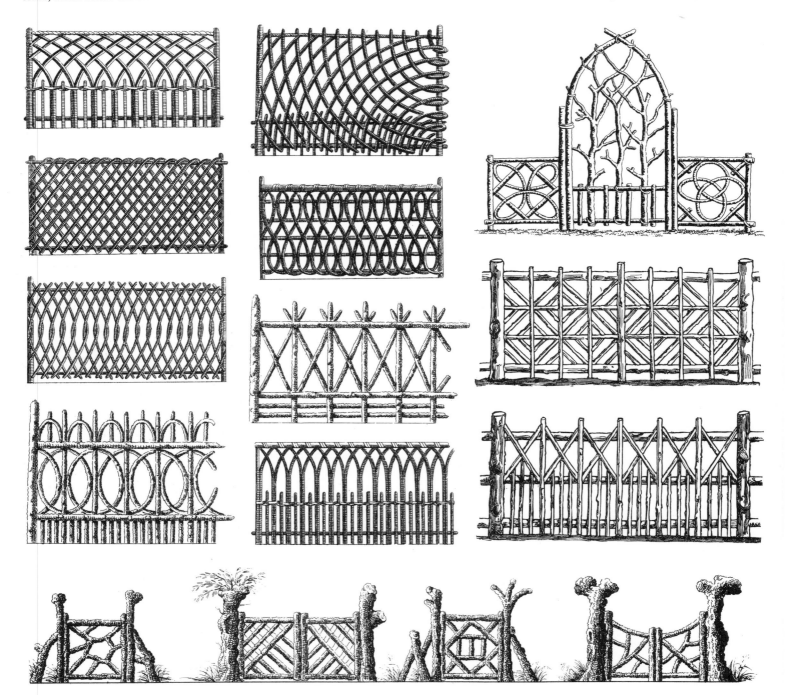

with a solid full-length door or a half-high gate. There is, however, one intriguing gateway in the 16th-century German illustration shown below worthy of the most romantic of the 18th-century, rustic style gates. The posts of gnarled, living tree trunks are trimmed to form a twisted arch. The gate is hinged in the center and on one post with what appear to be vines or, perhaps, leather straps. Stills,like the one pictured in this woodcut, were used to produce essential oils for perfumes, medical remedies, and flavoring agents.

Colonial Wattle Fences Early settlers in the American colonies relied on wattle fences to protect their gardens until more substantial fences of palings or rails could be built. In sparsely wooded areas, particularly in the

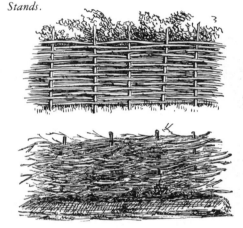

western states, wattle, or wicker, fences were a common sight until well into the 19th century.

English Wattle Fences At the beginning of the 20th century, wattle fences were still being made in the English west country. In 1926 Rural Industries, Ltd., in Cheltenham advertised prefabricated wattle fences in two sizes: those 6 feet long and 4 feet high sold for 42 shillings per dozen, while those 6 feet long and 3 feet high sold for 30 shillings per dozen. Custom-made fences could be ordered as well as wattle garden houses, furniture, wheelbarrows, and dovecotes.

FINIALS *See Sculpture.*
FISHPONDS *See Water, Natural Uses.*
FLOWERPOTS *See Plant Containers, Plant Stands.*

FLOWER BEDS *See Bed Design.*
FOLLIES *See Garden Houses, Gazeboes, Grottoes, Ruins, Towers.*
FONTS *See Bird Houses, Feeders, and Baths.*
FOOTBRIDGES *See Bridges.*
FORCING HOUSES *See Plant Houses.*

FOUNTAINS

The word *fountain* comes from the Latin *fons*, meaning spring. In ancient Greece, springs were held in deep veneration and were believed to be the haunts of water nymphs. The grounds around these springs were beautified with trees. Often marble basins were provided to catch the water. Later such springs were covered to prevent contamination, and the first architectural fountains in the Western world were created.

When Alexander the Great conquered Persia and established the Hellenic Empire, Asiatic influences began to be felt in the West. Fountains became elaborate and secular, losing most of their religious association. Generally, they were built into walls in the form of half-round niches and were decorated with statues and colorful mosaics. Such were the fountains that the Romans built in their small city gardens, often with the addition of a flight of marble steps, down which the water flowed into a shallow pool. Others were freestanding—a pedestal supporting a basin somewhat like a bird bath, out of which a single jet rose from the center.

Ancient Fountains From Pliny we know a little about the fountains of the great villa gardens of the Roman Empire. He tells of water gushing from under a marble seat into a cistern, filling a marble basin that was also used as a watery picnic table. Larger dishes were placed around the rim of the basin, while "the smaller ones swim about in the form of little vessels and water-fowl." Near that was a fountain that "throws [water] up a great height." Scattered about the gardens were marble seats: "near each seat is a little fountain; and, throughout the whole hippodrome, several small rills run murmuring along . . . watering here and there different spots of verdure, and in their progress refreshing the whole."

In medieval gardens a fountain was often the single decorative feature. Pictures in illuminated manuscripts show them to have been made of colored marble and often touched with gilt. Some were massive and architectural, while others were tiered basins embellished with carvings. The fountains often had four or more outlets that fed little channels leading to pools scattered throughout the garden or directly into planting beds. Some fed into pools that were used for bathing, a custom brought back from the East by the Crusaders. *See also Swimming Pools, Bath Houses.*

Spanish Fountains Some of the greatest fountain builders in history were the Arabs who invaded Persia and North Africa in the seventh century and Spain in the eighth. The garden style they brought with them was a mixture of elements appropriated from the people they had conquered, but their use of water was almost purely Persian. Their art lay not in huge displays such as those of Renaissance Italy but in extracting maximum effect from very little water. Water was the central element of every garden, and their fountains were made of rich and precious materials. In Morocco and especially in Spain good examples are still in place.

One of the most spectacular of these Moorish fountains is in the Lion Court at the Alhambra, shown in one of the photographs below. A great alabaster basin with a single central jet is guarded by eleven crudely carved but impressive marble lions. The fountain is encircled by a shallow channel, built to catch the water that overflows the rim of the basin and spouts from the lions' mouths and is carried off in four radiating channels.

Fountains more representative of Moorish style are small, have stone or marble basins set on pedestals or directly on the ground, and a single jet of water rising from the center. Others are built as small pools set in the pavement at the crossings of paths. Some have curbings from several inches to a foot and a half in height, others are flush with the pavement. These pools are lined with polychrome tiles, in zigzag or wavy patterns to give an illusion of depth and movement to the water. Most Moorish fountains are designed to overflow. The gleam of water on marble and tile and the small running rills and channels are extravagances in an otherwise hot and dusty climate.

Renaissance Fountains If there was an ideal time and place for fountains, it was Renaissance Italy; the country surrounding Rome and Florence was well supplied with water. In the year 1429 a manuscript entitled *De aquis urbis Romae* was found in the library of the monastery of Monte Cassino. *De aquis* was written in the first century A.D. by a Roman Commissioner of Water, Sextus Julius Frontinus. In it he gave detailed instructions for the construction of aqueducts and castella, the settling tanks used at distribution points, as well as methods for plumbing fountains. Because of Frontinus's manuscript, sophisticated

fountain technology was available to match the ambitions of 16th-century builders.

The Medici princes in Florence were the first to make use of these resources. The Villa de Castello, laid out in 1540 for Cosimo I, was named for the ancient Roman castellum that was incorporated into the water system. The central feature of the garden was a large three-tiered fountain surmounted by the statue of a woman wringing water from her hair. It is known as Florence Rising from the Waters and is shown in the photograph below.

The Boboli gardens, begun a year later by Cosimo's wife, Elenor, contain many magnificent fountains. The engraving below shows the Isoletto with its balustraded pools sur-

rounding a 24-foot diameter granite basin surmounted by the heroic figure Oceanus and three seated figures, representing the Nile, the Euphrates, and the Ganges. These were but forerunners to the great gardens of the Villa d'Este, the Villa Lante, and the Villa Aldobrandini, to name only a few. In these gardens water was displayed in many forms: shooting skyward in powerful jets, rushing down cascades and ramps, trickling over the brims of mossy basins, and reflecting clouds and cypresses in dark pools.

Italian fountains were copied throughout Europe, and many books were written detailing their construction. In Germany G. A. Booecklern published his *Architectura curiosa*

nove, showing hundreds of quaint fountain designs. The French, too, admired the Italian water gardens, but it was seldom possible to duplicate their lush effects in the gentle, less watered French countryside. French castles at that time did not lend themselves to the unified garden plans developed in Renaissance Italy. As a result, in the early years of the 16th century, the French simply added Renaissance surface decorations to what were basically medieval gardens.

The Fountains of Versailles In the mid-17th century Louis XIV began to build the gardens at Versailles and initiated the next great garden style. Since the supply of rushing water used so effectively in Italian gardens was not available, the fountains at Versailles were interspersed with huge reflecting pools and canals. The work at Versailles spanned a period of fifty years, during which time the garden was expanded and changed many times to accommodate the whims of the king and his current mistress.

While plans were under the direction of Le Nôtre, teams of sculptors, fountain engineers, and architects all contributed to the effort. As Louis's power grew, he adopted the sun disk as his symbol. The legend of Apollo, the sun god, became the motif for many of the large fountain groups. The Latona fountain, honoring Apollo's mother, was placed directly in front of the main palace. Below it, at the head of the mile-long grand canal, came the beautiful fountain depicting the sun god in his chariot, rising from the ocean with four Tritons blowing jets from conch shells.

The Marais, or marsh, was designed by the king's favorite, Madame de Montespan. It featured a tree in the center of a rectangular pool. Water spouted from every branch and leaf, while jets rose from metal bulrushes around the perimeter.

Many of the fountains were concealed in bosquets and side alleys, and by 1689 there were so many that the king published a guide for visitors to follow so that none would be missed. The tour took most of a day to complete.

Water supply was always a problem at Versailles, one that was never resolved. Despite cisterns and aqueducts that were built over the years, it was not possible to maintain sufficient water pressure to run all 1,400 jets at one time. As a result, a system of hidden paths was devised to enable unseen technicians to keep track of the king's progress. Thus fountains he had passed were turned off while those ahead could be turned on for a showy display.

Victorian Fountains From the mid-18th to the early 19th century, water appeared in gardens only as mountain torrents, winding streams, and ponds. Landscape gardeners of the period considered fountains to be artificial, contrived, and passé. In the early years of the 19th century, however, there was a gradual return to the use of formal elements, and fountains once again became popular. Pierre Boitard published designs for fountains from every period and style as well as fantastic inventions in pseudo-Egyptian, Moorish, Etruscan, and rustic styles. Inexpensive cast iron fountains became available for use in the most modest gardens and were popular in Europe and the United States up through the early 20th century.

Modern Fountains At the beginning of this century Gertrude Jekyll introduced fountain designs to complement her small and informal cottage style gardens. Her fountains were usually only simple jets rising from small pools or issuing from walls. She believed that "water needs to be employed very simply in small ones [gardens]. Little pools and rills and fountains, with their water not too vigorously 'jallissantes,' need to be disposed with a sparing hand."

At the same time, in the United States, a number of large gardens were built to rival the great gardens of Europe in their use of water. One of the most successful is the Italianate water garden at Longwood in Pennsylvania, where the fountains still display a full repertoire of effects. Nighttime shows include organ music and colored lights. Many less elaborate fountains, smaller antique fountains, fine reproductions, and contemporary designs are also found at Longwood.

Today, reproductions of Victorian cast iron fountains are still available as are components for some of the simpler Renaissance and 18th-century types. Antique fountains are occasionally available from dealers who specialize in garden furnishings. Modern designs, those developed in the last ten to twenty years, often rely more on manipulation of water than on sculptured basins and figures. Some of the most attractive of those designs are the clustered jets that resemble dandelion heads.

FRUIT HOUSES See Utility Buildings.

58

78

FRUIT WALLS

No one knows which gardener first discovered that fruit would ripen more quickly when the tree was trained against a sunny wall, but by the early 17th century fruit walls had become important in many European gardens. Over the years, there were innovations to protect the trees and to speed ripening. There were serpentine and zigzag walls; the trees were planted at the apexes of these walls, with the branches trained back on either side on the premise that in a cold snap or in driving rain only half of each tree would be damaged. Walls were sometimes built in a series of bays to provide protection and to increase the planting area. Other devices included curtains and sliding glass panels that could be drawn over the trees. Some walls were honeycombed with flues, then in cold weather the furnaces were fired up, and hot air was forced through the fruit walls.

Brick has always been the preferred material for fruit walls as it lends itself to hollow construction. Often walls are built with a cavity extending at least 2 feet above ground level to keep the wall warmer and reduce absorption of moisture from the soil. Brick also facilitates the attachment of the wire or lath grids on which the trees are trained. Wide overhanging copings protect the trees from heavy rain, or, in the absence of copings, iron brackets are fixed into the wall to hold protective boards and provide a place to attach bird netting as the fruit ripens.

Many espalier forms have been developed for the purpose of improving fruit size and quantity and for conserving space. As decorative and exotic as they may seem, they are completely practical. Many are still used today by commercial growers.

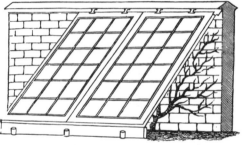

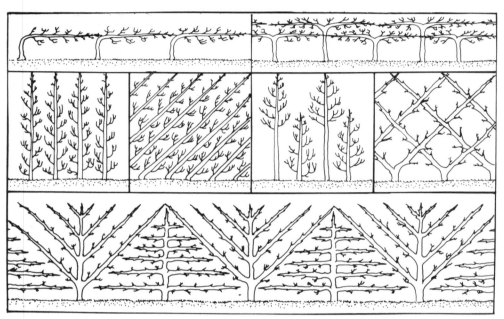

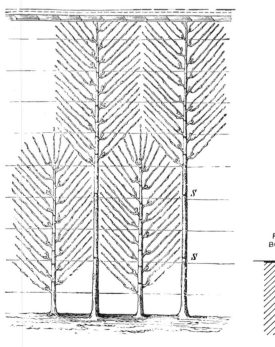

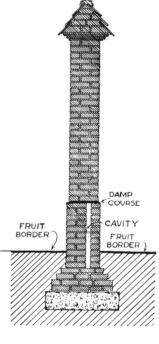

DAMP COURSE

FRUIT BORDER

CAVITY
FRUIT BORDER

FURNITURE
Stone and Masonry Furniture

Carved marble and stone have made graceful garden seats for centuries. The classic Italian Renaissance bench with trestle supports is most familiar, and variations of this design may be seen around the world in gardens large and small. Hand-carved stone furniture is no longer readily available, but good reproductions are made in cast stone and concrete. Both are surprisingly versatile plastic substances, which in skilled hands may be formed into almost any shape—from the sculpted modern to the rustic, which imitates rough tree branches and trunks.

Common cement, the binding agent for the sand and aggregate in concrete, is gray in color, but it is also made in white, which with the addition of marble dust can be used as a finish to simulate marble. Other additives can be used to imitate red or gray granite or other stones.

Concrete is shaped in several ways—in wooden forms or in molds of sand, metal, or fiberglass. Even carved polystyrene is used to form intricate designs. Another method of forming concrete is a technique called *ferro concrete*, used to build boat hulls but equally well suited for making garden furnishings. Here a stiff sand and cement mortar is shaped over wire mesh forms, much as a sculptor coats an armature with clay, until the desired shape is achieved.

47

Benches and seats are also made of brick; these can be freestanding or built in shallow alcoves as part of a garden wall. In Spanish gardens masonry seats are faced with polychrome tiles, which are smooth and cool to the touch, attractive qualities in furniture for a hot climate. The tiled solid fronts of these seats are slanted backwards to give foot room. Sometimes the wall behind a bench is tiled to look like the back of the seat.

Metal Furniture The 19th century was the "iron age" of garden furniture. With industrialization came the ability to mass-produce cast iron pieces of great intricacy. Once the original molds were made, cast iron chairs, settees, and tables could be produced inexpensively, furnishing the suburban gardens of the growing middle class. Some metal furniture was wrought by hand in the 18th century and was patterned after the elegantly restrained designs of the period. But these were

as nothing to the blossoming of cast iron during the Victorian era. And blossom it did; lilies of the valley, fern fronds, morning glories, and grapevines were all cast in lifelike detail as the backs, sides, and legs of furniture. Only the seats were made in flat, open-work patterns or of wood in consideration of the comfort of the sitter.

Iron was cast in the pointed arches and quatrefoils of the Gothic revival and in the rustic style as well, duplicating the discomfort of

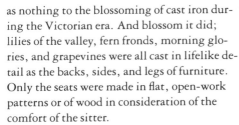

unbarked tree limbs in an even less resilient medium. Slightly less ornate were the garden settees that had wooden seats and backs. Only the side pieces of these bases were of patterned ironwork.

Cast iron fell out of fashion after the Edwardian era, but in recent years there has been a renewed appreciation of these exuberant Victorian designs. Some of the best of this garden furniture is being reproduced in cast iron or aluminum.

Wirework is delightfully frivolous furniture in which the intricate curves, so typical of Victoriana, were interpreted in scrolled wire, creating pieces that were light and airy and almost lacelike in appearance.

Wicker Furniture Wickerwork is defined as something made of plaited or woven twigs, sometimes of fruitwood, often of osier (wil-

low). However, *wicker* has also become a general term describing woven furniture of such materials as rattan, cane, reed, willow, raffia, rush, and other materials.

Wicker furniture is the offspring of the art of basket weaving, and is very likely as ancient. Pieces 4,000 years old have been found in Egyptian tombs, where the dry air of the desert has preserved them. Pliny described the Roman cultivation of the willow that was used to make carts, baskets, and furniture; and a third-century Roman carving shows a woman sitting in a wicker chair very like one that could be bought today. Basket, or "beehive," chairs of rush and peeled willow, so called because they resembled woven bee skeps, were in common use throughout medieval England and Europe.

Each culture has used the materials at hand for wickerwork, but the most common is rattan, an east Asian palm that grows the way vines do. It is valued because its long thin stems are strong, flexible, and naturally water resistant. It is used either whole or split to make cane for weaving seats.

Surprisingly, most of the wicker furniture so popular in America from the 1850s until the 1920s was made on the East Coast rather than in the Orient as might be supposed. Rattan was first imported to this country early in the 18th century, and a flourishing wicker furniture industry sprang up. The pliancy of rattan lent itself to the convolutions of Victorian design, and many pieces that might be termed "art wicker" are now valued antiques.

Wicker furniture is also imported from the

98

Orient. The fan-backed, "peacock" chair, with its hourglass base, is an example. Reproductions of Victorian designs are available as imports. Recently wicker furniture has again become popular and is now manufactured in traditional and contemporary designs.

Rustic Wood Furniture There is nothing truly rustic about rustic furniture or, indeed, any of the rustic styles that come into fashion periodically. They are the result of the apparently universal yearning of sophisticated people to return to nature, to get away from formality.

What we now describe as rustic style originated in the 18th century as a revolt against the excessive formalism of French and Dutch garden design and extended even to those small adjuncts of the landscape: garden furniture. By mid-century rustic furniture was highly popular. Like the Chinese furniture cunningly made of the convoluted roots of grape in which the sitter could imagine himself almost a part of a tree, the rustic furniture of the period was hardly natural; it was a highly articulated product of the craftsman's art. The materials were crude—branches of yew, apple, and pear were favored—but the results were most sophisticated. The vogue for rustic furniture was supplanted briefly at the end of the 18th century by renewed interest in classical Grecian forms.

Rustic furniture was revived as a byproduct of the romanticism of the early 19th century and once again late in the same century when it became fashionable for well-to-do Americans to spend their summers at camps in the woods. This latter-day furniture was more crude than the elegant designs of the 18th century, usually straight lined and rough hewn, but well suited to the character of the camp, where any hint of formality was banished.

It is necessary to distinguish between *rustic* and *country* furniture. The latter is made by country craftsmen for their own use. Examples include the handmade ladder-back rockers and bent willow chairs so typical of the southern mountain regions of the United States. But the distinctions have blurred as copies of this sort of furniture are now manufactured in many parts of the country and are as likely to be found in a city living room as in a country garden.

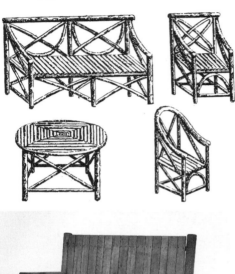

94

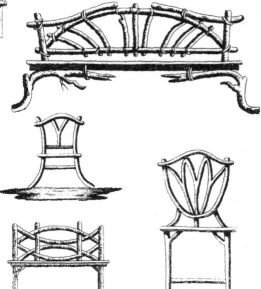

Formal Wood Furniture In the early days of the garden there was no special furniture made for outdoor use. People simply took tables, benches, and stools from the house when they wanted to dine or sit outside. Until the days of the Renaissance, even household furniture was sparse. Only the lord and lady of the house had armchairs; everyone else sat on benches or stools. Home furnishings included large chests and cupboards, often built in, and a trestle table for dining. These solid tables and benches of oak were well suited to a garden setting; their modern counterparts, the rectangular picnic tables with matching benches, are only scaled-down versions of refectory furniture that might have been found in an 11th-century abbey.

Much wooden garden furniture has kept to these plain designs; stylistic changes have been relatively restrained and confined to the design of the back and arms of chairs and settees. A good example is the 18th-century fretwork-backed garden furniture that is being reproduced today.

Redwood is the most popular wood for outdoor furniture because of its weather-resistant properties, although some oak and teak are still used. Much modern outdoor furniture is left in its natural color and treated with a clear preservative. If furniture is to be painted, white is the traditional color, chosen because it contrasts so pleasantly with background greenery. Wooden furniture that is to be left outside in a permanent location should have a footing of bricks or cement blocks, which can be sunk to ground level to be inconspicuous. Such footings protect the legs from rot and keep them from sinking into the ground.

GALLERIES *See Arbors.*

GARDEN HOUSES

If the urge to make a garden is a universal one, the urge to find a corner of it and build a little place of one's own is just as common. Garden houses are found in apparently endless variation in almost every culture with a garden history. As is the case with many other subjects in this book, terminology is traditionally used with some abandon, with descriptive names being applied without any perceptible distinction between them. We have sorted the subject into what we hope are logical categories and labeled each with one of the more evocative names. Here, *garden house* refers to a group of substantial structures intended to provide shelter from extremes of temperature and, in some cases, serve as short-term living accommodations. Other categories of structures are to be found under the headings: *Gazeboes, Pavilions, Sheltered Seats, Summer Houses, Tea Houses, and Temples*.

Chinese Garden Houses The tradition of the garden house in China is an old one. It goes back to the early poet-scholars who retired to rustic huts, called *chai*, in the mountains to write of the joys of life in the bosom of nature. The painting below is dated 1572, during the Ming Dynasty. In practice, however, the chai was not always a rude hut, nor was it always off somewhere in the wilds. They were as often found in gardens and, like the little house shown in the drawings below, were fully enclosed and quite elegant little structures. This garden house is in Soochow and has a formal-looking interior and latticework screens over the door and windows.

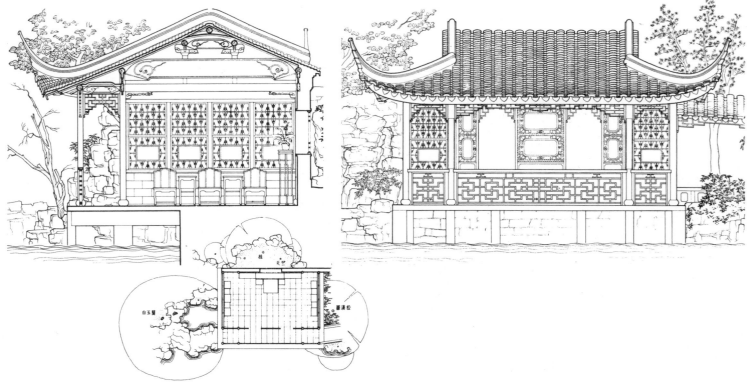

The Garden House in Italy The Romans built elaborate garden retreats where they could retire from the busy life of their villas and palaces. Pliny describes a garden house at his Tuscan villa that was made of "exquisite marble, the doors whereof project and open into a green enclosure; as from its upper and lower windows the eye is presented with a variety of different verdures. Next to this is a little private recess (which, though it seems to be distinct, may be laid into the same room) furnished with a couch; and notwithstanding it has windows on every side, yet it enjoys a very agreeable gloominess, by means of a spreading vine which climbs to the top and entirely overshades it. Here you may recline and fancy yourself in a wood . . . not exposed to the weather."

The Italian Renaissance palace was so integral a part of the garden that often the only additional shelter was provided by pergolas and grottoes. Occasionally a small building, called a *casino*, fulfilled the function of a garden house.

Banquet Houses Banquet houses were separate buildings where after-dinner wine and sweets were served in Renaissance Europe. The word *banquet* originally referred not only to a sumptuous meal, as it does today, but also to a collation of sweets served in a separate location. The practice began in the Middle Ages, when the entire household ate together in the great hall of the castle. When the meal was finished, the tables had to be removed before any further activities were possible, so it was the custom for the family and guests to stand and drink sweet spiced wine while the servants cleared the room. As domestic architecture became more sophisticated, a withdrawing room was provided for this purpose. By the 16th century, banqueting rooms in roof turrets, tree houses, or in separate buildings were common amenities in large establishments.

Many beautiful banquet houses were built in England in the Tudor period. The matched pair at Montacute are perhaps the most famous. One of them is shown in the photograph below. They are made of soft, yellow stone, their ogee-shaped roofs topped with little obelisks. Leaded-glass bay windows light all four walls. The lower rooms were used for storage of tools and fruit, while the upper rooms opening onto the terraces were used for banqueting and sometimes for lodging guests. Most such buildings were furnished with fireplaces or some other method of heating. A banquet house at Melford Hall in 1578 had a furnace in the lower room and flues to carry the hot air up through the walls.

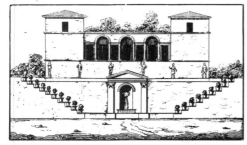

Secret Houses After-dinner entertaining was not the only use for garden houses. Some were built overlooking bowling greens or fish ponds to provide shelter for players and storage for bowls and fishing gear. Larger garden houses were used as secret houses, or hideaways, where one might retire away from the bustle of the household for several days at a time. John Woolridge in his book *Systema Horticulturae*, 1677, writes "that which crowns the pleasure of a Garden, is a place of repose, where neither Wind, Rain, Heat, nor Cold can annoy you. This small Edifice . . . may be made at some remote Angle of your Garden: For the more remote it is from your House, the more private you will be from the frequent disturbances of your Family or Acquaintances, and being made at an Angle, part within your Garden, and part without, you will have the privileges and advantages of Air and View, which otherwise you will want, and which render it much more pleasant than to be without them."

The Follies As English estate gardens became larger, the garden house proliferated. By the mid-18th century the landscaped parks of some estates covered many hundreds of acres. These gardens were meant to be toured on horseback or in carriages and were usually designed with one or more circuitous roads leading from one viewpoint to another. Shorter walking circuits were usually provided as well. In either case the tour of the gardens often led visitors a considerable distance from the house and because there was always the risk of being caught by showers, garden houses were positioned along the way for emergency shelter or simply as an amusing way-station where one could stop for refreshments and warmth. In some cases these houses served as living quarters for retainers as well, and a room would be set aside for the reception of guests.

In addition to such practical uses, the advocates of the romantic school of landscape design saw garden houses as ideal vehicles to create sensational and exotic points of interest. A hermitage was considered one of the most desirable of these effects, and if it housed a "hermit," so much the better. A man of appropriate appearance, who was willing to let his hair, beard, and fingernails grow and remain mute for a specified number of years, could retire after his service with a comfortable nest egg. The hermitages were grotesque little buildings; the walls were often made of twisted roots crudely filled with plaster, the roofs were thatched, and the floors were bare earth, or occasionally paved with sheep's bones.

Hermitages were not the only fantasies that appeared in these parks. Garden houses were built in the forms of battlemented Gothic castles, Greek temples, and Chinese *t'ings*. The English styles soon became the rage of all Europe: in France and particularly in Germany, garden houses were built in ever more exotic disguises. When the novelty had worn off the Gothic, the Greek, and the Chinese, they moved on to Egyptian, Moslem, and Swiss. Then when such geographic wandering had run its course, there was a return to nature; and garden houses were built as rustic cottages, mills, and woodsmen's huts.

American Garden Houses American garden houses dating from the mid-18th century reflect little of the European taste for exotic style. More often they harked back to the older Georgian idiom. The little octagonal garden house at Mount Vernon shown in the photograph opposite was used as a schoolroom. The exterior walls are made of wood, grooved to simulate brick. Fishscale shingles cover the graceful ogee-shaped roof.

Because there were few architects outside major cultural centers, early 19th-century

builders often worked from pattern books. When required to build a garden house, they would use only an element of a larger building, such as a cupola or steeple. Another common practice was to reduce architectural features and simply build a small version of a larger house. The small neoclassic garden house at Rosedown Plantation in Louisiana with its pillared portico was used as an office by the plantation doctor.

By mid-century the Gothic style reached a peak of popularity in the United States. The widespread use of wood for these buildings instead of the brick or stone favored in England lent these constructions an air of lightness and frivolity. The playhouse in the garden of General Vallejo's house at Sonoma, California, is one of the more fanciful examples of these carpenters' Gothic garden houses.

GATES *See Fences, Walls.*

GATEWAYS

Even though we have included many gates within the various sections on fences and walls, there are some gateways that by their very size and importance seem to require special treatment. They are the ones that give notice in a very special way of the beauty and grandeur within. In *Garden Ornament* Jekyll says, "The stranger entering a door or gate inevitably looks to it for an index of what and who awaits him beyond; the passer-by of what lies within. A good gateway should put the stranger into the state of mind in which he will see what he approaches to the best advantage; it should excite him and prepare him like the overture to an opera. Overstatement and understatement are alike undesirable. . . . An honest relation must exist between the entry and what is entered."

English Gateways Some of the gateways shown in medieval woodcuts suggest that they were derived from the fortified gatehouses of castles. The imposing entrances to many English estates of the Tudor period certainly owed their design to the early castle barbicans. Long after the need for such defenses, gateways were built with flanking towers and a room over the opening, as though to house the machinery for raising and lowering a portcullis. Gradually the fortress-like appearance was modified and the fortifications were reduced to a decorative parapet.

By the 17th century the arched gateways were replaced by two high piers that were sometimes flanked by wing walls, sometimes not. The piers were made of brick or beautifully detailed stone. The faces were often decorated in the Renaissance manner with bands of rusticated stonework, carved panels, and niches. Edwards, in *English Garden Ornaments*, suggests that the latter were provided as places for visitors to sit while awaiting admittance to the grounds. Obelisks, urns, heraldic beasts, or other appropriate statuary crowned the massive piers. Gates and overthrows of

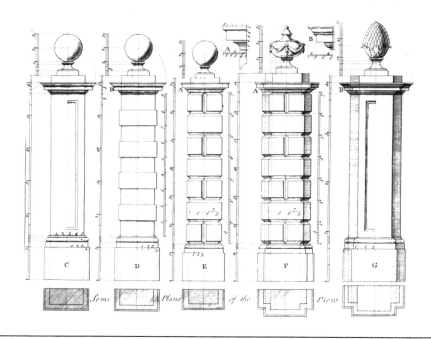

lacy wrought iron allowed a clear view of the avenue, or forecourt, and mansion within.

Italian Renaissance Gateways The great entrance gateways of the Renaissance palaces and villas were dramatic and decorative, exuberant promises of the grandeur to be seen within. Their towering pediments and sweeping wing walls were lavishly decorated with urns and statuary, one more example of the virtuosity and daring of Renaissance builders. In contrast to their elaborate stonework, the wrought iron gates were relatively plain and unpretentious.

American Gateways The lovely gateways of 17th- and 18th-century England were carefully copied in Colonial American gardens but

were generally reduced in scale and were of simpler design. Later, as the country absorbed influences from elsewhere, gateway styles became diverse, generally reflecting whichever architectural inclination was to be found in the accompanying house and accessory buildings.

In the photograph below, the plain brick piers and wing walls and lacy wrought ironwork of the entrance gate at the Elizabethan Gardens at Manteo, North Carolina, form a pleasant frame and screen for the flower beds located within. Also shown is the smaller but equally impressive gateway at Filoli near San Mateo, California. Here the ironwork is cast, and the gate is under the scrutiny of the

matched eagles that perch atop the piers. Additional American gates and one remarkable Victorian wooden gateway can be found in the sections on *Fences* and *Walls*.

Lych Gates Lych gates are descendants of the roofed gates used in medieval gardens. From the 16th century on they were used in England almost exclusively at the entrances to churchyards. The wide overhanging eaves provided shelter for the bier and pallbearers while the burial service was read. In the early 19th century they again became popular as garden gates, primarily for smaller, less formal estates and suburban villas, many of which were in the Gothic style.

GAZEBOES

The origin of the word *gazebo* is something of a mystery. Some garden historians insist that it is a Dutch word. However, Webster's dictionary gives a different and more amusing explanation of its source. It suggests that the word is an amalgam of the English word *gaze* with the Latin suffix *ebo*, making it "I shall gaze," a sort of 17th-century pig Latin. Because *gazebo* originally referred to the small structure that overlooked the walls of an enclosed garden, this makes some sense. The fact that the old English gazeboes were copied from or at least influenced by Dutch designs may account for the belief that the word was Dutch.

The Dutch gazebo was a small, solidly built structure placed at the corner of the property where it was bordered on one or both sides by canals. It was really more akin to the buildings we have categorized as garden houses. It was used as a banquet house and as a comfortable vantage point from which to watch the world go by on watery highways. An English traveler in the 18th century found them a doubtful pleasure. He reported that "every flower that wealth can purchase diffuses its perfume on the one side, every stench a canal can exhale poisons the air on the other."

While the word *gazebo* has retained the implication of a building with a view, modern usage refers to a more open, airy structure, and it is with this in mind that we have used gazebo. We have included in this section the Oriental versions as well: the Chinese *t'ing* and the small Japanese buildings that are used as viewing shelters. *See also Garden Houses, Pavilions, Tea Houses, Temples*.

The Chinese T'ing In Chinese landscape paintings the two dominant features are mountains and water. Where those are present, there is usually a small open building, or *t'ing*. As Maggie Keswick says in her book, *The Chinese Garden*, the t'ing "symbolises man's tiny but essential place in the natural order: just as without man nature lacks a focus, so too a garden landscape can scarcely exist without a *t'ing*." The Chinese t'ing is a small open building that may be placed on a rise where it commands a view, in the center of a bridge, at the top of a rockery, by the edge of a pond, or in the heart of a bamboo grove, anywhere that one might want to idle away an afternoon enjoying the scenery or the sound of lapping water. The t'ing is usually raised on a stone platform two or three steps above ground level. An overhanging roof of glazed tile is supported by heavy beams and posts. Occasionally they are enclosed but more often open, encircled by a low wall with a slanted balustrade that also serves as seating.

Japanese Open Shelters Early Japanese gardens were usually designed to be viewed from one principal vantage point, the hall or veranda of the major building. But the development in the 15th century of the tea garden with its meandering "dewy path" influenced the design of gardens unrelated to the tea house. These gardens were meant to be viewed from various points, and small shelters were provided for that purpose. The structures were made in various degrees of refinement but always of simple materials. The roofs were thatched or shingled with bark; the walls were of plaster or unfinished wood. The more refined versions had raised floors covered with matting, but generally they were paved with stone or tile. They were furnished with built-in wooden benches or porcelain tubs for seating. These little shelters, which are still popular today, are built at the crest of a hill or near a waterfall or stream, where the sound of rushing water can be enjoyed. Some are built on pilings over a pond, a place to sit and admire water lilies and carp or the reflection of the moon. Such shelters are given names alluding to some ancient legend or that suggest the beauties to be admired, such as "The Arbor of Reddening Foliage," "The Cascade Viewing Arbor," or "The Heart-Cleansing Arbor."

18th-Century Gazeboes and Kiosks

Throughout the landscape and Anglo-Chinese gardens of Europe in the 18th century, small open structures were introduced to provide shelter. Many were styled after the t'ing, which was a prominent motif in Chinese porcelains and paintings being imported at that time. These European gazeboes only superficially resembled the Chinese models. The application of fretwork balustrades, up-curved eaves, bells, and dragons to basically Western structures was, in most cases, as close as they came to the originals.

The taste for unusual styles did not end with the Chinese. Gazeboes were soon built in every exotic architectural style that a fertile imagination and a blithe disregard for authenticity could invent. This may be the period when the word *kiosk*, or in French *kiosque*, came into popular use for garden shelters. The word is derived from the Turkish *koshk*, meaning pavilion, which is derived from the Persian *kushk*, meaning palace. Persian palaces were always set in gardens. The kiosks were generally smaller than other gazeboes and most often reflected a flavor of the Near East with mosquelike roofs, Moorish arches, and Arabic symbols, though there were kiosks built in the "Gothick" and "Rustic" manner as well.

Colonial American garden designers rarely copied the more fanciful styles popular in England and on the continent. They were content, on the whole, with the more conservative Dutch-English models, though an occasional note of exoticism crept in. A small gazebo at Williamsburg with a Chinese balustrade and a matched pair of "Gothick" gazeboes at Gunstan Hall (see photographs below) reflect, if only faintly, the rampant romanticism of the period.

Victorian Gazeboes Exotic garden buildings continued to be popular well into the 19th century, but the rustic, the Gothic, and a style called either German or Swiss, along with the ubiquitous classic temple, predominated. In England members of the newly affluent middle class, created by the industrial revolution, were beginning to build their own gardens. The emphasis of garden design also was changing. Flowers were becoming more important than architectural embellishments. As a result, less pretentious and less expensive structures that could be built by amateurs or country carpenters were in demand. The rustic style was most adaptable for this purpose and consequently one of the most popular. Victorian rustic gazeboes were generally less complicated than their 18th-century predecessors.

In America both Gothic and Swiss designs appeared in builders' pattern books, but the old Dutch-style gazebo never lost its popularity. The same basic square and octagonal buildings were retained and fancied up with scrollwork brackets, turned finials, and latticework panels.

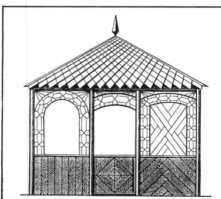

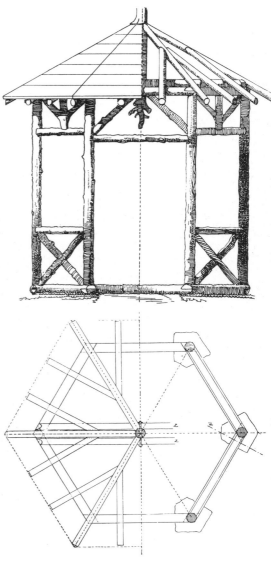

Modern Gazeboes After the turn of the century, gazeboes of a more substantial nature were occasionally built. J. C. N. Forestier's solid and rather austere little buildings with their tile roofs reflected his predilection for Spanish-style gardens. Two examples are shown in the renderings below and to the right. Inigo Triggs designed a half-timbered gazebo, tying it into architectural continuity with the house. But the gazeboes that have retained their popularity to the present day are the reproductions and adaptations of the old 18th- and 19th-century designs. Despite the simple, unornamented balustrade and posts, the modern gazebo, designed by Thomas Church and built on a platform, retains a distinct resemblance to its flamboyant ancestors.

GLASS HOUSES *See Plant Houses.*
GLORIETAS *See Pleached Trees and Shrubs.*
GREENHOUSES *See Plant Houses.*

22

GROTTOES

Ancient Grottoes Garden grottoes in Europe originated with the classic Greek nymphaeum. Certain sites, often a rocky cave with dripping water and ferns and a hint of mystery, were set aside as places to make offerings to nymphs. Artificial nymphaea copied the natural grottoes, and these later became a staple in ancient Roman gardens. Strabo wrote of the natural caverns along the Tyrrhenian Sea that were transformed into elegant cool chambers for the Roman villas built along the coast. Such a cavern discovered at Sperlonga in 1957 is believed to be part of the first-century villa of Emperor Tiberius. The grotto had a large pool, and the walls still bear traces of the paint, stucco, mosaics, and inlaid seashells that decorated it.

Chinese Grottoes Rocks of strange and irregular form were important in Chinese gardens as symbols of sacred mountains. Grottoes, formed in artificial hills or rocks "oddly heaped together," had Taoist and magical associations. These grottoes never achieved the architectural excesses of their European counterparts; the rocks themselves were enough decoration. Gothein quoted Hsi-Ma-Kuang's 11th-century description of the grotto in his garden, which "makes a kind of irregularly-shaped room with an arched ceiling. The light comes in through a . . . large opening hung round with wild vine and honeysuckle. Rocks serve as seats, and one gets protection in the blazing dog-days. . . . A small stream comes out on one side and fills the hollow of a great stone, and then drops out in little trickles to the floor."

The photograph shows an early 20th-century grotto in a Hong Kong garden. The bold concrete stairs visible through the archway would never have been used in a traditional Chinese garden; rather they would have been made of rough stone and artfully concealed.

European Grottoes Italians of the early Renaissance attempted to re-create the glories

of ancient Rome. The 15th-century architect Leon Battista Alberti designed grottoes "because the ancients had them." Grottoes in many extravagant forms were an important part of garden architecture: as separate structures, in the ground floors of buildings, or under terraces. The exterior was usually of normal appearance. The inside might simulate an underwater cavern with mosaic shellwork and strange fish. Other grottoes were decorated with tufa in grotesque forms. Water was always present, in drips, gurgles, fountains, and water surprises.

By the mid-16th century every large garden in Europe had its grotto. Most unusual was one designed by Pallisy for the Tuileries garden of Catherine de Médicis. It was filled with lifelike animals and lizards, glazed, then fired as in a huge kiln so that the interior shimmered with an iridescent enameled finish. Guernieri's engraving, 1706, shows another kind of grotto, with a wild and rocky facade concealing an opulent interior.

Later 18th- and 19th-century versions were rustic and grottoesque both inside and out. Most of the drawings shown on these pages are from this later period.

Modern Grottoes Grottoes are not entirely things of the past. A modest but effective one was made in the 1920s in the garden at Blake House, now the official residence of the president of the University of California. Here a small chamber is set into a rough stone retaining wall. It is fronted by a shallow raised pool and is flanked by curved stairways leading to the wooded hillside above. Although small, it shares the qualities of ancient grottoes—contrast of bright sun and cool darkness, the gurgle of underground water, and just a hint of an otherworldly presence.

HA-HAS *See Walls.*

HEDGES

Hedges have served as alternatives to masonry walls and fences since the earliest times. In climates that encouraged the lush growth of trees and shrubs, they were probably the first form of garden enclosure. The Romans used clipped hedges to outline flower beds and paths and as boundaries and divisions within the garden. A ditch and a high thorn hedge made a common and effective enclosure for medieval gardens when they were first built outside castle fortifications. In Renaissance gardens hedges were at first used in much the same manner as they were in Roman times; often cut into fanciful shapes. Low box hedges outlined the geometric knots and parterres and bordered terraces. High hedges lined the avenues and formed backdrops for fountains and statuary. *See also Bed Design, Topiary.*

French Hedges The architectural use of hedges reached its zenith in the great French gardens of the 17th century. At Versailles, Marly, and Saint-Cloud, high hedges were clipped and shaped so precisely that they scarcely resembled living plants. They lined miles of allees cut through dense groves of tall trees and walled the innumerable bosquets of the Sun King's vast domain. They were shaped to simulate porticos and pilastered walls and formed niches for statues and fountains. An army of gardeners on wheeled platforms were needed to keep them trimmed.

Dutch Hedges The French garden style was soon emulated throughout Europe, but in the Netherlands it underwent a transformation. The high winds and shallow soil of the lowlands made the culture of large trees impractical, and, as a result, Dutch gardeners often had to rely on hedges alone to create arboreal effects. Because land was scarce and divided by canals, everything had to be simplified and reduced in scale so that a variety of decorative effects could be fitted into a small space. As a result, topiary art and fancifully clipped hedges and trees retained their popularity in Holland long after they were considered passé elsewhere in Europe.

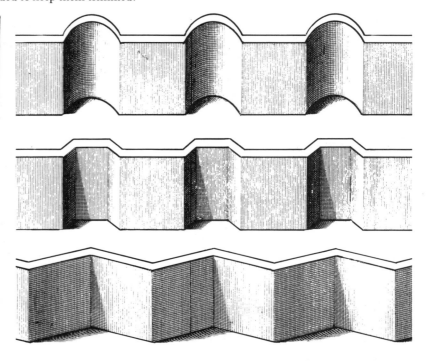

English Hedges The French-style gardens came late to England and with a strong Dutch influence, for it was during the reign of William and Mary that many of the great English estates were remodeled in "the grand manner." Smaller gardens were more often done in the Dutch style with clipped hedges of holly, box, or yew and ornamented with topiary specimens. It was these more modest gardens that English colonists in the New World copied. We see this influence in the prim, clipped hedges and borders of the restored gardens at Williamsburg and plantations throughout the southern United States. These hedges are most often of holly or box because yew did not transplant easily, and many of the oldest have been allowed to grow freely until

they have billowed well beyond their original boundaries.

In England only a few of these magnificent hedges escaped the axes of the landscape gardeners in the mid-18th century who considered them one more example of the abominable "Dutch busyness." The only hedges tolerated were those used to screen an estate from the public road or to conceal an enclosing wall, and they were left unclipped.

Modern Hedges Through the 19th century there was a gradual return to more formal elements in garden design. Enclosed geometric gardens were often found nearest the house with less formal landscaped areas beyond. By the early 20th century Italian, Tudor, and Dutch-style gardens had all reappeared, and

with them clipped hedges in all their various forms. Gertrude Jekyll, writing during this period, had this to say about that favorite of all English hedging materials, the yew: "Hedges of yew with turf alone have an extraordinary quality of repose—of inspiring a sentiment of refreshing contentment. . . . Compared with the yew no tree is so patient of coercion, so protective in its close growth, or so effective as a background to the bright bloom of parterre or flower-border. Its docility to shaping into wall, niche, arch and column is so complete and convenient that it comes first among growing things as a means of expression in that domain of design that lies between architecture and gardening."

Japanese Hedges Clipped hedges are

used in Japan both for outer enclosures and for divisions within the garden. Camellia, cryptomeria, and ilex, prized for its cedarlike scent, are popular hedging materials. Hedges are often used in combination with fences and walls, or with other hedges, that is, a low hedge of one material backed by a high hedge of another.

HERBACEOUS BORDERS *See Bed Design.*
HERMITAGES *See Garden Houses.*
JARDINIERES *See Plant Containers, Plant Stands.*
KIOSKS *See Gazebos.*
KNOT GARDENS *See Bed Design.*
LABYRINTHS *See Mazes.*
LAKES *See Water, Natural Uses.*
LATH HOUSES *See Plant Houses.*

LIGHTING

Decorative Lighting Lanterns are the most commonly used decorative fixtures, and they are often reproductions in brass or iron of antique gas and oil lamps. They are mounted on walls, on gate piers, or on posts of wood or cast iron or aluminum, and are generally used as entrance lights. Hanging lanterns are also used in the garden, and temporary strings of colorful paper lanterns have long been popular for garden parties.

Low-standing spread lights, seldom more than 3½ feet tall, are useful for illuminating a general area, especially steps. Path or border lights, usually less than 2 feet high, are shielded to direct light downward so as not to compete with other landscape lighting. These come in a variety of designs and are usually finished in green to better harmonize with plants.

Concealed Lighting Concealed, or landscape, lighting offers a number of possibilities for illuminating the garden. There are many different fixtures that can be used to create varied effects: lights that shine up, those that shine down, spotlights, lights that are buried in wells, and lights that are used singly or in combinations. All are designed to be as unobtrusive as possible and are usually hidden in shrubbery or trees.

Japanese Stone Lanterns The distinctive garden lanterns of Japan were originally patterned after the hanging bronze lanterns used in Buddhist temples and shrines. Similar designs, carved in stone, were introduced into the garden by tea masters in the 15th and 16th centuries. Supplied with small oil lamps, they were used to light the way for guests at evening tea ceremonies. Individual styles are still known by the name of the temple where the design originated or by the name of the tea master in whose garden they first appeared. Custom dictates the use of a particular type of lantern for a given site, the lantern always harmonizing in size and shape with the character of the garden. The use of these lanterns has become more decorative than functional, but even so, in the formalized design of the Japanese garden they are rarely placed except where light would be needed: by a gate, by a water basin, or to mark the turning of a path, and usually in artful combinations with stones, shrubbery, and trees.

The principal forms of the stone lantern are: the buried lantern, or *ikekomegata*, whose shaft is sunk in the ground (a variation of this form, which is in the form of a thatched-roof cottage, closely resembles some Western lanterns); the open-legged, mushroom-roofed *yukimigata*, or snow-viewing lantern, so called because of the attractive way its broad roof bears a mantle of snow, is usually placed where its light reflects in the water; the smallest lantern, the *okgata*, is used near pathways; the tallest, the pedestal lantern, or *tuchi-gata*, has ornamental carving on the base and lamp housing and a hexagonal, curved roof with up-turned scrolls at each point.

91

95

91

78

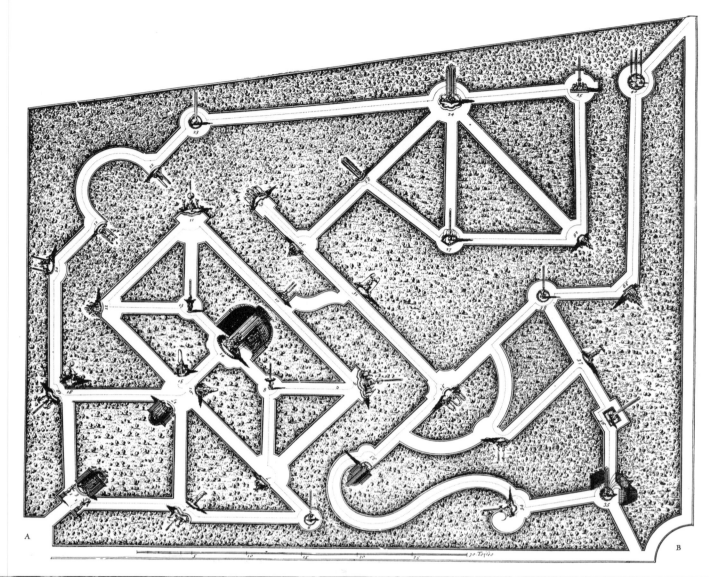

MAZES

A maze, or labyrinth—the terms are used interchangeably—is a network of paths or passages through which it is difficult to find the way. The origin of the maze is obscure, reaching far back in time even before the fabled Cretan labyrinth was built. They may once have had some mystic, or perhaps defensive, purpose, but since the Renaissance the principal use of maze and labyrinth has been as decoration and diversion in the garden. Some mazes are planned so that by simply following the turnings of the path one may arrive at the center; others are more complex and challenging, with numerous dead ends. In either case the goal at the center may be a pavilion, an arbor, a fountain, or a tree.

Hedge Mazes Some hedge mazes were only 3 to 4 feet high, but by the early 17th century higher hedges were being used because they provided more sport. Lawson advises, "Mazes well framed, of a man's height, may perhaps make your friend wander in gathering of berries till he cannot recover himself without your helpe." The maze at the Villa Garzoni in Tuscany had an extra fillip. In the grotto at the center was a tap that activated water jets along the paths. The first person to find the grotto had the pleasure of turning them on and wetting everyone still lost in the maze.

A famous and elaborate labyrinth was designed by Le Nôtre for the gardens at Versailles. The plan is unusual in that it is not made in concentric rings or geometric shapes but rather as wandering paths. The puzzle was to find all forty of the painted lead statuary groups with fountains illustrating Aesop's fables. This maze was built in a bosquet, with paths bordered by green latticework backed by high hornbeam hedges.

Garden mazes reached America in the late 17th century, and one was set out at the Governor's Palace at Williamsburg. Mazes continued to be planted as amusements in public resorts until the late 19th century. The circular maze in the photograph (opposite) was planted in 1892 at the Hotel Rafael, in San Rafael, California, by a Mr. Ulrich, who also designed a square maze for the Del Monte Hotel at Pebble Beach, California.

Floral Labyrinths Some of the early mazes were just another form of parterre design worked out in low-growing herbs or flowers. Thomas Hyal, in his book *The Profitable Arte of Gardening*, suggested that these mazes be planted with winter savory, "time," "issop," lavender, and "majerome." There was little challenge to these fragrant mazes because they usually consisted of only a single path, and, in any case, one could easily step over the divisions.

MONOLITHS *See Rockwork.*
MONUMENTS *See Sculpture.*
MOSS HOUSES *See Summer Houses.*

MOUNTS

The use of mounts, or artificial hills, in gardens is almost as old as gardens themselves. As early as 2200 B.C. the Sumerians made entire gardens in the form of mountains. These ziggurats were stepped pyramids built of clay bricks, planted with trees, and watered by an elaborate irrigation system. On the top was a sacred grove and a temple. The Hanging Gardens of Babylon, built some 1,500 years later, were probably very similar in form to the early Sumerian mounts.

European Mounts The mounts built in Western gardens were never intended to imitate natural scenery. In medieval gardens they fulfilled several functions. Early ones served as convenient watchtowers in time of war, and in peaceful periods as pleasant aeries from which to view the countryside and catch a summer breeze.

In Renaissance gardens mounts provided high vantage points from where the intricate patterns formed by parterres and knot gardens could be seen to best advantage. They were particularly popular in areas where the terrain was flat and were only rarely found in the terraced gardens of Italy. Renaissance mounts were usually built of bricks or stone, covered with earth, and planted with trees or shrubs. Some of these artificial hills were free standing, often as the central feature of a maze and topped with a light arbor or, in colder climates, with a substantial garden house. They were provided either with straight flights of steps up one or more of the sides or with a spiral path to the top.

Another form of mount was built against an enclosing wall that provided a balustrade for the top platform. These were usually rec-

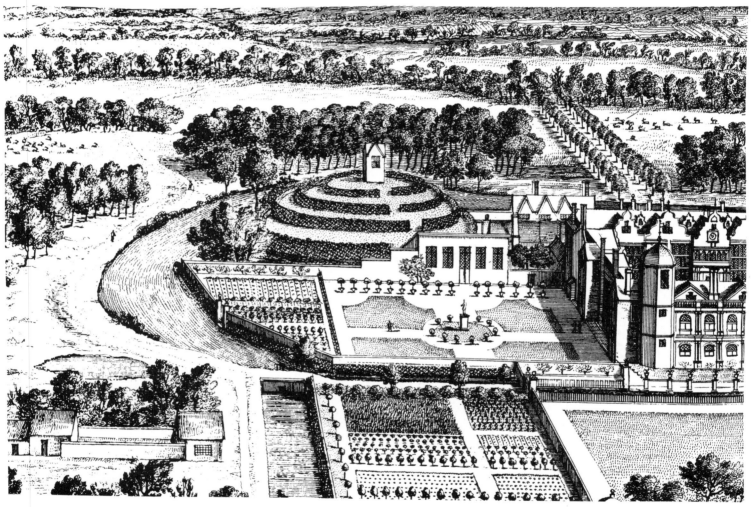

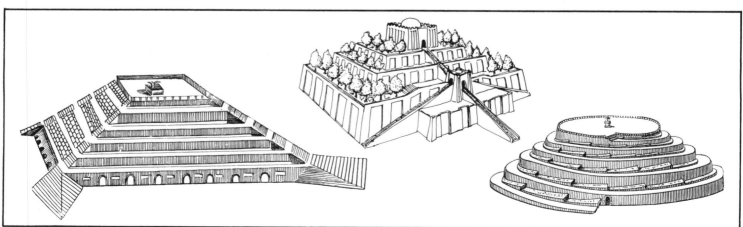

tangular and terraced. The banks were made of bricks or were sodded and had a single stairway ascending the front slope. Olivier de Serres, a French garden designer, in his influential book, *Le théâtre d'agriculture*, 1600, showed two plans, one square and one round, for terraced mounts to be used as botanical gardens. The stated advantages of these forms were that they would save space and money and provide different exposures for a variety of medicinal and ornamental plants. Grottoes underneath the mounts could be used for storage and to shelter tender species during the winter months.

American Mounts In the American colonies mounts were still popular long after they were no longer used in English gardens. The pleasant tree-shaded, ivy-covered eminence in the photograph is located in the garden of the Governor's Palace at Williamsburg. It overlooks the maze and formal parterres and was practical as well as decorative for it concealed an icehouse in its base.

The "cockleshell" mount shown below is topped with a rustic gazebo; it stood in the grounds of Thurlow Lodge, a 19th-century California mansion. One wonders if the builder thought of it only as a novel form of rock garden or if he was consciously following the ancient tradition.

Oriental Mounts The mounts in Oriental gardens are meant to suggest actual mountain scenery. In Chinese gardens they are made of water-eroded sandstone rocks fitted and cemented together and laced with tunnels and grottoes. These intricate, and often grotesque, constructions may seem totally artificial to Western eyes but are, in fact, only slightly exaggerated re-creations of the fantastic shapes found in the peaks and caverns of Kweilin. These mounts became popular garden features in the first century B.C. when the Han emperor Wu-ti built a miniature range of mountains on his palace grounds. They were meant to replicate the mountains that were the legendary home of the Immortals. He hoped to lure these magical beings into his garden, then learn from them the secret of their longevity.

Chinese garden styles were carried to Japan, where they underwent gradual changes. The mountains became more realistic, and hill gardens were made to suggest a variety of landscapes, from rugged sea cliffs to distant hills. Some of these artificial mountains are meant to replicate specific scenes; for example, Mount Fuji, considered the ideal shape for a mountain, is often represented. Some are topped with gazeboes, where one can rest and enjoy an view of the garden. Others are placed so as to limit the extent of borrowed scenery or to block the view of undesirable elements outside the garden.

NYMPHAEA *See Grottoes.*
OBELISKS *See Sculpture.*
OBSERVATION TOWERS *See Towers.*
OIL JARS *See Plant Containers, Plant Stands.*
ORANGERIES *See Plant Houses.*
OUTBUILDINGS *See Utility Buildings.*
PAGODAS *See Towers.*
PALISADES *See Fences, Close Board.*
PARTERRES *See Bed Design.*

PATHS

European Paths In the formal garden, paths fulfill specific functions. At the most practical level they divide planting beds into segments, providing convenient places to stand or kneel while tending the plants. More largely they direct the eye and the foot to specific goals and define the structure of the garden. In Western gardens, until the mid-18th century, paths were usually straight, leading directly from one place to another. An occasional garden might be laid out with circular paths, and, of course, mazes often followed serpentine courses, but these were exceptions.

Formal and rectilinear gardens eventually gave way to the serpentine lines of the landscape school. One of the earliest hints of this revolution in design can be seen in the convoluted walks set forth in Batty Langley's *New Principles of Gardening*. Still, these mazelike paths, winding through dense plantings of trees and shrubs, were contained within a balanced, geometric garden plan.

From the mid-18th century until well into the 19th century, straight lines were entirely abandoned in landscape gardens in favor of the curve. The fashion was carried to such extremes as to provoke a good deal of ridicule. In the play *The Clandestine Marriage* by Coleman and Garrick, 1766, the newly-rich Mr. Sterling brags of the improvements he has made on his estate. "Ay—here's none of your strait lines here—but all taste—zig-zag—crinkum-crankum—in and out—right and left— to and again—twisting and turning like a worm, my Lord!"

Lord Ogleby replies, "Admirably laid out indeed, Mr. Sterling! One can hardly see an inch beyond one's nose any where in these walks.—You are a most excellent economist of your land, and make a little go a great way.—It lies together in as small parcels as if it was placed in pots out at your window in Gracechurch-Street."

The excessively twisted paths continued to elicit protests into the early 20th century. Blomfield, in *The Formal Garden in England*, accuses the typical landscape gardener of deliberately "planting trees and bushes in the way, to give him an opportunity of winding his path, and then taking credit to himself for subordinating his paths to 'nature.' " On a more folksy level, Henderson, in *Gardening for Pleasure*, tells of a gentleman who so lengthened the walk from the street to his front door with a curved path that "it was hard on the butcher's and grocer's boys; and it was said that even book-peddlers, sewing-machine agents, and lightning-rod men looked ruefully at it and left him in peace." *See also Pavings.*

Chinese Paths The paths in Chinese gardens are winding and to some extent resemble those of a Western landscape garden. Early reports of Chinese gardens were welcomed by the English garden designers as confirmations of their own ideas, yet in reality there was little similarity of intent between the two. Although there are two types of pathways in Chinese gardens, both have the same purpose: to reveal the garden by degrees, for it has been said that a Chinese garden should be seen in

the same way as a scroll painting, with the winding and turning of the path producing the same effect as the slow unrolling and re-rolling of the scroll.

The open paths that thread their way around rocks, along the edges of pools, and up miniature crags are often deliberately difficult. Liu, author of *Soochow Gardens*, in speaking of the irrationalities found in Chinese gardens, says, "Then there is the narrow and serpentine footway which covers the longest distance between two points, and the slippery, almost perpendicular rock hill so precar-

ious as to discourage climbing." He goes on to speak of the labyrinthian complications of the garden. "To play to the full on the hide-and-seek motif, the visitor's movement in the puzzle would be ever so often deviated and sidetracked. But it matters little. Is it not so much more enjoyable to travel than to arrive?"

The other form of walkway is virtually unique to the Chinese garden. It is the covered path, or *lang*. The lang, like the open path, follows the contour of the ground as it twists and turns about the garden. Crossing water, it becomes a covered bridge. Maggie

Keswick, in *The Chinese Garden*, describes the lang as "that distinctive centipede of the Chinese garden, the roofed and open-sided gallery. . . . [They] wind up and down hills connecting pavilions and gateways, and at the same time dividing up the spaces like a screen." The roof of the lang is supported on a series of pillars that are connected under the eaves and at knee level by latticework lambrequins and balustrades, which act to frame each successive view as the visitor strolls along.

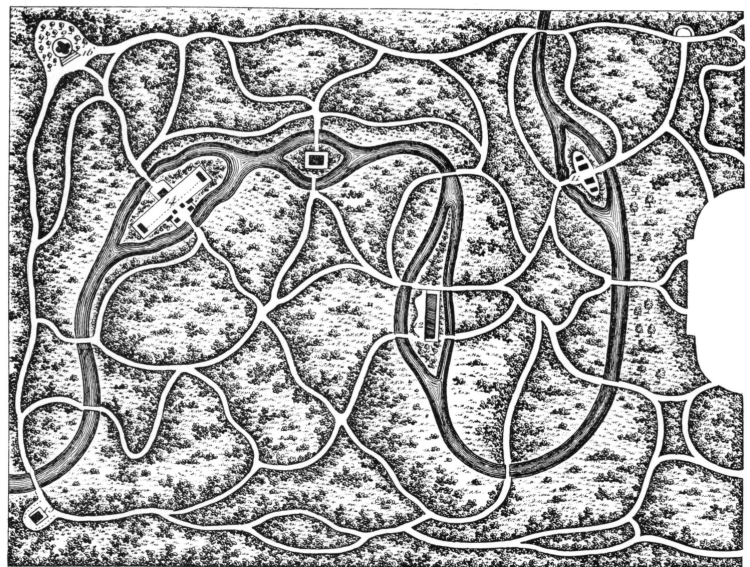

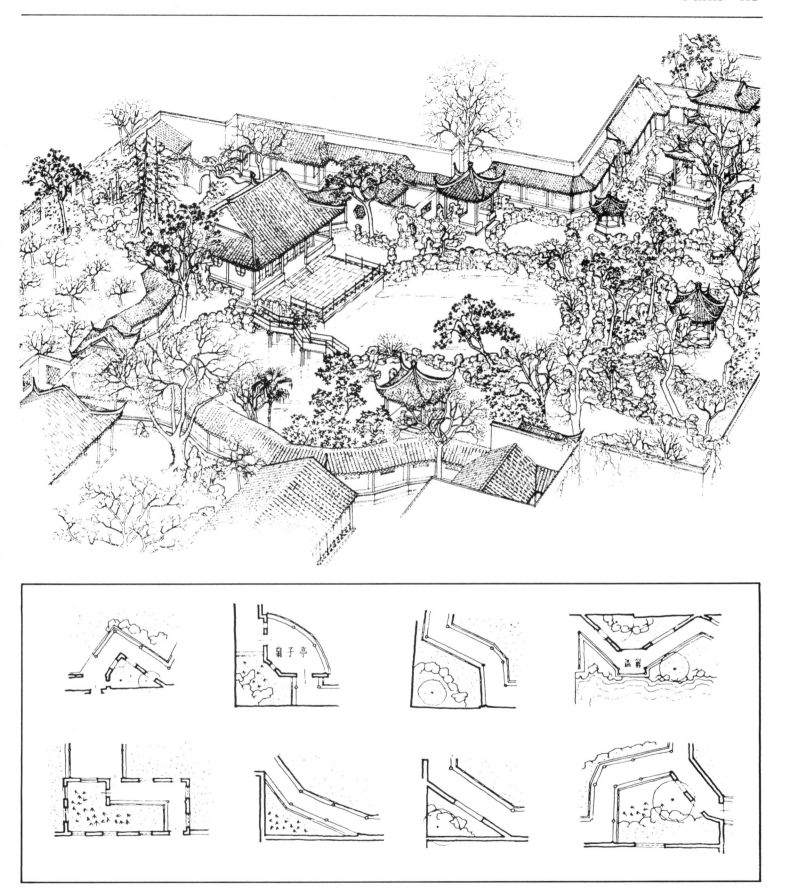

Japanese Paths Japanese paths may be made straight and fully paved, or they may be curved and made of sand, gravel, stepping stones, or a combination of all of these. Fully paved paths are made in several degrees of refinement to conform with the nature of the surroundings.

A paving of cut stone is the most formal path and is generally used in the approach to a large public building or for the entrance to a house. It is particularly adaptable for use in conjunction with modern Western-style architecture. It is used only where it does not conflict with the more asymmetrical natural forms. In this type of paving, care is taken to avoid laying the stones so that the joints form a cross. Rather they are laid to form only T and L shapes.

Of less formality are the paths of a mixture of cut and natural stones. These too are laid with straight outside edges and the stones positioned to avoid the unwanted configuration of joints. Even less formal are the paths made entirely of natural stones—flat irregular flags or rounded boulders laid with uneven edges.

Paths made of large, thick stones are set in a bed of gravel and sand, but those made of small stones are laid in mortar over a concrete base. The joints are grouted with mortar that has been colored with charcoal ash to make it blend with the color of the stones. The grout surface is lower than that of the stones by at least one-half inch to create well-defined shadows.

The width of the paths varies according to use. The rule of thumb given by Katsuo Saito in *Japanese Gardening Hints*, 1967, is: "Paved areas may be as wide as six feet in heavily traveled places . . . but one and one-half feet usually suffice for ordinary domestic gardens. Tea garden pavements are rarely more than two feet wide."

Winding stepping-stone paths were widely used in tea gardens and subsequently in all gardens after the late 16th century. The approach to a tea garden is of major significance, for it symbolizes the journey from civilization and the concerns of the world to the hermit's hut, which represents the state of simplicity and detachment necessary to experience aesthetic and spiritual rebirth.

The placement and size of the stepping stones are carefully planned, not only for beauty but to direct the visitor's attention to certain views. A stone large enough for both feet indicates that one should stop and look around, while a series of small stones requires that one go slowly and admire the texture and color of the stones and the fresh mossy borders. Often there are two possible routes to

the tea house, in which case the host will choose the one to be followed and will place a barrier consisting of a small stone tied round with a rope to indicate the one that is closed.

Stepping stones are often used in conjunction with areas of straight-edged paved paths or with a pair of cut-and-finished rectangular stones, offset one from the other. The latter are called *tanzaku-ishi* after the paper on which poetry is written. More formal paths are made with cut stones such as the diamond-shaped ones set in sand and bordered with bands of cut stone at the Silver Pavilion.

Stepping stones may be used to cross streams or marshy areas that are too shallow or too narrow to require a bridge. The long crossing at the Heian Shrine in Kyoto, made of pilings from the old Sanjo Bridge, is a late-19th-century departure from traditional usage. See photograph below.

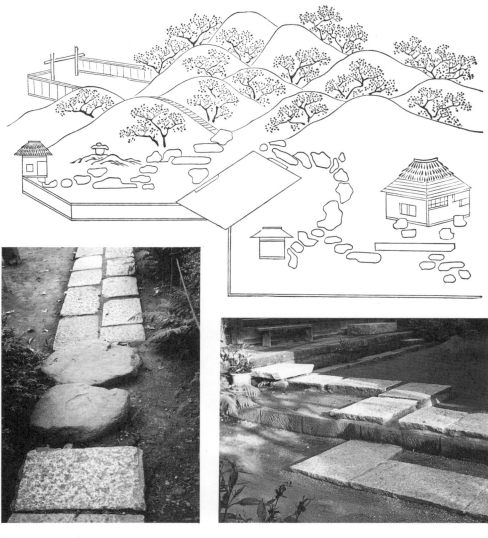

PATIOS AND COURTYARDS

Although the outdoor room is most often created by and is part of a building, it has a place in this book because it is also where the garden and home meet. Few urban dwellings are without some version of this amenity, and there must be as many versions of it as there are building designers. Here we will deal with the subject only in terms of its earliest history, though you will find examples scattered throughout this book, notably in the sections dealing with *Fountains* and *Water*.

It has been said that the courtyards and riads of Morocco are the direct descendants of the Roman atriums and peristyles. The resemblance between northern African houses and those that have been excavated at Pompeii is truly remarkable. The atrium of a Roman house was a large room, often two stories high, lighted by an opening in the roof through which rainwater was directed into a pool below. The interior courts of Moroccan houses closely follow this plan. The larger, more open peristyle of the Roman house has its counterpart in the Moroccan riad with its columned porticoes. We see these same forms in the patios and courtyards of southern Spain and subsequently in those of Latin America.

In Italy and northern Europe the tradition of the Roman peristyle was carried on in the cloisters of the Middle Ages. It has been suggested that because early Christian religious services were often held in private homes, the ancient architectural forms came to be associated with monastic buildings.

The city palace, too, of the Italian Renaissance followed the Roman plan in that it presented an austere and defensive facade to the street, while the living quarters faced inward on a colonnaded courtyard. This arrangement, ideal in hot, dry climates, is less often encountered in northern countries.

PAVILIONS

Tents The word *pavilion* has been used to describe a variety of very different structures, most of which are related to garden use. *Pavilion* is derived from the Latin word *papilio*, meaning "butterfly" and "tent," since the shape of a tent could be said to resemble that of a butterfly. In the Middle Ages Crusaders returning from the East brought with them the Oriental custom of using colorful little tents as garden shelters, hence, a garden pavilion.

The use of tents or tentlike structures in the garden enjoyed a revival in the 18th century. Designs ranged from medieval tournament tents to exotic Eastern confections. They were usually made of painted canvas and were supported by metal poles though some of the more elaborate were actually made of tin that was painted to resemble fabric.

18th-Century French Pavilions In 18th-century France the word *pavilion* re-ferred to more substantial buildings. These French *pavillons* were used as hideaways where one could escape the formality and restrictions of court life. Some consisted of only a few exquisitely paneled rooms that were used for entertaining small groups with musical performances or card games. Others were large enough to serve as guest houses or even as long-term living accommodations for a favorite mistress.

19th-Century Pavilions In the 19th century the word *pavilion* came to be used as it is today, for a temporary shelter such as a tent at a fair or for a large open-sided shelter of a more permanent nature. This sort of building is still sometimes found in public parks where people can sit and enjoy the air and view, picnic, or hold an informal dance on a summer evening.

Bandstands Because of their architectural form and the fact that they are most often to be found in public parks and gardens, we have included bandstands in the category of pavilions. Indeed, in Germany they are known as *musik-pavillons*, and even today no self-respecting spa is without one. The designs of these "temples of culture" ranged from Gothic ironwork to gingerbread to the ultimate expression of delightful nonsense, the lacy "Chinese" bandstand in the heart of midwestern America.

PAVINGS

Brick Paving Bricks are one of the most popular garden pavings, and with good reason, for the color and texture of bricks blend well with most plant materials. Their versatility and ease of handling make them ideal for amateur work; however, the more intricate designs and sharp curves require precision cutting to achieve close-fitting joints.

A great variety of effects can be had with bricks simply by laying them in different bonds, or patterns, or by using them with the narrow side exposed. Where large areas are to be covered, several different bonds may be used, or decorative panels can be introduced to lend interest and prevent monotony. Often a separation of wood, cement, or cut stone is desirable where pattern changes occur.

Edgings can be used to create variation in effect. Narrow curbs of bricks set on edge or in a sawtooth manner are informal and countri-

Brick Paving

fied. Broad decorative borders create a more finished and formal appearance.

The type of brick used as well as the width of the joints left between them have much to do with the degree of formality achieved. Closely fitted or precisely spaced and mortared joints and the use of smooth, more uniform "face" bricks produce a refined paving suitable for the most formal settings. Used bricks with their residue of old mortar or common bricks with their rougher texture and less uniform shape look more casual and rustic.

Concrete Paving Concrete has been used for paving since Roman times. Examples excavated at Pompeii were made of pounded tile mixed with lime, producing a red matrix into which small black-and-white marble tesserae were set to create patterned fields and borders. This method was used for both interior and exterior paving, but where it was to be exposed to the weather, it was waterproofed with a mixture of oil and lime.

Modern concrete—a mixture of cement, gravel, sand, and water—is one of the most versatile and inexpensive garden paving materials. While plain slabs have a glaring, utilitarian appearance, there are a variety of treatments possible to render it attractive enough for most situations. Grids formed of brick or wood not only provide expansion joints that prevent cracking but create interest and pattern. Slab installations can be grooved or stamped to simulate flagstone, brick, adobe, or cobblestone. Coloring agents, either premixed or applied, reduce glare and help the concrete blend with its surroundings. A variety of surface treatments are possible. Concrete may be scored or brushed to produce a rough-textured, nonskid surface, or it may be scrubbed while still plastic to expose the aggregate within the mixture. A stronger pebbled surface can be produced by seeding, or sprinkling, the surface with pebbles after the concrete has been poured.

Precast concrete units offer further possibilities for garden paving. Such pavers have been used in Europe for many years and have recently become available in the United States. Units of open-work blocks are now available in which grass or other ground covers can be planted and maintained even under heavy usage. Entire paving systems have been developed with compatible units to create not only a variety of paving patterns but gutters, steps, curbings, and retaining walls as well. While more expensive than poured concrete, their versatility and design are strong recommendations. At Longue Vue in New Orleans, imaginative use of decorative blocks laid as pavers and filled with asphalt produced an elegant and durable surface for a parking area visible from the garden.

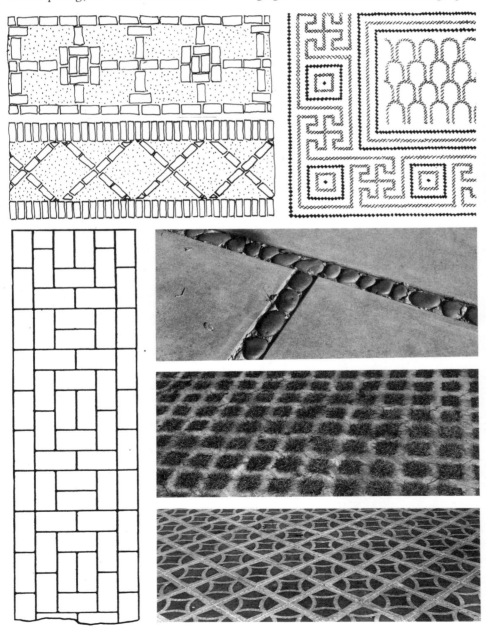

Flagstone Paving Flagstone, while initially expensive, is one of the most durable and attractive garden pavements. The degree of formality desired determines whether uncut flags are laid with uneven edges, with aligned edges, or with borders of cut stone. The closer the joints are, the more finished the effect will be.

Cut flagstones, in random or uniform sizes, are appropriate in the most formal gardens. Unusual effects are achieved by combining flagstones with bricks or cobblestones to give line and form and to prevent monotony in large areas of paving.

Flagging may be laid directly in the ground if the stones are at least one and one-half inches thick. If the flags are set slightly lower than their surroundings, turf grass may be grown between and around them. The turf can be clipped by running the lawn mower over them. Large areas of flagging should be

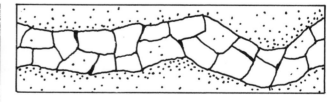

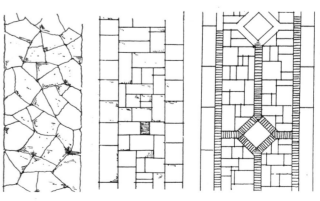

set on a foundation of concrete over a layer of cinders or gravel.

Pebble Paving It is not surprising that pavings made of pebbles are found in most cultures. The smooth elegance of rounded river stones and sea shingle presents a medium that cries out to be used in decorative pavements.

Pebble pavements are often found in old Chinese gardens. They may be used to surface an entire courtyard, for the paths that wander through rockeries, or for the pavings of roofed langs. Geometric patterns, simple floral shapes, and free-flowing pictorial motifs are all employed. The patterns and figures are outlined with sections of straight and curved roof tile set on end and filled with pebbles of different colors. Intricate representational mosaics may incorporate crushed stones and bricks as well.

The ancient Greeks used pebble pavements for interior and exterior floors, and that practice spread throughout the Mediterranean world. Regional styles were distinctive. In the Greek islands leaf, bird, and scroll motifs predominate. Portuguese pavements are usually made in bold, abstract designs worked out in two shades of gray. On the island of Majorca pebble pavements are divided into simple geometric shapes outlined with cut-stone blocks and filled with pebbles of random size.

Spanish pebble pavings are more regular and refined. Stones of uniform size in shades of gray, white, and purplish blue are used to create a variety of geometric patterns, some of which are quite intricate. Occasionally, pictorial panels representing coats of arms or heraldic beasts are inserted; but these are rare, particularly where Moorish influence predominates. Pebbles are sometimes combined with materials such as tile, brick, or cut marble slabs. Traditionally, such pavements were made by setting the stones in a mud made of sifted clay soil and water. The pebbles were set on end, slightly high, then pressed into the mud to a uniform level.

Modern American examples of pebble paving often reflect the influences of the past. In the photographic detail below a panel of round stones set against a border of white granite resembles the treatment often found on the banks of Japanese garden ponds. At Dunbarton Oaks an ornate medallion of mosaic pebbles set within marble scrolls surrounds the base of an 18th-century stone vase. The Spanish theme of the gardens at Longue Vue is reflected in the extensive use of a simple crosshatched pattern of dark stones against a lighter-colored pebble paving as a background for Moorish-style fountains.

Tile Paving Historically the use of tile for exterior paving has been associated with the hot, dry countries of Asia Minor and Africa.

The early Persian garden paths and pools were paved with colorful tiles. With the Moslem conquests the style spread to India, northern Africa, and southern Spain.

The enclosed gardens, or riads, of Morocco often follow the classic Persian form—a square or rectangle divided into four equal parts by tiled paths—with a fountain and, perhaps, a kiosk where the paths cross. The paths, raised well above the level of the planting beds, are paved with mosaic tiles laid in patterns. Mosaic tiles are made in many different shapes, each a different color, which are fitted together to form intricate designs. Larger marble slabs are sometimes combined with the mosaic tiles to provide more variety of effect.

Similar paving was used in Moorish Spain until the 14th century when a method for making polychrome tile was developed. These *azulejos* were larger, either square or rectangular, and were decorated with multicolored designs that were fired into the surface. Azulejos

were used throughout the garden for edgings around flower beds, stair risers, wainscots on enclosing walls, and linings and decorative surrounds of pools and fountains. In paving they were used as scattered inserts with unglazed tiles or bricks.

We have mentioned the use of roof tiles set on edge to form outlines for pebble paving in Chinese gardens, and they were occasionally used in the same way to form the main body of paving. This method of using tile for paving is found in widely disparate cultures. A 17th-century Chinese garden manual shows a flame pattern that was worked out in roof tiles. In Japan we found an informal path incorporating plain roof tiles and ridge and eave tiles (see photographic detail). Gertrude Jekyll, in *Gardens for Small Country Houses*, shows several paving plans that use sections of tile set on edge in combination with bricks and flat-laid tile. She describes one plan as "a tracery of sections of half-round tile connected with small pieces of roofing tile, with filling of another

material." She gives no hint of what the other "filling" should be, but one may speculate that it might be pebble mosaic, gravel, or exposed aggregate.

Today one can find a large selection of tiles that are suitable for garden paving. Unglazed tiles are generally used for this purpose, except the Spanish-type insets, because they provide a safer, less slippery surface when wet than do the glazed varieties. A wide range of colors, shapes, and textures offer many design possibilities. The colors in unglazed tiles are either intrinsic to the materials used, derived from additives, or are from surface flashing. For general use, however, the natural earth tones are most compatible with flowers and foliage. Machine-shaped tiles, with uniform, crisp edges, are appropriate for use in clean, modern designs. Hand-molded tiles, with small variations of shape and softer outlines, create a feeling of long use that blends well in traditional settings.

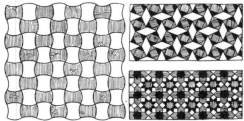

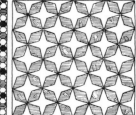

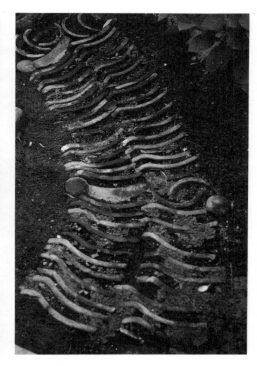

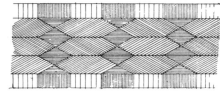

Wood Paving Paths made of wood are a modern addition to the area of garden design. Wooden walkways are often raised above ground level, serving as extensions of decks and achieving a formal architectural effect.

Railroad ties may be used in a number of ways for exterior paving. They may be used full length, laid directly into the ground, or into a bed of gravel, or they may be cut into short lengths and laid in a basket-weave pattern. A totally different effect may be produced by cutting them into blocks and laying them with the open grain facing up. A more casual, woodsy paving is made by laying redwood rounds in sand. It is a good idea to presoak any wood that is to be set in the ground in some preservative solution.

PERENNIAL BORDERS *See Bed Design.*
PERGOLAS *See Arbors.*
PIGEON HOUSES *See Dovecotes.*

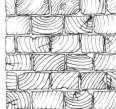 

16

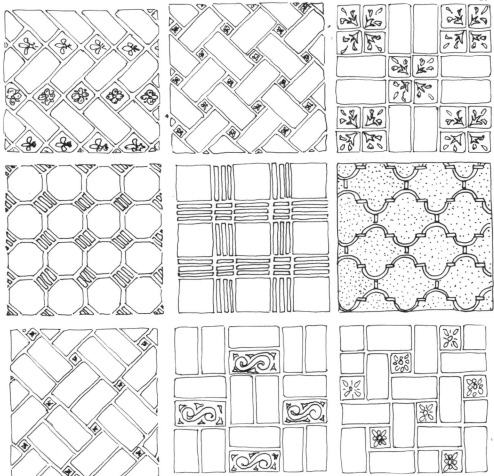

PLANT CONTAINERS, PLANT STANDS

Plant Containers Container gardening is said to have originated in ancient Greece, where during the Festival of Adonis, women planted quick-sprouting seeds in earthen pots, which they then placed around a statue of Adonis that was on the roof of the house. In the hot sun the plants grew and quickly died; they were symbolic of the brief life of Aphrodite's handsome young lover.

There are several styles of garden where plant containers play a vital role. Most important and with lasting influence has been the formal Italianate garden. In these highly architectural settings citrus and oleander trees in ornamental containers line paths and terraces. Stone or terra-cotta vases for smaller plants are placed at intervals on stone bases made especially for them around pools and along balustrades, walls, and stairways.

Plant containers are also important in Spanish and other patio gardens, but they are used in a much more informal way. There may be rows of matching pots on walls or stairways, but it is more usual to see a cheerful mélange of pots and tubs of assorted shapes and sizes clustered wherever a touch of color or greenery is wanted.

Ceramic Containers The majority of plant containers are *ceramic* which is a general term that includes everything from the ordinary clay flowerpots, often condemned as "fit only for stacking," although they are neat, plain, and quite at home in informal settings, to the huge china bowls, which are glazed with multicolored designs that seem too ornate for outdoor use. Glazed or colored pots seldom look right in a garden. The best planters are made of terra cotta, a fine quality earth-

enware. These are available in numerous vase, tub, and box forms.

Metal Containers Lead was the most commonly used metal for garden ornaments beginning in the 17th century and particularly in the early 18th century. It is well suited for outdoor use since it is unaffected by weather. With age it develops a fine silver gray patina that harmonizes well with plants. In the old gardens, however, lead was often gilded, painted, or coated to resemble stone. Lead vases were usually modeled in classic forms, with leaf decorations and mythological sub-

jects. Fine examples are the two vases at Hampton Court in England with seated nymphs emerging from the handles.

Cast iron supplanted lead in the 19th century, and iron vases and urns became staple decorations in the Victorian gardens. Iron is long lasting but must be treated regularly to prevent rust. Many old cast iron designs are available as reproductions.

Stone Containers Carved stone has been the traditional material for architectural and decorative elements in many formal gardens. Alberti recommended the use of stone vases

for plants in the 15th century. Stone is much more appropriate for garden use than marble, although marble ornaments did appear in princely gardens. Marble is too clean and cold to harmonize well with plants and flowers. Stone has a certain warmth even when newly cut and soon achieves with age an attractive air of antiquity. Carved stone pieces are still made, principally in Italy, but they are often replaced by cast stone or concrete, which, if artfully made and artistically aged, can have much the same character as stone at considerably less cost.

78

Wooden Containers Wood is the material most suitable for large planters that must be moved periodically. Wooden planters were first used extensively in conjunction with the orangeries that were so typical of 17th- and 18th-century gardens, where sometimes hundreds of citrus trees were kept for the winter. Large wooden tubs and drum-shaped cases were used, but most were boxes on short legs, usually ornamented at each corner with rounded finials. An 18th-century refinement was to make boxes with sides that could be re-moved for root pruning and the addition of soil. Assembled, the sides were held in place with metal bars. Such cases are still made; some have been used as pleasing accents in the restored 18th-century gardens at Williams-burg, Virginia (see photograph).

Plant Stands A plant stand can be any sort of an elevated base intended for the display of one or more potted plants. Usually only plants of lush growth or those in full bloom are used. Stands are made as stepped shelves of wood or metal, tiered so that each plant can be seen. In the 18th and 19th century stands were made in the form of pyramids or even garden houses where hundreds of plants be-came walls of cascading flowers. A modern version of the plant stand is the three-tiered platform in the garden at Strybing Arboretum in San Francisco where wooden boxes and pots form a mass in an easily changed display (see photograph). Upright plant stands of metal are often made in the shape of a vine or tree, each branch holding a plant. These may be freestanding or made to attach to a wall.

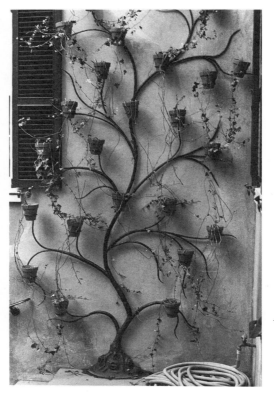

PLANT HOUSES

Shelters for plant protection and propagation became necessary as soon as gardeners attempted to extend normal growing seasons or when they tried to grow plants beyond their usual climate range. There is evidence that forcing houses were used in ancient Rome and that the principles of greenhouse practice were understood at least 2,000 years ago.

In the first century A.D. Seneca was growing grapes, cucumbers, and flowers out of season with the aid of hot-water pipes, and Martial complained that a friend's fruit tree was treated better than his guests. The plant house had glazed windows to protect the tree from the cold, the guest room did not.

Orangeries Oranges were introduced into Spain by the Arabs in the 12th or 13th century, and into Italy in the early Renaissance. Citrus trees are susceptible to frost, and in order to grow them in cool climates, winter protection is necessary. So began the Italian custom of growing orange and lemon trees in containers that could be moved inside during the cold season. Special buildings were made for wintering the trees, and these orangeries became an important part of the garden plan, often used for summer entertaining when emptied of plants.

By the 17th century citrus trees were cultivated throughout Europe, and orangeries became quite grand. The best architects were commissioned to design them; Christopher Wren planned the orangerie at Kensington Palace, and Mansart designed the imposing structure at Versailles. They were not at all like later glass houses, but simply large rooms with good-size windows and a stove for winter heating. Henri Cause's 17th-century illustrations show the interiors of "winter-plaats" in Holland, with containers designed to be carried on poles.

The brick building with paired chimneys (see photograph) is an example of an American orangery of the 18th century, one of the more important structures at George Washington's estate, Mount Vernon. It was not until the 19th century that the need for more light in plant growing was fully understood and the glass greenhouse and conservatory supplanted the orangery.

Conservatories *Conservatory* is a term generally applied to a decorative glass house permanently attached as an extension to a house. Conservatories became fashionable in the late 18th and 19th centuries as display houses for the many new and exotic plants being introduced in Europe from all over the world. These were not intended for use as propagation or forcing houses, although tender plants might be wintered in them, but rather as indoor garden rooms or winter gardens.

On large estates and, later, in public gardens where there was an over-size collection of plants, the conservatory might be a separate building, but the attached conservatory was the most usual. Humphrey Repton, in *Theory and Practice*, 1803, wrote that "amongst the refinements of modern luxury may be reckoned that of attaching a greenhouse to some room in the mansion." He was concerned with visually linking these additions to the house. The old orangeries had solid roofs and could be built in conformity with the house, but the new plants required more light, and it was "difficult to make the glass roof of a conservatory architectural, whether Grecian or Gothic." One of his solutions was to copy the chapter rooms of Gothic cathedrals, where the ribs of the octagonal roof were supported by a slim pillar in the middle, but he substituted cast iron for stone and filled the "interstices" with glass.

The problem of architectural harmony is simplified today by the use of new materials and building techniques. Conservatories in all sizes and shapes are now available.

Greenhouses A greenhouse is a glass-enclosed structure where the atmosphere can be controlled with a careful balance of heat, moisture, light, and air to suit the kinds of plants to be grown there. Unlike conservatories, they are primarily growing places rather than showcases, although they may serve as both for the home gardener. Greenhouses come in a wide range of sizes and shapes, from the frankly utilitarian lean-to, just large enough for a few flats and some tomato plants, to large and decorative structures.

Many greenhouses are now equipped with thermostats that control heating units and automatic vent openers that are operated either

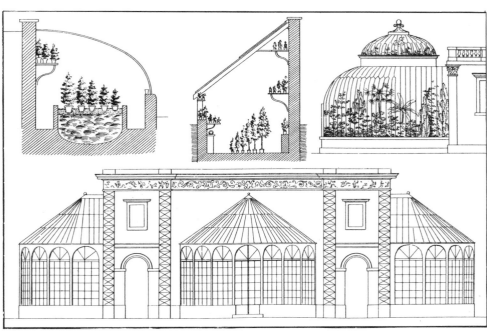

electrically or hydraulically. Some have automatic misting systems to control humidity; some even have an alarm system that is triggered when the automatic system breaks down. All are useful devices to save time and to protect the plants.

A story is told of a hapless gardener at the Austrian Schönbrunn Palace, where there were a large number of greenhouses. Expeditions were sent to South America and the West Indies to collect rare plants. Those plants were carried by ship to Italy, then overland on the backs of mules to Austria. The plants and trees flourished and were much admired. One night in 1780 there was a heavy frost, and the gardener forgot to light the stoves. In the morning, hoping to remedy his error, he built hot fires; the sudden change of temperature killed most of the plants. One can only speculate on the fate of the gardener.

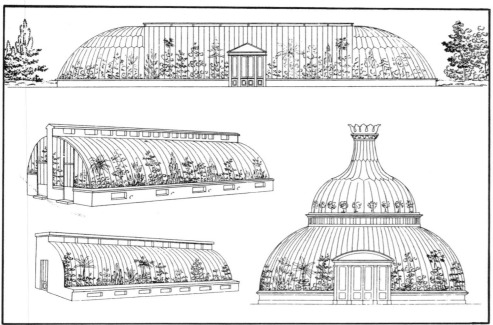

Lath Houses Lath houses are simple structures made of lath or narrow strips of wood for the purpose of shading plants. A lath house may be used as an intermediary stop for seedlings grown in greenhouses before they are set out in the garden or as a decorative display area for shade-loving plants. Lath houses can be attractive structures. The lath, usually spaced the width of a lath apart, produces interesting patterns of sun and shadow. These shelters can also be made in more ornamental latticework designs so long as the pattern does not cut out too much light.

Frames Frames are boxes with glass roofs sloped to catch maximum sunlight. Some are of wood or metal, often portable so they can be placed as needed over planting beds. Others are permanent, like the series of handsome brick frames in the kitchen gardens at Mount Vernon shown in the photograph. Lean-to frames were sometimes used for seasonal pro-

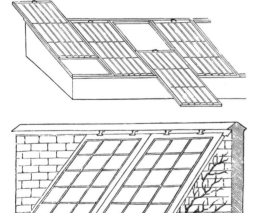

tection of espaliered plants on walls.

Cold frames are used to give seedlings an early start, for winter shelter of plants, and to harden off, or acclimate, greenhouse-grown plants to outside life.

Heated frames, or hot beds, are more versatile for starting and maintaining tender plants. Traditionally, warmth was provided by a two-foot layer of fresh barnyard manure. The manure was put under where the frame was to be placed, then covered with a layer of soil. The manure gave off heat as it decomposed and fermented. That process was efficient and economical when the stable was next door to the garden. Now some frames are heated by electrical cables.

PLANT STANDS *See Plant Containers, Plant Stands.*

PLANTING WALLS *See Walls.*

PLATFORMS *See Decks and Platforms.*

PLAY HOUSES *See Garden Houses.*

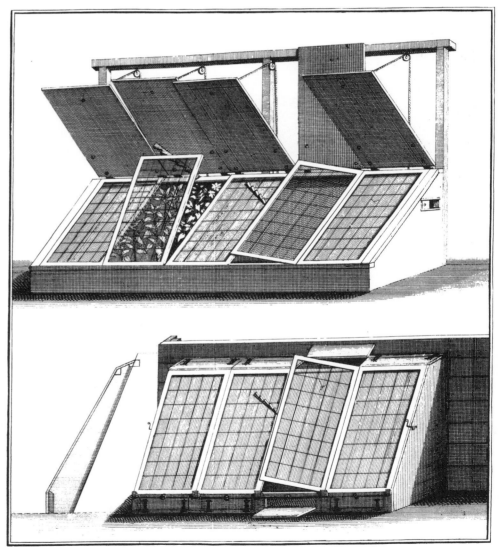

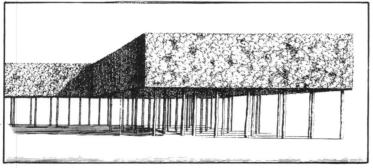

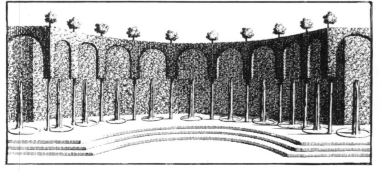

PLEACHED TREES AND SHRUBS

Pleaching is a technique used for training and shaping trees and shrubs into forms they would not naturally assume. It is done by bending and intertwining the branches and clipping them to a more or less smooth contour. This definition could in some cases apply equally to topiary, and, indeed, the distinction between the two is fuzzy. We have used the word *pleached* to refer to the more architectural forms and *topiary* for those that are more purely decorative.

Pleaching is used in the formation of palissades, alleys, arches, and outdoor rooms where the main support for the structure is provided by the trunks and branches of the plant material, not by a fabricated framework. This is not to say that artificial supports are never used, for in the initial training, light supports are often employed then either removed or left in place to be covered by greenery. *See also Arbors, Topiary.*

Palissades A major use of pleaching is to form palissades. One of the most common types, often called a *pole hedge* in England, is formed by planting a row of trees at regular intervals, their trunks left bare to a height of eight to ten feet and the branches above intertwined and clipped to resemble a hedge. In others the foliage is allowed to grow from the base of the trunk to form a series of arches. Still others are trained to form a hedgelike wall pierced by windowlike openings. In some cases shrubs are planted at the base of the trees and both are clipped to form a continuous green wall. These combination plantings can be grown to great heights without the lower foliage dying away.

Palissades were used extensively in French gardens of the 17th century. According to Dezallier d'Argenville, they were useful to cover the walls of enclosures, as well as to obstruct or limit the view at certain points so that the whole extent of the garden was not seen at once, and to correct and improve the turns and angles of the walls.

Pleached Alleys One of the oldest uses for pleaching is to form alleys, which are made by

planting a double row of trees or shrubs and allowing them to grow to a good height, then pulling the upper branches together, intertwining them, and clipping the whole structure into a smooth green tunnel. Pleached alleys were often used in medieval gardens in place of the supported "carpenter's work" galleries (*see also Arbors*). In England, alleys were made of box, whitethorn, or, most commonly, yew, which was highly prized for its velvety texture. These alleys were permitted to become very dense to provide shelter in rainy weather. There was usually sand or gravel underfoot, and little openings pierced the foliage from time to time to provide light and views of the garden. Wider spaces or little rooms at the intersections of two alleys were furnished with seats.

The lofty pleached alleys that were so popular in French gardens in the late 17th century were formed with elms, limes, or hornbeams. Some were allowed to grow freely once the ini-

tial archway was formed; others were strictly controlled and cut into stylized architectural shapes—the results scarcely resembled living plants. This latter technique soon spread to England, and the fashionable team of garden designers, London and Wise, provided detailed instructions for the formation of pleached alleys. The trees were to be planted ten feet apart and allowed to grow until they were sixteen feet high. Then the trunks were clipped bare to a height of six feet, and the branches were bound close to the trunks and clipped. Wooden hoops fixed between the trees were used to train the top branches into precise arches. Small tufts of foliage left between the spandrels were trimmed into the shape of apples "or any other form you please."

Pleached Arches Arches made by pleaching were often used in Spanish gardens. Cypress, cedar, and arborvitae were used for this purpose, the tips of two trees being tied to-

gether over a light framework and clipped into a smooth archway of greenery. Such arches were used singly, in a series, or interlocked to form a green glorieta.

Yew arches were a common feature in 17th-century English topiary gardens. They were often used over the entrance to an enclosed garden to frame the vista or in a series over long walks.

Victorian gardeners were particularly fond of pleached arches at entrances. Frank Scott recommends evergreens for this purpose and claims that "with patience and annual care, these can be perfected within about ten years, but they will also afford most pleasing labor from the beginning; and the infantile graces of the trees, which are year by year to be developed into verdant arches, will probably afford quite as much pleasure in their early growth as in their perfected forms."

Pleached Summer Houses Maggie Keswick, in *The Chinese Garden*, tells of a second-century scholar who planted bamboos in a circle to look "like a jade ring," then tied all the tips together to make a leafy tent and called it his fisherman's hut. That early pleached summer house is but one of many recorded in history. The medieval garden described in the anonymous *Flower and Leaf* had a room with the walls and roof cut out of a hedge "as thick as a castle wall," which suggests that the room was pleached rather than framed with carpenter's work. There is, too, an intriguing 16th-century description of a temple made of living trees for Catherine de Médicis in the Tuileries. Bernard Palissey, in *Recepte veritable*, advises that young elms should be planted to form the outline of a small temple. The branches are to be lopped off to the proper height to form columns, and at the top and bottom the bark is slashed. As the tree heals, the protruding scar tissue forms capitals and bases. The branches that shoot out from above the capitals are then woven into a decorative frieze to complete the temple.

The medieval tradition of pleached summer houses was retained in Holland long after they were passé in the rest of Europe, and the style was reintroduced into England along with other Dutch elements when William of Orange came to the throne in 1689. Topiary gardens, popular during this period, often included a pleached bower such as the one at Solihull, Warwickshire, with the topiary peacock perched on the roof (see drawing).

Pleached summer houses enjoyed renewed popularity in the Victorian era. Scott recommends planting six hemlocks, one at each corner of a hexagon of ten to twelve feet in diameter. When the trees are twelve feet tall, they are tied with a rope several feet from the top and drawn together toward the center until they are about six feet apart. When the trees have grown another six feet in that position, the tops are tied together. The inside branches are sheared close to the trunks, while the feathery growth on the outside is trimmed to form a smooth mosquelike dome. Scott warns against impatience, because the process may require as long as fifteen years to complete. "In this, as in most other things in life, it is well to remember Shakespeare's lines— 'What's won is done; joy's soul lies in the

doing.' " Scott goes on to point out that less formal bowers may be produced by planting deciduous trees such as hawthorn and sassafras and keeping them trimmed to a height of twelve feet until they spread to form a thick canopy, "a cool summer resort for smoking or reading, a place to take tea, or a children's playhouse."

Edward Kemp tells of a lime bower at Knowle Park in the mid-19th century. "Besides other strange and striking examples, there is an old Lime tree on one of the lawns, the branches of which, having naturally bent downwards toward the earth, have there struck root, and it is now surrounded with myriads of tufted trees of various ages and sizes, covering altogether an immense surface."

PONDS *See Water, Natural Uses; Water, Japanese Uses.*

POOLS *See Water, Formal Uses.*

PORTICOES *See Hedges, Treillage.*

POTS *See Plant Containers, Plant Stands.*

POTTING SHEDS *See Utility Buildings.*

PRIVIES *See Utility Buildings.*

PUMPS *See Wells.*

RABBITRIES *See Utility Buildings.*

RETAINING WALLS *See Walls.*

ROCKWORK

Chinese Rockwork The use of rocks as garden decorations has been a characteristic of Chinese garden design since ancient times. In addition to the use of rocks to build mounts and grottoes, rocks are displayed singly and in groups in much the same manner as is statuary in Western gardens. Some of the most highly prized are the water-modeled sandstone chunks dredged from the bottom of Lake T'ai. These fantastic pitted and convoluted monoliths are often set on pedestals and are admired as *objets d'art*. Overhanging stones, a form often found in Chinese paintings of mountain scenes, are particularly valued. *See also Walls*.

Japanese Rockwork Stones are important in the Japanese garden also, but here they are used in a more unobtrusive and naturalistic manner. Rock arrangements are often meant to represent mountain scenery with peaks, chasms, and waterfalls. In dry gardens, which were popularized by Zen monks in the 15th and 16th centuries, stones may simulate landscapes or they may form an entirely abstract design open to the interpretation of the viewer.

There are traditional guidelines for the placement of stone that have been followed, though never slavishly, for many generations. According to Josiah Conder, five basic stone shapes are commonly used. Three types of vertical stones—the *tall vertical*, or *statue*, stone; the *low vertical* stone; and the *arching* stone—and two types of horizontal stones—the *flat* stone and the curved *recumbent ox* stone—

make up the group. Various combinations of two, three, and five of these types may be used, depending on their placement. Single stones of exceptional beauty are featured in much the same way as in Chinese gardens.

Another form found in both Chinese and Japanese gardens is the inscribed stone. It may be hewn or natural, the inscription being a descriptive name, poetry, or some historic reference that adds significance to the spot.

Western Rockwork Even though the Romans built artificial grottoes and Renaissance designers embellished their fountains, grottoes, and cascades with tufa, it was in the picturesque gardens of the late 18th century that the first attempts were made to imitate natural rock formations. In those gardens wild nature, "awful" crags, precipices, and caverns

became the order of the day. If none of these desirable elements were present on the site, they were built, sometimes entirely of natural stones and sometimes in combination with reconstituted stone that was sculpted to look like natural rock formations.

The introduction of new plant materials such as alpines, ferns, and California annuals in the 19th century gave further impetus to the use of rockwork, particularly in England. Rock gardens that not only replicated the natural habitat but brought the plants up to eye level where they could be examined at close range became the rage. Some of them were mere piles of stone composed of odd and unrelated elements. One of the earliest rock gardens built in a glass house at the Chelsea Physic Garden was made of stones from the Tower of London, lava rock from Iceland, flints, and chalk. Others incorporated bits of broken china, glass fragments, and seashells on the theory that those objects added richness.

The best rockeries were built with great care to give the appearance of natural strata. The chapter on rock gardens in Jekyll and Weaver's *Gardens for Small Country Houses* was contributed by Raymond E. Negus, who gives this advice: "Every stone in the garden should bear the semblance of having been in its place from time immemorial. The first principle of rock gardening is, 'Adopt a definite scheme of stratification and carry it out uniformly throughout your garden.' . . . The stones used should be of the largest possible size compatible with convenience of handling. It is of the utmost importance that a stone once placed in position should never be moved; moreover, large well-placed rocks are a joy in and for themselves . . . whereas small ones almost invariably look scrappy. . . . The best all-round kind of rock to employ is weather-worn limestone, which is beautiful in itself. Natural stone should be used wherever it occurs in the district. Sandstone crumbles somewhat rapidly, but the grit thus produced is a valuable rooting medium. Avoid, as you would the plague, all manner of brickbats, clinkers, concrete and tree trunks. Always lay the stones with their broadest face downwards. If these simple rules be obeyed, the rock garden will appear to be something inherent in the soil, and not a mere fortuitous medly of stones."

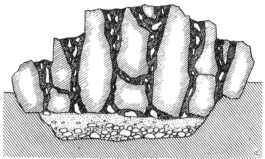

RUINS

Sham ruins were a distinctive feature of the picturesque landscape in the 18th century. They were another expression of the romantic revolution that swept away every hint of regularity in gardens and sought to return to the freedom of nature. Gardens at that time were expected to evoke imagination and sentiment, and artificial effects were added to insure they did.

"Ruins," wrote Whateley in *Observations on Gardening*, 1765, "are a class by themselves, beautiful as objects, expressive as characters, and particularly calculated to connect with their appendages into elegant groupes . . . contiguity is not necessary . . . but straggling ruins have a bad effect."

A fortunate few had real ruins to create a sensation of pleasurable melancholy: *Bless'd is the man, in whose sequester'd glade, Some ancient abbey's walls diffuse their shade. . . . Bless'd too is he, who 'midst his tufted trees, Some ruin'd castle's loftly tower sees* (Richard Payne Knight, *The*

Landscape, A Didactic Poem, 1794). Most people had to build their own. Some copied from the ancients; Sir William Chambers designed the ruined Roman arch at Kew Gardens. Another Roman "ruin" was built as a termination of one of the side avenues at Schönbrunn in 1776. These ruins satisfied both sentimental and archaeological tastes. A growing interest in the Middle Ages led to the creation of Gothic ruins as well, and "mouldering remnants of obsolete taste" in the form of knightly castles and monkish cloisters appeared. The more practical landholder followed plans for building cattle sheds that were designed to look like ruined abbeys. Others, with even less taste, simply built a thin facade on an existing farm building.

The fashion for ruins continued for some time. As late as 1914, Phebe Humphreys decried "an absurd fashion [on] the estates of millionaires whose lack of good taste is in proportion to their great wealth . . . is that of counterfeiting ancient ruins."

SCULPTURE

Statuary In the Western world the Greeks were the first to use statuary for garden ornaments. Marble likenesses of heroes and gods decorated academy, gymnasium, and sanctuary gardens. The Romans copied the Greek practice and imported Greek statuary and sculptors as well as producing vast quantities of their own work to ornament their villa gardens.

In the early 15th century great numbers of these statues were excavated. The Renaissance princes and merchants who were avid collectors of Roman works soon ran out of house

space and started to display them in their gardens. By the end of the century, ancient and contemporary statues were used in a variety of ways in the garden. The most spectacular pieces were incorporated into fountains, grottoes, and water theaters. (They are discussed elsewhere in this book.) In addition, statues were often displayed in a series, the figures placed on the piers of terrace balustrades or in fours, marking the corners of each division of a parterre. Statuary was often used to mark an important path intersection or the termination of an axis or vista.

Statuary was, if anything, even more im-

portant to the decorative scheme of the great gardens of 17th- and 18th-century France. Gleaming marble figures lined the broad alleys. Gilded bronze figures stood against great expanses of sky or were reflected in bright sheets of water.

In England the styles of Italy and France were never adopted wholeheartedly, and the use of garden statuary was modest and restricted. For one thing, marble and bronze have never been popular with the English gardener. Blomfield says, "Marble statuary is a mistake in an English garden. To attain its full effect it wants strong sunlight, a clear dry

78

78

light, and a cloudless sky. In the soft light and nebulous atmosphere of the north marble looks forlorn and out of place. It does not colour like stone, and the qualities of which it is most capable—such as refinements of contour and modelling—are simply lost under an English sky." He puts forth much the same argument against bronze statues. "They do not lend themselves to the modelling of nature; they do not grow in with nature, as stone or lead." Blomfield advocates Portland stone statuary for the English garden because "it is hard and weathers well, and few if any stones profit so much by exposure to the sun and rain. The harshness of its outlines becomes

softened by time, and it will take on the most delicate colours, from the green stains of the pedestal to the pure white of the statue that gleams from under the deep canopy of yew."

The most popular medium for English statuary from the early 18th century on was lead. Not only was it plentiful and relatively inexpensive, but it was easily cast. Most important, it weathers to a silvery gray, ideally suited to the tones of an English garden. As W. R. Lethaby says in *Leadwork*, "lead is homely and ordinary and not too good to receive the *graffiti* of lovers' knots, red letter dates and initials." These "homely" statues depicted the usual nymphs, Herculeses, Pans,

and Cupids as well as a whole new complement of milkmaids, country swains, hunters, buccaneers, and even cows. Many of these same themes, along with the ubiquitous "stags at bay" and "faithful dogs," were carried over into the cast iron statues of the Victorian era.

Minor Sculptures Small carved or cast figures, covered urns, carved vases of fruit or flowers, finials, and small obelisks are used in much the same settings as those in which statuary is used to provide accents and points of interest in the garden. The smaller-scale ornaments and statuary are extremely useful in the restricted space of most modern gardens. As

Jekyll states in *Gardens for Small Country Houses*, "So far from formal treatment [of sculpture] being suitable for great gardens only, it seems to be peculiarly applicable to little spaces. Where a garden scheme extends over several acres a designer can afford to be severely simple in the details of his conception. . . . A little garden, however, if too simply treated, soon exhausts our curiosity. The more the designer lacks space, the apter should he be in making us forget his garden's limitations. Ingenious pleasantries of treatment here and there arrest the interest. By concentrating it they make the visitor oblivious of the smallness of the theater which yields so much diversion. This is not a plea for many ornaments, still less for any one that stands out markedly from its surroundings; no more is it claimed than that ornament of the right kind is even more welcome in small gardens than in big."

Monuments and Tombs In the late 18th century, at the height of the romantic era, monuments in memory of national heroes and famous literary figures, market crosses, wayside shrines, and, in some cases, actual tombs and mausoleums found their way into the garden. Such reminders of the transitory nature of fame and mortality were held to induce an emotion of gentle melancholy, which was considered necessary for the proper enjoyment of the garden scene.

SHADOW HOUSES *See Summer Houses.*
SHELL HOUSES *See Grottoes, Summer Houses.*

55

55

SHELTERED SEATS

The landscape gardens of the late 18th century and the early 19th century were designed for walking. The serpentine paths often caused visitors to wander a good distance from their starting point and presented them with a series of scenic views. Seats, often roofed for shelter from the sun and sometimes partially enclosed, were provided at strategic points along the way. These sheltered seats were built in all the exotic styles favored for the more substantial garden house. Small umbrellalike covered seats—the earliest were often in the Chinese style, and the later ones in the rustic mode—were highly popular for these casual little resting places. Such minimal shelters are occasionally found in modern gardens. Originally, a swing seat hung under the roof of this canopy with lacy wrought iron supports (see photograph).

SMOKEHOUSES *See Utility Buildings.*
SPRINGHOUSES *See Utility Buildings.*

STAIRS

Prior to the 16th century, stairways were seldom used as decorative elements in the garden. In Roman gardens they were simple necessities for passage from level to level on hillside sites. But in the Renaissance garden the grand stairway became a major focal point. Long flights flanking cascades, curved sweeps embracing fountains, and balustraded switchbacks climbing from terrace to terrace provided architectural unity.

In the less precipitous French and English gardens stairways never assumed such great prominence in the overall design but were used to good effect in less dramatic ways. A series of stairway plans based on the designs of Le Nôtre appeared in the highly influential book *The Theory and Practice of Gardening* by Dezallier d'Argenville, first published in France in 1709 and in England in 1712.

In the landscape gardens of the next century stairways were again reduced to unimportant necessities or completely eliminated, causing Walpole to crow, "How many Frenchmen are there who have seen *our* gardens, and still prefer *natural* flights of steps and shady cloisters covered with lead! Le Nôtre, the architect of the groves and grottoes at Versailles, came hither on a misson to improve our taste. He planted St. James's and Greenwich parks—no great monuments of his invention. . . .

"Fortunately Kent and a few others were not quite so timid, or we might still be going

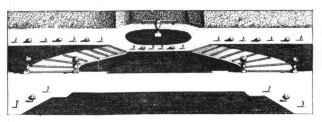

up and down stairs in the open air."

Despite Walpole and the 18th-century landscape architects, we are still going up and down stairs out-of-doors. Steps, whether to be treated unobtrusively in the wild garden or as a featured element in the formal garden, have certain basic requirements. Safety and comfort demand that the risers be of uniform height and that the treads be of uniform width and relatively flat. The risers should be no more than six inches high and the tread no

less than twelve inches wide. A good standard is a six-inch riser with a fifteen-inch tread. If the riser is lower, the tread should be proportionally wider, that is, a five-inch riser and a seventeen-inch tread or a four-inch riser and a nineteen-inch tread. When the treads are wider than nineteen inches, they should then be wide enough to accommodate a normal stride before stepping onto the next tread. On a long stairway a landing every eight to ten steps helps to avoid the forbidding prospect of

a long, uninterrupted flight of stairs.

Formal Stairs In the formal garden where stairways are treated as major architectural elements there are many design possibilities. A single flight at right angles to the slope or terrace wall is the simplest approach where the drop is neither too long nor too steep. Longer flights may be run parallel to the wall and may be broken by a landing at the halfway point. Strong decorative statements may be made by using double stairways that diverge

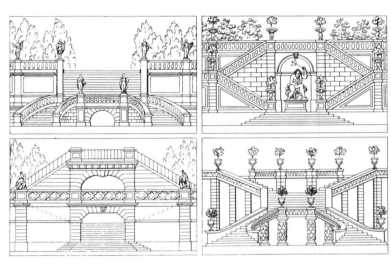

from a single path, either at top or bottom. The space created between the stairways can be used for a fountain, statue, or niche. Where steps descend to a large paved area or to divergent paths, the lower steps are often opened out into a wide curved base, indicating a spreading traffic pattern.

Informal Stairs Informal stairways, where the object is to make them as unobtrusive as possible, usually are sunken slightly, following the contour of the bank or hillside. Materials, such as local stone, used brick, railroad ties, or redwood rounds, that blend into the

surroundings are most satisfactory for this use. Where the terrain is uneven, a series of steps broken by gently sloped ramps is often employed. On steep slopes curved switchbacks not only ease the climb, but by concealing the destination of the stairs, they add a little mystery and adventure to the garden. Uneven edging and planting that overhangs and frames the passageway can further create an atmosphere of informality.

STATUARY *See Sculpture.*
STEPPING STONES *See Paths, Pavings.*
STEW PONDS *See Water, Natural Uses.*

STILES

A stile is the country dweller's device for getting over a fence, wall, or hedge where there is no gate. The principal advantage of a stile is that it allows passage for pedestrians at the same time it doesn't provide the chance for a careless passerby to leave a gate open and let the cows out. Stiles are still often used where public footpaths cross pastureland, and they are useful wherever children take short cuts that involve climbing over or under a fence, to the detriment of both fence and clothing.

The simplest stiles are a pair of ladders on either side of the barrier, sometimes with a platform at the top and hand holds to make climbing easier. More refined versions have steps, railings, and a larger platform that makes a pleasant place from which to observe one's surroundings.

More decorative stiles were built rather like steep bridges. The two rustic stiles shown in the drawing below are 19th-century English designs. Both are basically a pair of ladders, one with a platform at the top, but the rustic railings make them quite suitable for garden use. Swinging stiles, on the order of the turn-stiles used in subway stations, were also made. They served the same purpose as step-stiles in letting people, but not animals, pass.

SUMMER HOUSES

A summer house is the type of garden building where one might sit on a warm day and read a book, sew, or write long, chatty letters to old friends. It is more enclosed and private than a gazebo, larger than a sheltered seat, yet more informal and airy than a garden house. An old name often used in England for such a structure was *shadow house*, and they were traditionally set at the end of a long walk. Before the 18th century summer houses usually followed the style of the main house, but the romanticism of the mid-18th century affected these structures, just as it did every other aspect of the garden. Summer houses blossomed in a full range of fanciful styles. The decoration of their interiors was often taken over by the women. Shell mosaics that completely covered the walls and ceilings were a favorite project, requiring many hands and long hours of happy occupation.

Victorian Summer Houses By the mid-19th century wall decoration was often done with moss and the summer house itself was apt to be built in the rustic mode. These buildings were usually constructed by amateurs or country carpenters, using materials at hand. They were decorated by jamming colored mosses between closely set battens to form a pattern "not unlike that of a Turkey carpet." (Critics complained that such wall coverings were good only for harboring noxious insects and providing nesting materials for all the birds in the vicinity.) The popularity of rustic construction was due in part to its being inexpensive. Industrialization had created a new social class. Such people could afford to buy and improve small country estates but, unlike the old aristocracy, might contemplate selling their property at some point rather than passing it on to their heirs. As J. C. Loudon, the guru of Victorian garden design, warned in his book *The Villa Gardener*, expensive brick or stone temples and garden houses added little to the market value of a property. "Ornamental buildings, therefore, are chiefly to be valued for the enjoyment they afford the proprietor during his lifetime; and, unless a part of this enjoyment consists in knowing that these buildings will descend to his posterity, prudence dictates that they should be built so as not to occasion great expense. In all that respects the introduction of ornamental buildings, however, much must be left to the particular taste of the proprietor; and, as most proprietors take pleasure in having at all times some structure, alteration, or addition, going forward, this is an additional argument in favour of structures of temporary materials, erected for picturesque effect, and as occasional resting-places; or for affording shelter, and not intended to last longer than the verdant scenery by which they are surrounded."

In America, particularly in the southern states, airy retreats were a necessity during the summer months. Construction details changed very little from the mid-18th century on. The little summer houses shown in the photographs below, with their quaintly shaped roofs, were not only decorative but completely practical. The lattice walls, which add to their grace, provide shade without blocking any breath of cooling breeze.

Modern Summer Houses In the last years of the 19th century and the early 20th century a number of large gardens were developed in England and the United States that incorporated the better features of many garden styles. These eclectic gardens usually combined areas of landscaped parkland with more formal areas, which drew upon the past for inspiration.

Summer houses were again built to match the style of the house, particularly if they were in close proximity. Mawson shows several designs for summer houses and comments, "Such erections must be designed in strict relation to their surroundings, and the amount of elaboration or rusticity of treatment which is necessary will usually be determined by their nearness to or remoteness from the mansion. Nevertheless, however rural their surroundings, nothing can justify that spurious rusticity which marked the designs of the Early-Victorian era. . . .

"A primitive summer-house or arbour is often required for a position in the wild garden, along a woodland walk or in specially interesting spots to which short excursions are made, and being away from the dominating architectural features of the residence, may be constructed of any material ready to hand. In a stone district, rough, rubble-built dry walls might be used and the roof covered with thatch of straw, gorse, or bracken, or it may be shingled or slated. . . . Such erections, if built in the simplest and most direct manner and no attempt is made to improve them by applied ornament of any kind, whether of twisted oak or virgin bark, will generally provide a summer-house rustic in character, possessing all the charm which such a retreat is capable of lending to a woodland scene, and the rusticity would be real and not of the sham description previously referred to."

Summer houses today are generally designed with the architectural style of the house in mind. Do-it-yourself instruction books, companies selling detailed building plans, and manufacturers of prefabricated garden structures offer a wide choice of period and contemporary designs.

SUNDECKS *See Decks and Platforms.*

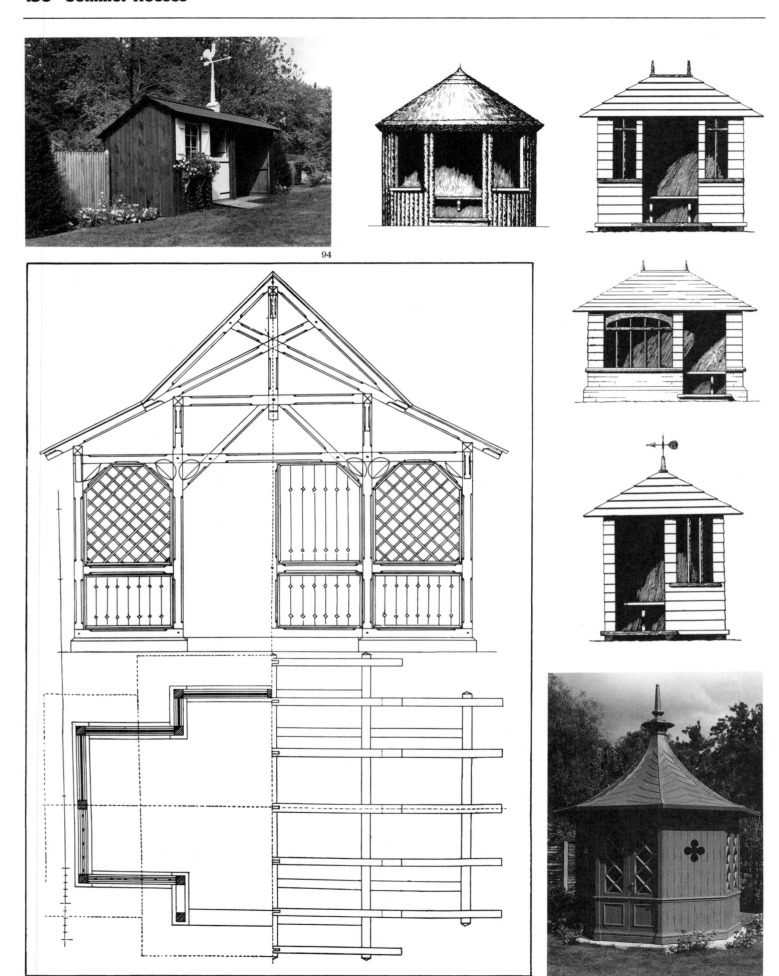

94

49

100

SUNDIALS

A sundial is an instrument for marking the passage of time by means of the position of a shadow cast by the sun. Sundials have been used since at least 1500 B.C.

The principal parts of a sundial are the *dial face*, with the hours marked, and the *gnomon*, which is a fixed object whose shadow serves as the indicator. The straight edge of the gnomon that casts the shadow line is called the *style*. This shadow-casting edge must point to the celestial pole and must form an angle with a level plane equal to the latitude of the place of intended use. These are the basics of telling time by the sun, which can be interpreted in many different ways.

Designing sundials was of particular interest in the 16th century. At that time clocks were scarce and not very accurate, and a new understanding of mathematics made possible precise calculations for sundials. Craftsmen

and mathematicians, who guarded their secrets carefully, made sundials in every imaginable size and shape. There were pocket-size dials and dials on gimbals for use at sea. Sundials were made on gravestones and on church walls and found their way into the garden as useful ornaments.

Horizontal Dials These are the most familiar dials. They are made with a flat circular plate, usually of bronze, have a triangular gnomon, and must be designed for a particular location. They are usually set on pedestals of varying degrees of ornamentation or are supported by figures—a kneeling slave in lead, Father Time assisted by Cupid—and were set as a central piece in the garden. Most had an appropriate inscription engraved on the dial: "Tempus fugit" or "I mark only the sunny hours." A sundial at Ladew Gardens in Maryland reads "I am a sundial, and I make a botch, of what is done, far better by a watch."

Vertical Dials These are similar in construction to horizontal dials but are made to be mounted on a wall or column. Pillar dials, which were often placed in town squares for public use, had four vertical dials, one on each side. They indicated not only the time but direction, for each dial must face a cardinal point of the compass.

Armillary Spheres These are spheres formed from a series of solid rings and were originally used as astronomical models. For use as sundials, the inner surface of the ring, representing the equator, serves as a dial plate. A thin rod, usually in the form of an arrow, lies parallel to the earth's axis and serves as a gnomon. These dials can be adjusted to give accurate solar time at any latitude.

Equatorial sundials are rather like streamlined armillary spheres. The rings are not closed to form a circle but are left open. Some have only a half-circle ring as a dial plate. These, too, are adjustable for latitude.

Floral Sundials Floral dials are made on the ground, using growing plants to form the dial face and usually the gnomon as well. In the 17th century they were used as another sort of parterre decoration. The illustration showing the date A: 1696 is especially interesting; it shows a small circular dial with a triangular gnomon. There is also a great checkerboarded dial face, ornamented with astrological signs and other obscure symbols. The garden must have belonged to an astrologer or someone versed in occult matters.

The Noon Cannon Cannon dials were made as early as the 17th century. A miniature cannon is mounted on a dial; it is fitted with a lens, or burning glass, which can be adjusted to focus the rays of the noon sun on the touchhole of the cannon. When the touchhole is primed with black powder, there will be a very satisfactory boom at lunch time.

100

97

SWIMMING POOLS, BATH HOUSES

Bathing Pools Modern swimming pools began with the practice, common until the 18th century, of taking baths in the garden. In an earlier age Roman engineers had developed plumbing to a high degree and made indoor baths for comfort and outdoor pools for pleasure. Roman villas with these facilities were built throughout Europe and Britain, wherever the Pax Romana extended, but these amenities did not long survive the fall of Rome. Winston Churchill, in *A History of the English-Speaking Peoples*, affirms that in the Roman period "well-to-do persons in Britain lived better than they ever did until late Victorian times. From the year 400 till the year 1900 no one had central heating and very few had hot baths. . . . Even now a smaller pro-portion of the whole population dwells in centrally heated houses than in those ancient days. As for indoor baths, they were completely lost till the middle of the nineteenth century."

Outdoor bathing pools were a feature of medieval gardens, which, according to Crisp, could be traced "directly to Oriental influence." The "Orient" at that time included the Middle East, and Crusaders returning home brought elements of Eastern garden craft.

Sir Robert Ker Porter, an early 19th-century traveler, gives us an idea of what those Eastern bathing pools might have been like. He described, with evident relish, a summer bath at a Persian palace: "this bath-saloon, or court . . . is circular, with a vast basin in its centre, of pure white marble . . . and about sixty or seventy feet in diameter. This is filled with the clearest water, sparkling in the sun, . . . rose-trees, with other pendant shrubs bearing flowers, cluster near it; and . . . throw a beautifully quivering shade over the excessive brightness of the water." The ladies of the harem "so fond are they of this luxury, they . . . remain in the water for hours. . . . The royal master . . . has only to turn his eyes to the scene below, to see the loveliest objects of his tenderness, sporting like naiads amidst the crystal stream. . . . In such a bath-court, it is probable that Bathsheba was seen by the enamoured king of Israel."

The Biblical story of Bathsheba was the inspiration for many of the medieval and postmedieval illustrations of garden baths. Artists

portrayed her in the gardens of their own time, and she appears in varying stages of undress in all sorts of basins and pools. In the wood engraving reproduced on the opposite page, she sits in a half-bath below a fountain while King David, we assume, peers out a window under which is the date 1519.

Bathing pools were usually placed where they would catch the overflow from fountains. Sometimes the fountain basin itself served as a bath. Mixed bathing was acceptable and apparently was as much a social occasion as is the modern hot tub, complete with wine and music.

As the garden grew beyond the confines of the medieval enclosure so, too, did the ideal pool enlarge. Sir Francis Bacon described "a fair receipt of water, of some thirty or forty foot square, but without fish, slime, or mud . . . the bottom . . . be finely paved, and with images; the sides likewise. . . . The main point is . . . that the water be in perpetual motion, fed by a water higher than the pool . . . and then discharged away underground." Bacon's essay *On Gardens* was published in 1597. A pool of this size must have been intended as much for pleasure as for washing.

To *bathe* means to "immerse in water," not necessarily for cleaning purposes, so it is not clear at what point a *bathing* pool became a *swimming* pool. Long after the bathtub had moved back into the house the bathing pool remained as a recreational feature in the garden, according to Thomas Mawson, for the "increasing number of persons who delight to begin the day with a vigorous cold plunge taken in the open air."

Bath Houses A bath house, sometimes called a *cabana*, can be a useful and decorative accessory to a swimming pool, particularly if the house is any distance away. They were first used solely as changing rooms, sometimes with fireplaces to ease the teeth-chattering cold of a spring-fed bathing pool. Bath houses still serve as changing rooms and storage areas for pool equipment and are often equipped with bathrooms and cooking areas for entertaining, which allow them to serve as guest houses as well.

TEA HOUSES

In the 16th century the famous tea master Sen-no-Rikyu developed what can be considered the prototype for the traditional Japanese tea houses. Tea-drinking gatherings had been popular entertainment among the upper classes for many centuries. Contests were held and prizes given to the guest who was able to identify the greatest number of different types of tea. The Zen masters transformed tea drinking into an aesthetic experience of studied simplicity, designed to teach the four basic virtues—urbanity, courtesy, purity, imperturbability.

Within the tea garden are two major buildings, the waiting shed and the tea house. The waiting shed, where the guests sit until they are invited to enter the tea house, is a narrow, open building, little more than three walls and a roof sheltering a plank bench. These structures are made of the plainest materials and paved with rough stones.

The tea house, too, is made of plain materials, and the roof is thatched or shingled with bark. The woodwork is finely crafted but left unpainted to show the grain. Walls are plastered but they, too, are left unpainted. The tea house is fully enclosed, and the windows are covered with paper so that no outside influence may intrude upon the ceremony. The door is often small and low so that guests must enter on their knees, a symbol of humbleness and the equality of all participants.

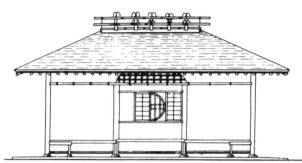
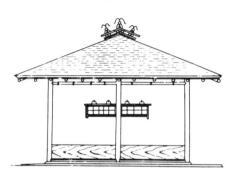

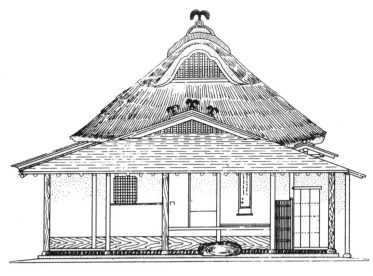

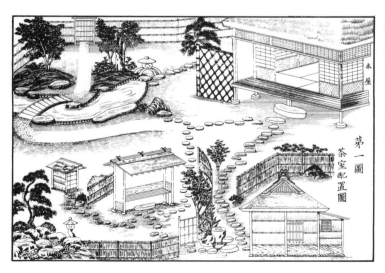

TEMPLES

The most popular type of building in the 18th-century landscape garden was the temple. These structures ranged from relatively accurate interpretations of classic models to spurious imitations to strange hybrids called "Gothic temples." Stowe, one of the earliest and most admired of the landscape parks, boasted a full complement of temples scattered over its five hundred acres. There was The Temple of Concord and Victory, modeled after the Maison Carrée at Nîmes; The Lady's Temple, with its grand Corinthian portico and statuary groups honoring womankind; The Temple of Venus; The Temple of Ancient Virtue; and a ruin, satirically named The Temple of Modern Virtue.

Many buildings of this type were open rotundas of columns supporting domed roofs, of little practical use in a northern climate. They were little more than eye-catchers, placed to terminate a vista, provide a romantic point of interest on a distant hill, or be reflected in a still lake. Others of more substantial and enclosed design housed art collections, baths, or hideaways. Humphrey Repton relates in *The Art of Landscape Gardening* the history of one such building on an estate he remodeled: "Both the form and the colour of a small house in Langley Park rendered it an object unworthy of its situation; yet, from peculiar circumstances, it was not deemed advisable either to remove it or to hide it by plantations. I therefore recommended a Doric portico to cover the front; and thus a building formerly unsightly, because out of character with the park, became its brightest ornament, doing honour to the taste and feelings of the noble proprietor, who preserved the house for having been a favourite retreat of his mother, and which, thus ornamented, may be considered as a temple sacred to filial piety."

Temples continued to be popular in public parks and private gardens throughout the 19th century. Even today temples are available in reproductions or through dealers of antique architectural components.

TENTS *See Pavilions.*

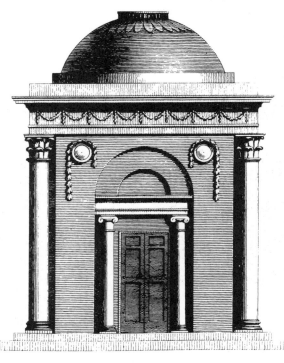

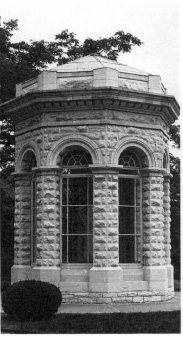

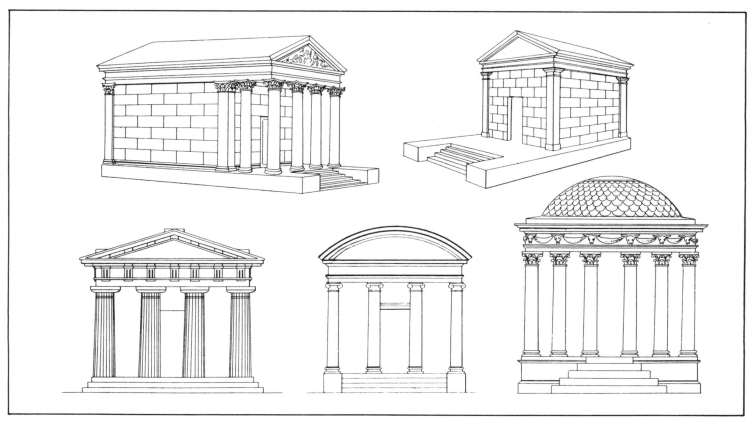

TERRACES

Ancient Terraces The terrace is an ancient garden form that came about as a result of both practical and aesthetic needs. Terracing has been used not only to control the flow and retention of water and to prevent erosion but to provide vantage points from which the garden can best be enjoyed. The ruins of the ziggurats of ancient Mesopotamia and descriptions of the Hanging Gardens of Babylon give us only a hazy picture of these early terraced gardens.

The remains of the great garden tomb of Hatshepsut and written descriptions of its planting offer a more tangible idea of this

early example. It rises against a mountain side in three broad terraces. The top one, containing the shrine, is excavated from solid rock. The terraces are formed by high retaining walls fronted with pillared corridors and connected by broad ramps leading from terrace to terrace. Descriptions by contemporaries of Queen Hatshepsut tell us exactly how the terraced gardens were treated. The most important plants were Boswellia trees, brought by ship from Punt, or Somaliland. The gum of the Boswellia was used to make frankincense. The trees were planted in pits filled with Nile mud; a low wall of mud was raised around the holes to form a basin that retained water. The

terraces were further embellished with geometric flower beds and pools where lotus and water lilies were grown.

Though this magnificent garden was undoubtedly known throughout the Mediterranean area, there are no remains or records of such a unified garden plan in Roman Italy. The Romans did build grand hillside villas with elaborate gardens on descending terraces. But so far as we know, Roman terraces were conceived as unrelated elements. Access from one level to another was provided by randomly located stairways, often virtually concealed by plantings and other garden features.

Renaissance Terraces It remained for the Italian garden designers of the late Renaissance to surpass the Egyptians by reviving and producing unified terraced gardens. In these the stairway again became a dominant architectural feature. High terrace walls with open-work balustrades, one above the other, producing strong horizontal divisions, were unified by the axial line of wide central avenues, cascades, and stairways. The terrace walls provided surfaces to be decorated with niches for statuary and fountains or to be tunneled through for grottoes. Upper terraces served as viewing points from which to admire the intricate designs of the parterres below. The terrace balustrades, a prominant feature in many Renaissance gardens, were carved of gleaming marble. The line of balusters was often broken by piers supporting statues, urns, finials, or huge vases holding clipped orange trees.

French Terraces The terracing in French gardens of the 17th and 18th centuries, while less dramatic and precipitous than Italian gardens, was essential to the rigid and orderly shaping required in these gardens.

English Terraces English garden designers were influenced by Italian and French styles, but extensive terracing, such as was practiced in those countries, was seldom feasible in England. High terraces were rarely needed and strict Parliamentary control of the king's purse strings prevented the building of royal gardens on the scale of Versailles.

English gardens of the Tudor period often had narrow terraces raised along one or more sides of the enclosing wall. These accomplished the same purpose as a mount, affording a view of the countryside and providing an eminence from which to enjoy the patterns of knot gardens and parterres. Other terraces extended along the facade of the house, with broad flights of stairs leading down to the garden. Stone balustrades were topped with urns or finials in the Italian manner. Pierced stone and arcaded balustrades produced a heavier more ornate appearance.

The landscape architects of the 18th century shunned terracing as unnatural, and as a result, many a grand house stood bare and stark on a grassy hill. With the subsequent return to formal plans in the 19th century, such estates were often remodeled and the sites again terraced and balustraded. The drawing of the Palladian mansion at Foots Cray Place shows dramatically this change in style. The balustrading of such later terraces is often made of cement castings rather than carved stone and when softened by age and weathering does not appear appreciably different form earlier counterparts. Brick open work is sometimes used to achieve much the same effect as Tudor pierced-stone balustrades.

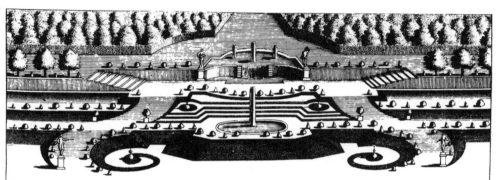

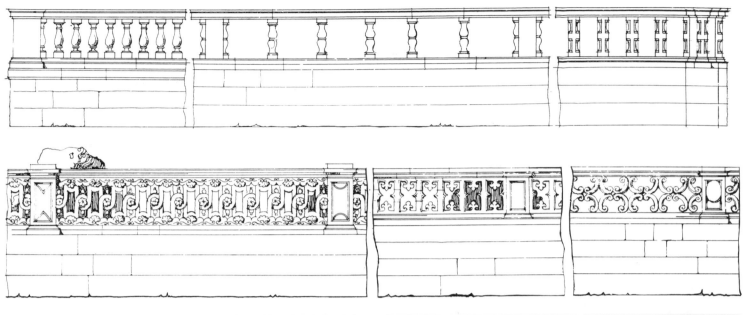

THEATERS

Teatro di Verdura The *Teatro di Verdura*, a permanent theater formed of trees and shrubbery, was a wonderful element of the Italian villa garden of the Renaissance and Baroque eras. These garden theaters, some just large enough for an audience of a dozen or so, were ideally suited for entertainments performed by traveling players or by family and guests for their own amusement. They were an appropriate setting for the pastoral dramas created by poets of the Italian Renaissance, with their tales of lovelorn shepherdesses and Arcadian bliss, and for the improvised humor of the commedia dell'arte.

The stages were designed so that no architectural element intruded; stone retaining walls supporting the stage were hidden by clipped box. The floor was turfed, and neatly trimmed hedges of ilex, cypress, or box formed the back, sides, and wings. All was contrived of greenery. For decoration there might be several life-size statues, mute actors to occupy the stage when no play was in progress.

Some of the green theaters were made as another of those separate and private "rooms" so characteristic of these gardens; the oval theater at the Villa Gori was hidden by tall hedges at the end of a long tunnel of ilex (see page 171). Others were a more important part of the garden plan. At the Villa Segardi the theater (also shown) formed the fourth side of the courtyard opposite the house and could be seen from the windows. The perspective of the overlapping wings gave an illusion of considerable depth, accenting the group of statues and creating a cool and pleasant view.

European Garden Theaters Italian garden theaters were often copied in 17th-century Europe, even in the comparatively small gardens of Holland. The illustration shows an elaborate example at Westerwyck with a proscenium arch of pleached hornbeam and a backdrop of treillage. It is interesting to note that permanent garden theaters did not become a significant part of French gardens until late in the 18th century when Le Nôtre's influence was fading. In his classic gardens of

the late 17th and early 18th centuries, there was little need for them; his designs were in themselves giant stage sets for the outdoor life of the French court. For special occasions, temporary theaters would be set up in various parts of the grounds. Many of Molière's comedies were first performed in the gardens at Versailles, and Louis XIV, clad in pink tights with a headdress of ostrich plumes, danced outdoors in a ballet by Lully.

There was, at Versailles, a magnificent semicircular "water theater" with numerous dancing jets that was sometimes used as a background for entertainments, but it was the dazzling display of water that was the main attraction.

The photograph with dancers shows a side view of the theater at Dartington Hall, Devon, England, center for arts and crafts. Although the hedging may seem unimpressive from the perspective in the photograph, from the point of view of the audience the lapped wings and backdrop would seem to be a solid wall of green that is higher than the dancers' heads.

American Outdoor Theaters Many outdoor theaters, both public and private, were built in America in the early years of this century, where the home garden theater was much less formal than in Europe and was often designed to seem like a natural woodland glade. Frank Waugh, in *Outdoor Theaters*,

1917, described an appropriate entertainment for this setting. A pretty girl in white sat beneath a tree and played Mendelssohn's "Spring Song" on the harp. "In response to this music there appeared from the dark recesses of the surrounding wood a group of fairies—children dressed in brown who danced on the green."

TOMBS *See Sculpture.*
TOOL SHEDS *See Utility Buildings.*

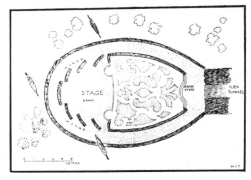

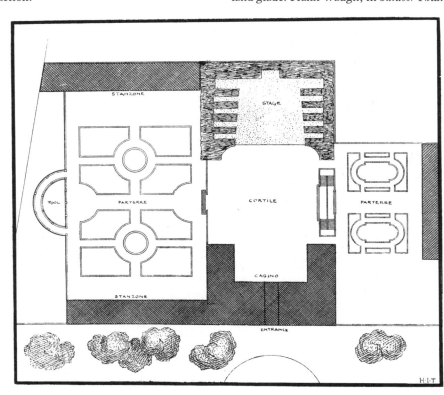

TOPIARY

Topiary is the art of shaping and clipping trees and shrubs into unnatural decorative forms. Several methods are used to achieve this end. The figures may be formed primarily by the judicious use of shears. Occasionally supports are used during the initial stages of training. Another method, often used in the 17th century, is to use lathwork forms of the shapes desired and clip the plant material to conform. Modern topiary is often made of ivy or other climbing plants trained over a three-dimensional wire frame. The advantages of this method are twofold. The figures can be more complicated because there is no need for structural support from the plant material itself. The frames can be attached to a wire planting basket that can be sunk in the ground or in containers. Thus the topiary figure can be moved if necessary.

Ancient Topiary Topiary is first mentioned in descriptions of Roman gardens and is said to have been invented in the first century A.D. by Cnaeus Martius, a Roman soldier and friend of the Emperor Augustus. More than a century later when Pliny wrote the description of his gardens at Tusci, the art had reached a high degree of refinement, for he tells of walks enclosed by hedges clipped into the shapes of animals, obelisks, ships, and "letters expressing the name of the master."

European Topiary Topiary work was apparently carried on to some extent throughout the centuries following the fall of Rome, and examples appear in medieval garden illustrations in the form of small trees clipped into tiered pompoms that were used as the central feature surrounded by geometric flower beds.

By the early 16th century more elaborate

topiary pieces, rivaling those of Pliny's time, were again popular garden ornaments. Colonna's *Hypnerotomachia Poliphili* illustrated some of the more fantastic shapes that could be achieved. Jovianus Pontanus, in *De Hortis Hesperidum*, 1500, waxed eloquent on the subject. "Plant young shoots, and arrange them in fixed rows, support them with bast, that from the start they know what they have to do, each in its own proper place. When the tree, owing to the gardener's constant care and attention, begins to put out its branches and unfold its leaves, then choose the task for each, and make the formless mass into shapes of beauty. Let one climb to high tower or bulwark, another bend to spear or bow; let one make strong the trenches or the walls; one like a trumpet must wake men to arms and summon hosts to battle; another shall throw stones from slings of brass, storming the camp, sending the foe back to their ruined walls. In those ruins the hosts go forward, and stand at the open gates; the conquering army presses into the town. Thus shall you by skill, time, native strength, and careful nurture, convert the tree into many new forms, even as a thread of wool is woven into divers figures and colours in a carpet."

While such peculiar ornaments lost their popularity in Italian gardens at the height of the Renaissance, they became increasingly popular in the rest of Europe. German and French princes enclosed their elaborate parterres with clipped hedges topped with heraldic beasts, initials, dates, and hunting scenes. The entrace to one German garden was through an arch formed by the legs of a topiary Colossus. Topiary work was especially popular in the Netherlands where the scarcity of land required a form of miniaturized garden design. Trees of any significant size were often impossible to grow because the roots soon reached water. Small topiary forms were an excellent substitute.

English Topiary Topiary, or *antike worke*,

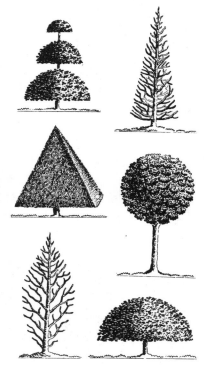

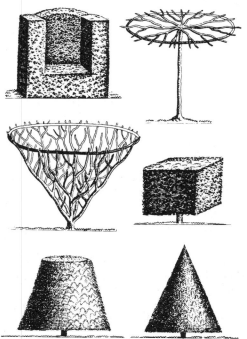

reached England, probably through Holland, and was at the height of popularity in the 17th century. Gervase Markham, in *The Countrey Farme*, gives patterns for forming "fine curious hedges made battlement-wise in sundrie forms according to invention." The hedging material, a mixture of whitethorn and sweetbrier, was entwined through wooden forms and trimmed to follow their shapes. Freestanding pieces, birds, beasts, chessmen, and jelly-mold shapes, were sculptured in yew and box. These were often set in a wide circle of sand to protect them from the scythes used to cut surrounding lawns.

The passion for topiary work eventually ran its course in England as it had in France, and the excesses resulting from the practice became a point of ridicule. Alexander Pope's famous article on the subject delivered the coup de grâce. In it he gave a list of greens for sale by an imaginary nurseryman: "ADAM and *Eve* in Yew; *Adam* an little shatter'd by the fall of the Tree of Knowledge in the great Storm. *Eve* and the Serpent very flourishing. St. GEORGE in Box; his Arm scarse long enough, but will be in a Condition to stick the Dragon by next *April*. A *green dragon* of the same, with a Tail of Ground-Ivy for the present. N.B. *These two not to be Sold separately*. A *Pair of Giants*; *stunted*, to be sold cheap. A Quick-set Hog shot up into a Porcupine, by its being forgot a Week in rainy Weather. NOAH's *Ark* in holly, standing on the Mount; the Ribs a little damaged for want of Water."

After the mid-18th century topiary was found only in cottage gardens or an occasional Dutch-style garden, spared from the improving axes of the landscape gardeners. Topiary enjoyed a brief revival in the 19th century when, in the eclectic spirit of the era, several major topiary gardens were planted in England and in Scotland.

American Topiary Long after the use of topiary died out in England, it remained popular in American gardens. At Williamsburg

and on the James River plantations little cones and pyramids of clipped box still punctuated the parterres and knot gardens. Farther north, in New York and New England, yews were still cut in the old manner. The restrained geometric designs of these topiary pieces no doubt account for their continued popularity. At the end of the 19th century, however, a garden incorporating some of the more extravagant forms was started by Thomas E. Brayton in Rhode Island. The topiary figures at Green Animals, now belonging to the Preservation Society of Newport County, include sixteen different animals executed in California privet and numerous geometric forms in box (photograph page 172 and large photograph below). Other American gardens utilizing topiary figures are Ladew Gardens in Maryland and Longwood Gardens in Delaware.

TOWERS

Prospect Towers Prospect, or belvedere, towers were quite characteristic of English landscape gardens in the 18th and early 19th centuries. They were usually situated on a hill commanding a panoramic view from which on a fine day "you could see seven counties." They were built as memorials, to commemorate a historic event, or simply to outdo a neighboring tower. They were round, square, pointed, castellated, Gothic, Italianate, and lighthouse shaped. Towers ranged in height from a mere 8 feet or so to over 150; any structure rather tall in relation to its width may be considered a tower. It is the intent of the builder that determines the case rather than architectural specifics.

Pagodas In 1761 Sir William Chambers designed a ten-story pagoda for Kew Gardens based on his own drawing of a *Ta* in Canton, China. It was the first major reproduction of an authentic Chinese building; until then only Chinoiserie decorations had been used in architecture. It was so strikingly different that it was to be copied in English and European gardens for the next fifty years. The pagoda at Kew, rising out of a clump of trees, is shown in the engraving below. The elevation shown in the accompanying drawing is one of the many designs that followed.

Windmills and Water Towers Windmills and water towers serve practical purposes; one pumps water, the other stores it at a sufficient height so as to give the required "head" of pressure for home and garden use. Water towers often had a belvedere at the top for viewing the scenery, a garden room on the ground level, and sometimes a clock on the tower as well.

Folly Towers One definition of a *folly* is "a foolish building built on the estate of a wealthy eccentric." Most garden structures do not qualify, for they lack what Barbara Jones, in *Follies and Grottos*, 1953, describes as "that essential dispensation of reason which distinguishes the folly." By her definition, a good one, all privately built towers have crossed the borderline of unreason to join those other garden eccentricities—grottoes—in folly land.

TREE HOUSES

A tree house may be anything from a few boards nailed together by ambitious children after reading *Swiss Family Robinson* to a guest house designed by an architect. They have been called *arbors*, *bowers*, *crow's-nests*, *roosting places*, *tree seats*, and *tree rooms*. The common factor is that all are made above ground level and in or around a tree.

Tree houses seem to have been most popular in the 16th and 17th centuries, for it is from travelers of this period that we learn of many curious examples. They were common in Italy, sometimes as an elaborate sort of "water surprise," with jets hidden among the branches to give climbers a thorough drenching. At Pratolino there was an oak so large that two persons could walk side by side up the spiral staircase twined around its massive trunk.

Tall trees were used as observation points: Celia Fiennes visited the estate of the Duke of Bedford in the late 1600s, where "there is a Seate up in a high tree that ascends from Ye green 50 steps that Commands the whole parke round to see the Deer hunted, as also a Large prospect of the Country."

Pleached Tree Houses The art of pleaching was as necessary as carpentry in building some arborial rooms. Montaigne described a "little chamber made amongst the boughs of an evergreen tree of . . . luxuriant growth" at Castello. "It is entirely clipped out of the green boughs of the tree," so dense that windows had to be made by clearing away branches. "In the midst of the chamber, from pipes which are concealed, rises a fountain which is set in the middle of a marble table. By a certain device the water made music."

In Europe and England summer banquet houses were made in trees that were clipped and trained to form a room seven or eight feet

above the ground. The trunk of the tree formed the central column, with branches bent to form the roof and sides. In the engraving of a Dutch garden of the 17th century one "bower" has columns supporting the outer edges of the floor, forming a second room beneath. Montaigne saw such tree houses in Germany and Switzerland and commented that "the tree brought into this form is a very beautiful object."

Parkinson was awed by an "arbour" at Cobham, Kent, "the goodliest spectacle" that ever he had seen. It was made in three stories, with branches plashed to form the roof of one and the floor of the next level. The whole structure was large enough for fifty people.

Persian Tree Houses Tree houses were not restricted to Western gardens; indeed, it is possible they originated in the East. Gothein wrote that "the love of trees is an inheritance for all Persians; as in ancient days, they still love to have little rooms fixed up among the branches, and steps to help them up into the tree." Who could fail to be impressed by the tree house shown in the mid-16th century Persian miniature reproduced below. The artist must have been dealing with a familiar subject, note the practical brace supports.

Modern Tree Houses Phebe Humphreys was one of the few 20th-century writers to treat tree houses as a serious subject, worthy of the attention of garden makers, and devoted a chapter of *The Practical Book of Garden Architecture*, 1917, to their design and construction. Humphreys felt that a tree house should be built away from the house and, therefore, in a less public part of the garden, where one could find "delightful seclusion up among the breezes in the shelter of tree branches." She distinguished between a real tree house and a crow's-nest: the real crow's-nest is never roofed over; yet a real tree house has a roof, walls, windows, and doors and might be fitted up with a cot, provide storage for bed linens and tea making apparatus—an ideal work room or study for adults.

Much of the appeal of tree houses lies in their variety, since the tree, or trees, available dictates the size and shape. They are best finished with barked slabs, poles, or shingles to make them look as much a part of the tree as possible. Stairs are necessary for less-agile grownups and small children.

TREE SEATS *See Furniture.*

TREILLAGE

Treillage is a French word that can be translated into English only as "trelliswork"; however, to do so is to miss the more subtle implications of the word. To fix an exact division between latticework construction and treillage is almost impossible, but the French word implies trelliswork of a highly developed nature and which is architecturally significant.

Dutch Treillage While there are earlier examples of lath construction that might be considered treillage, the art was developed to a high degree of refinement in the 17th century. The Dutch treillage illustrated by J. Van der Groen in 1669 are some of the less-elaborate constructions of this genre. The lath used in Dutch treillage was comparatively heavy; the details were simple and rather crude.

French Treillage French treillage was lighter and more elaborate than the Dutch. It was constructed of chestnut, oak, or ash lath that was one inch wide. The pieces of lath were lashed together with a single strand of iron wire. Thin iron supports, painted to look like lath, were used to strengthen vaults and uprights. Decorations of garlands, bouquets, and leaves that were cut from sheet iron then

painted or gilded were often added. Dezallier d'Argenville lists some of the uses for treillage: "Arbors, Porticos, Galleries, Cabinets, Summer-Houses, Salons, Niches, and Shells, adorn'd with Columns, Pilasters, Cornices, Pedaments, Jambs, Pannels, Vases, Corbels, Frontispieces, Domes, Lanterns, and other Ornaments of Architecture." He goes on to advise that "a just Proportion ought to be observed, and every Part of the Ordonance should be regulated and determin'd by a Module, as though it were a Building."

The popularity of treillage was due in part to the fact that it could be designed and built

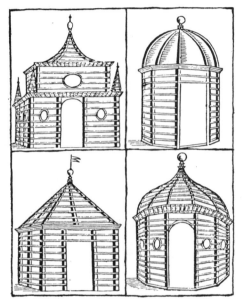

quickly and provided finished effects long before hedges or trees would grow to desirable height. This was an advantage in a period when the whims of royalty might dictate that a garden be planned and executed within a short period of time.

Modern Treillage Due to the ephemeral nature of the materials used, 17th- and 18th-century treillage constructions are known to us only through illustrations of the period. Examples of 19th-century and modern treillage, however, are not hard to find, for it is still a useful and popular kind of garden construction. As John Belcher points out, "Such a medium may be to the Architect what clay is to the Sculptor; in it he may venture to give shape to some poetic dream of ethereal architecture which has visited his brain, or at any rate (if this seems too large a flight of fancy) he may realise, if only temporarily, some playful fancy for his own satisfaction in work, which from the very nature of its material cannot be taken seriously, or raise great expectations. It is the ease and facility with which daring experiments can be made which render it valuable. It can be altered and shifted at pleasure until the desired effect is obtained in a way which more solid and valuable materials prohibit."

One of the more fanciful of these poetic dreams is found in the rustic screen at Dunbarton Oaks with its trompe l'oeil niche and inlaid abalone-shell fountain. More traditional types are exemplified by the relatively simple half-round arbor seat at Montalvo and the magnificent screen at the M. H. De Young Memorial Museum in San Francisco. From the 17th century to the present treillage has commonly been used to mask the surrounding walls of city gardens. Here trompe l'oeil effects are particularly valuable as they create the illusion of space in an enclosed area.

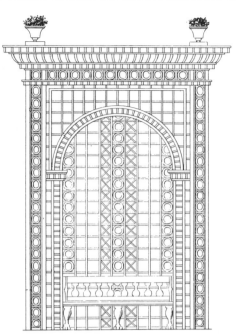

TRELLISES

Trellises are simple structures used for supporting, training, and displaying plants. They are necessary in the kitchen garden for supporting vines such as peas, beans, grapes, and berries. In pleasure gardens trellises are used to support and display flowering vines and roses. They may be flat or three-dimensional, freestanding or used against a wall or fence. Though the term *trellis* is often used interchangeably with *arbor*, a trellis is primarily a supporting device; an arbor defines and encloses a space, making it, at least in part, a shelter.

Flat Trellises Flat trellises may be used freestanding or against a wall. Freestanding trellises are used to espalier plants in much the same way as fruit walls do. The attractive post-and-rail trellises at the Governor's Palace in Williamsburg support dwarf fruit trees (see photograph below). Metal posts strung with wires are the most common form.

Flat trellises for vines and roses were often used in 17th-century Dutch gardens. Old prints show highly decorative fan, cone, and obelisk shapes that were made of wood lath or a combination of wood and wire. Flat trellises were popular in American gardens throughout the 19th century and into the early years of the 20th century. They were used freestanding, against walls, and to screen windows and verandas. Designs ranged from simple to elaborate geometric arrangements.

Arches and Festoons Arched trellises are used in a number of ways. A single archway over a path can mark the division between two different areas of the garden or draw the eye to some feature of the distant landscape. A series of arches spanning a pathway can create much the same effect as a gallery. A row of arches, side by side, forming a circular enclosure around a central focal point such as a fountain, sundial, or statue, can give unity and vertical emphasis to a large, flat area of bedding. Boundary screens formed by a series of arched trellises are often used to form frames for borrowed scenery.

Somewhat similar to the latter treatment is

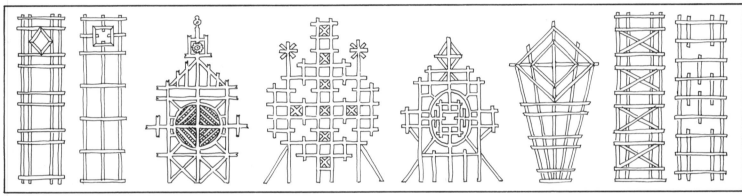

a line of pillars connected one to the other by loops of chain on which vines may be trained in festoons. These were particularly popular in 19th-century Germany, where the entire garden might be enclosed within a trellis of decorative wrought iron posts and festoons of roses. Indeed, all of the aforementioned supports were commonly used in rose gardens, because they provided the full exposure to the sun that is necessary for profuse blossoming. Mawson, however, recommends that the upright portions of such trellises be made of wood rather than metal so that the initial growth of the vines or roses will not be retarded by cold conducted through the supports.

Three-Dimensional Trellises Trellises in three-dimensional forms such as obelisks and piers were used in 17th-century Dutch gardens. Those illustrated at right, though relatively simple in design, presage the more complicated architectural forms of later treillage. Victorian examples of such trellises were often placed over the plants that grew up inside the structures. In the old photograph shown a crude country version filled with a tangle of honeysuckle provides a fragrant climbing structure for a small boy dressed in his Sunday best.

Utilitarian, yet no less decorative, trellises were made for use in kitchen gardens. At Williamsburg, hop poles supported by a maze of stringers create a corridor of green pillars. Vase-shaped grape trellises shown in a 19th-century German garden book are so decorative that one wonders how practical they actually were.

Bamboo trellises are often used in Japanese gardens. Umbrellalike structures are used to support the branches of ancient cherry trees. Another common form is a simple grid raised on poles to support wisteria vines. These are often extended out over water so that the blossoms may be enjoyed in reflection as well as firsthand.

TUBS *See Plant Containers, Plant Stands.*
URNS *See Plant Containers, Plant Stands; Sculpture.*

UTILITY BUILDINGS

European Buildings Utility Buildings—if one discounts the garden houses of the English Tudor period, which contained rooms on the lower level that were used for fruit and tool storage—were not allowed to intrude upon the garden until the 18th century. With the development of the picturesque garden and particularly the *ferme ornée*, or ornamental farm, in the mid-1800s, however, the utility building became one more excuse for romantic and fanciful architecture.

The English ferme ornée was a genuine attempt to combine the ornamental and the practical by disguising utilitarian farm buildings within exotic eye-catchers such as Gothic castles and Chinese temples. Odd corners of fields were planted with flowers and hedgerows, beautified with roses and ornamental trees. Winding gravel paths were laid out through the farmland, and small serpentine rivers were provided for the ducks and geese. The larger concept of the ferme ornée soon proved to be impractical; however, the idea of

decorative utility buildings remained popular through the 19th century. Books of designs for cow sheds, barns, rabbitries, and chicken houses, often in the rustic style, were circulated at this period. Privies, too, were housed in unusual and amusing structures. The four French designs shown here typify the extent to which some of these frivolities were carried. One of these "commodities" is concealed in the trunk of a hollow tree, another in what appears to be a stack of firewood.

American Buildings The southern plantations of Colonial America were, of necessity, largely self-sufficient communities. Most of the needs of the plantation were met by slave labor and a great number of utility buildings, kitchens, weaving rooms, carpenter shops, wash houses, dairies, stables, carriage houses, smoke houses, spring houses, and privies were needed to house these activities. Many of these out-buildings were, for convenience, located in close conjunction to the main house and, as a result, became important elements in the design of the grounds and gardens. Often built in the same architectural style as the mansion, they were generally arranged more or less symmetrically, flanking the house as at Mount Vernon, or were placed to one side of the house around a central service area.

Town houses and smaller, less remote country houses required fewer out-buildings but still needed a number of dependencies. These were usually arranged bordering the garden with the stables the farthest removed from the house.

Utility buildings in modern gardens are usually confined to potting and tool sheds. The stone tool shed built against a wall at Dunbarton Oaks (see photograph) is a substantial and highly decorative example of such structures.

VASES See *Plant Containers, Plant Stands; Sculpture.*

WALKS See *Alleys and Avenues, Arbors, Paths, Pleached Trees and Shrubs.*

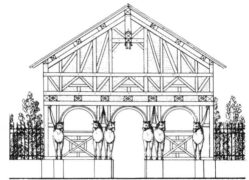

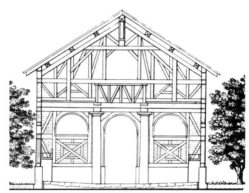

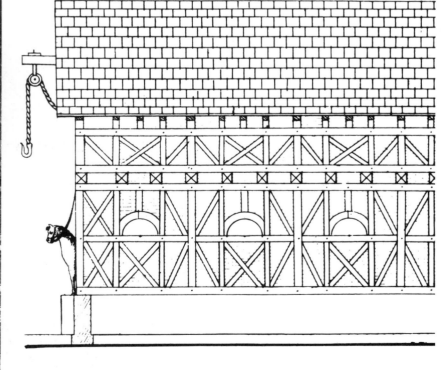

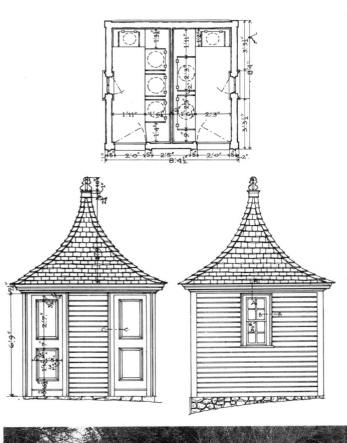

WALLS

Brick and Adobe Walls Brick, the oldest and most universal man-made building material, may have been in common use as much as 12,000 years ago. Ancient builders simply dried their bricks in the sun. The adobe block walls of Spanish America testify to the durability of unfired bricks. Adobe walls, while massive and substantial, retain a softness of outline, even when stuccoed and painted, that blends well with growing things. The traditional and most attractive copings for such walls are made of interlocking roof tiles, which are laid on a slope to shed water.

Over the centuries hundreds of ways have been devised to beautify brick construction; bricks have been glazed, carved, and embossed; the colors have been subtly changed by varying the composition of the clays. Scores of bonds, or laying patterns, have been used to give richness and variety to surface design.

The construction of brick walls, because of the very nature of the material, is lighter than that of stone. A straight, freestanding wall no more than two feet high may be built successfully only four inches wide, or the width of one brick; or it may be as high as six feet if it is curved. The serpentine wall, like the old worm fence, derives stability from its form; but, unlike its wooden counterpart, it is more economical in terms of materials than a straight wall, which would need a two-brick thickness. The invention of the serpentine wall, popularly but erroneously ascribed to Thomas Jefferson, was probably European. This type of wall was common in England long before those famous ones at the University of Virginia were built. Serpentine walls are laid out by establishing a section of the radius of a circle and continuing it in a joined series of reverse curves. They may be built in short, deep bays or in long, shallow ones, depending on the terrain and the effect desired.

Straight walls higher than two feet should be built at least eight inches thick, or the length of a common brick. Long stretches of wall are often reinforced with piers that are set at twelve-foot intervals. In the presence of piers and a solid eight-inch base, the panels between piers may be made in an open-work pattern four inches thick. This style of wall is useful in warm climates because it allows air to circulate and at the same time affords a certain degree of privacy.

Often the most decorative feature of a brick wall is the coping. Many methods were used by Colonial masons, some employing standard brick shapes and others using half-round or "beaded" bricks made for the purpose.

Rammed-Earth Walls Rammed-earth walls are made by stamping moistened earth mixed with bonding agents into a wooden form. When the earth is dry, the form is removed and the surface is plastered. This is one of the most common techniques for building walls in Oriental gardens.

In China the plaster is sometimes tinted in shades ranging from brick red to greenish brown, but, most often, it is white. White plaster was traditionally made of paper pulp and chalk and, after application, was rubbed with wax to give it a shiny surface. A wall plastered in this manner, with the tracery of bamboo or plum trees against it, has been compared to a brush painting on the white paper of a scroll.

Two types of copings are commonly used on Chinese walls: a peaked roof with wide overhanging eaves covered with ornate black, yellow, or deep blue glazed tiles and a simpler one consisting of layers of half-round tiles which form an open-work frieze that is sandwiched between two courses of flat tiles (see detail drawing). The most distinctive aspect of Chinese walls is that they tend to follow the contour of the land. They slide over hillocks, down into gullies, and wind along the banks of lakes as though squeezed from a tube. They seldom form sharp angles but curve and snake around obstacles. The Chinese garden usually has many dividing walls within the outer wall, forming a number of courtyards. The inner walls are pierced by windows that are cut in the shape of fans, fruits, or flowers. Doorways, too, assume shapes such as vases, gourds, and shells, as well as the familiar moon shape.

Japanese rammed-earth walls differ from the Chinese in that they are generally straight, enclosing precise square or rectangular plots. The more refined of these walls are made with a framework of heavy wooden posts and stringers; the panels between are filled with plastered and painted mud. These are, in effect, something between a wall and a fence. They are coped with a peaked-tile or wooden roof carried on brackets. The tiles may be of the ornate Chinese type or of a simpler wave-shaped type with a pronounced overlap, eliminating the need for half-round tiles to cover the joints.

Less-formal Japanese walls are heavier in appearance and generally set on a stone base to protect the plaster from ground moisture and road splashing. A third type of rammed-earth wall is often used to enclose temple grounds. This style of wall is left unplastered, the surface textured by courses of broken tile or thin stones embedded in the mud.

Stone Walls Stonework for walls falls into two general categories: ashlar and rubble. Ashlar work is made of carefully dressed stone of uniform size and shape. The face of the stone may be finished in any way, from finely polished to an extremely rough surface, but the joints between are no more than one-eighth inch wide when laid. Because of the expense and the painstaking nature of this work, it is rarely used for garden walls. When it *is* used, it is often confined to the decorative detailing around gateways; or it is used as a thin facing, applied over a rougher grade of stone or brickwork that forms the main structure of the wall.

Rubble construction covers an equally broad spectrum of stonework, from the crudest form of drywall to highly refined work closely resembling ashlar, differing only in the width of the mortar joints. Dry rubble walls, those put together without mortar, range from the very crude lines of stone cleared from the fields that are often seen along country roads to the massive, precision-cut-and-fitted bastions of Japan. Copings are not strictly necessary on dry walls because cracking due to freezing is not a problem and tumbled stones are easily replaced.

Mortared rubble walls may achieve different effects, depending on the type of stone used and the width and depth of the mortar joints. Round river stones or natural field stones laid with deep mortar joints produce much the same appearance as drywall construction, except that walls built in this manner must be coped to prevent water from seeping into the wall. The simplest way to protect the wall is with a solid layer of mortar spread along the top surface. Schist set on edge in mortar is effective, as is the overhanging shingle roof on the Pennsylvania fieldstone wall shown in the photograph below. A common and attractive finish is provided by slabs of cut stone carefully fitted and mortared. These copings are generally slightly wider than the wall so that they direct water away from the wall surface.

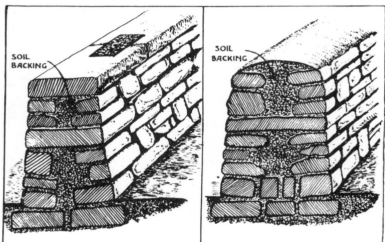

SOIL BACKING

SOIL BACKING

Planting Walls Planting walls, whether retaining a bank or freestanding, must be built with several requirements in mind. They must provide pockets of soil for planting and must be built so that water will reach the roots of the plants. A strong batter, or slope, and the elimination of an overhanging coping help to direct water into planting areas, but other measures should be taken as well. In rubble construction, the natural irregularities of the stone will catch the rain, but in brick walls the addition of a slightly projecting slate below each planting hole may serve that purpose. Good drainage must be provided to prevent puddling inside the wall. The planting soil and some plants are introduced during the building process. Further planting is done upon completion of the wall by rolling seeds in balls of moist soil and inserting them from the outside. If mortar is used, it should be made with river sand instead of beach sand to avoid buildup of salt in the planting soil.

Clairvoyées Triggs, in *Garden Craft in Europe*, says that the clairvoyée was, despite its French name, "a purely Dutch invention. Placed at the end of an alley, it consists of two or more brick piers with an ornamental iron grille between, to extend the garden view to the country beyond, perhaps to some church steeple or other feature of the landscape." He gives no explanation for his assumption that they were of Dutch origin, and, indeed, they were used in 17th-century French and English gardens as well. These early clairvoyées, like the grand gateways of the 17th century, were one more area where the wrought iron craftsman could display his skills. An interesting alternative to the clairvoyée is described by Dezallier d'Argenville. He suggests that a painted perspective might be substituted to cover "such Walls as terminate Walks that can be pierced no farther. They make handsome Decoration enough, and their fallacious Openings are very Surprizing. They are painted either in Oil, or in Fresco, and are secured above by a small Roofing, which throws off the Rain-Water that would otherwise run along the Wall, and quite spoil the Painting." He goes on to say that "the perspective at Ruel was so well painted that the Birds would be ready to break their heads against the Wall attempting to go through the Arch where the sky was Painted."

Later examples, like the circular clairvoyée at the Governor's Palace at Williamsburg, (see photograph), were more in the nature of windows. These smaller openings, where there was no danger of intruders, were often left ungrilled.

Ha-Has The ha-ha, a type of retaining wall, was one of the major factors in the development of the English landscape garden. Its purpose was not for terracing but to provide a concealed barrier between garden and pasture lands. It was formed by digging a sloping ditch on the pasture side, backed by a retaining wall that rose no higher than ground level on the garden side. Viewed at any distance from the garden, the entire contrivance was invisible and the sweep of lawn appeared uninterrupted. Stairs could be added without breaking the illusion if the landing was dropped several steps below the lip of the wall.

Some people regarded the ha-ha in this form a hazard to unsuspecting visitors. John Hughes recommends that a low parapet be erected along the top. This, however, he warned, constituted its own danger, "unless the distance at which it [the balustrade] can be seen is very short, or unless the slope can be made very long; for it is clear that if the distance be so great as to conceal the ditch, the balustrade will seem to be on the level, and will appear to be placed there on purpose to be leaped over," leaving one with the amusing picture of some 18th-century dandy, thinking to impress the ladies with a graceful vault over the railing and ending ignominiously among the cows.

WATER, ANCIENT USES

We know from tomb paintings that pools were an important feature in Egyptian gardens. They were a necessity for the storage of water, but they were a major decorative element as well. Some were simple rectangular tanks with deep sloping sides and stairs leading down to the water; others were extensions of a canal outside the walls and deep enough to accommodate boats. T-shaped canals with landing stages at the ends are pictured in some paintings that show they were planted with lotuses and were probably stocked with fish and waterfowl.

The Romans used water in many ways to embellish their gardens. Little remains today of the great villa gardens, but at Tivoli the half-ruined Canopus at Hadrian's Villa Ad-riana gives a clear picture of what their pools were like. Smaller Roman homes at Pompeii and Herculanium were built around courtyards. The *atrium*, or entrance court, where guests were received, usually contained a small pool, or *impluvium*, to catch rainwater from the roof. A larger court, the *peristyle*, was often planted as a garden and included pools, basins, and fountains. The Villa of Tiburtinus at Pompeii has a long narrow garden with a T-shaped canal behind the house. The crosspiece runs the length of the *triclinium*, or summer dining room, and the stem bisects the garden. Other gardens have square or rectangular pools that are fed by a center fountain or a marble water-stair. These early cascades consisted of five or six steps of about the same dimensions as a normal stairway. They were placed in front of a half-round niche and were decorated with mosaics and statues. Water gushing from the niche flowed down the steps into the pool.

Water was *the* most important element in the Persian garden. It was revered by the people of Mesopotamia as the source of all life. Their traditional garden form had a central tank from which four canals issued, dividing the garden into four equal parts, just as the four rivers of life were believed to divide the world. This form is often seen in the Moorish gardens of Spain and northern Africa as well as in the Mogul gardens of India, for Islamic gardens were derived from the ancient Persian prototype.

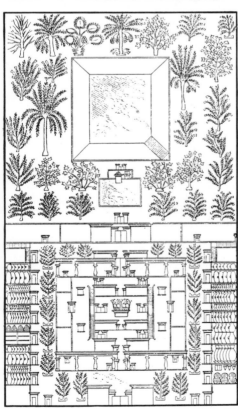

WATER, FORMAL USES

Spanish Pools and Canals A form often found in Spanish gardens is a single canal, the four-part division of its Islamic heritage suggested only by a cross-path. The main patio of the Generalife in Granada has such a pool. In the Patio de los Cipreses a U-shaped canal embraces two square flower beds and a small central pool (see drawing below). The jets arching over the canal are believed to be a Renaissance addition.

Italian Pools and Cascades Water in all its forms—still pools, bursting fountains, rushing cascades, and secret trickles—was the principal feature in Italian Renaissance gardens. In the early ones, those of the 15th century, pools were often still, centered with a fountain that was notable as fine statuary rather than for any exuberant display of water.

In the 16th century the use of water became more daring. At the Villa d'Este, in addition to fountains, water theaters, and mossy grottoes, there are four square pools of still water on the lower terrace. In the mid-17th-century engraving reproduced below, the pools seem relatively plain and unadorned except for the fountain piers and rows of lemon trees. But pictures from a century before present an entirely different view. In earlier drawings the two center pools are shown to have been decorated with elegant little kiosks, possible shelters for waterfowl, while the two outer pools were divided into parterrelike patterns and crossed by small arched bridges.

Water parterres, groups of geometric pools arranged in a unified design with a large central fountain, were popular during this period. One of the loveliest of these water gardens is the Isolotto at Boboli in Florence. Enclosed within a high ilex hedge is a large oval pool, in the center of which is an oval island. Incorporated into the carved-stone balustrade that surrounds the island are huge terra cotta pots containing orange trees. Figures of mermen on horses decorate the pool, and the gigantic Oceanus fountain dominates the island.

Cascades were often included in 16th- and 17th-century Italian gardens. At the Villa d'Este a rustic cascade constructed of huge boulders pours water from three different sources into a swirling pool. The water is then conveyed underground to appear again as the four pools mentioned above. These rustic cascades were frankly artificial and never intended to imitate natural waterfalls.

French Pools and Canals The use of water in large, still pools gave the French Renaissance garden its distinction. Medieval French castles were often moated or built in the loop of a river for purposes of defense. When these estates were refurbished and expanded during the Renaissance, the moats were incorporated into garden plans and became a strong element in the development of the distinctive national garden style of the next century.

Du Cerceau's drawings of chateaus of this period show garden after garden dominated by great canals and pools. One of the most spectacular was at Gaillon where the canal ended in a large pool with an island pavilion in the center (partially visible in the engraving below). Paralleling this canal is a second canal with circular pools at either end and a square pool in the center, a form strangely reminiscent of some Moorish designs. Such canals and pools were often used for elaborate water pageants where mock sea battles were fought.

Le Nôtre, Louis XIV's major garden designer, brought the French style to its zenith at Versailles. There, the great canal became the unifying feature of a vast garden. In the form of a cross, the main axis of the canal starts at the foot of the Grande Allée in front of the palace and stretches for a mile, seeming almost to reach the horizon (see engraving below). The side arms of the canal lead to the Ménagerie on the south and the Trianon on the north. At the eastern end is a square port where, in Louis XIV's time, a number of boats were moored.

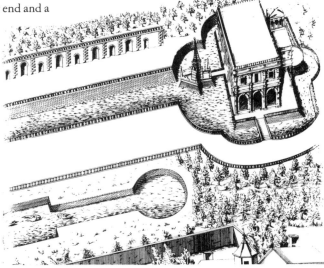

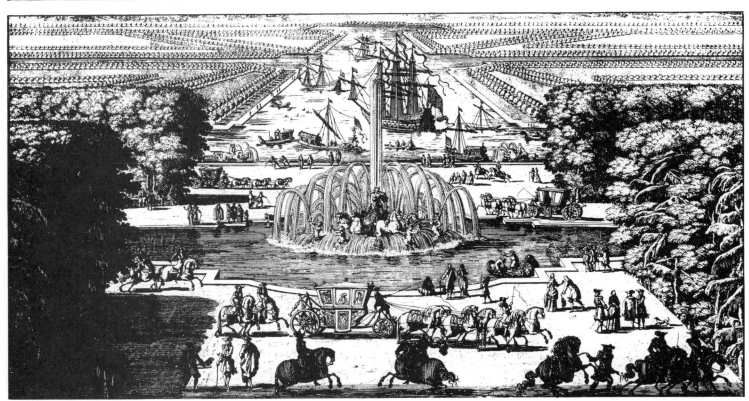

English Pools and Canals Despite Francis Bacon's complaint that "pools mar all, and make the garden unwholesome, and full of flies and frogs," the fish pond was a prime feature in English gardens of the 15th and 16th centuries. They were often less ornamental than practical, usually rectangular with sloping turf banks and a small tank, or stew, at one end where fish that had been netted could be kept until they were needed in the kitchen. Markham, in *Cheape and Good Husbandrie*, gives a plan for a fish pond to be made on marshy ground or where a stream runs through the property. "You shall dig your Pond not above eight feet deepe, and so it may carry not above six foot of water. You shall pave all the bottome, and bankes of the Pond,

with large Sods of Flotgrasse, which naturally growes under water, for it is a great feeder of Fish; and you shall aly them very close together, and pinne them downe fast with small stakes and windings. You shall upon one side of the Pond in the bottome, stake fast divers battens of Faggots of brushwood, wherein your fish shall cast their spawne, for that will defend it from destruction; and at another end you shall lay sods, with grasse sides together in the bottome of the Pond, for that will nourish and breed Eales; and if you sticke sharp stakes slant-wise by everie side of the Pond, that will keep thieves from robbing them."

As the influence of the French garden styles began to be felt the old fish ponds gave way to more ornamental pools. Long canals in the

manner of Le Nôtre, bordered by high hedges and statuary, while rarely on the scale of Versailles, were built in a number of English gardens. The Long Water at Hampton Court, laid out by French gardeners under Charles II, was three-fourths of a mile long. The narrow canals at Westbury Court, shown in the photograph below, are more typical of the smaller English water gardens.

Modern Pools and Canals With the revival of formal styles in the 19th century, geometric pools and canals came back into popularity and were prominent in the Victorian garden. In the early 20th century one of the most original and influential garden designers, Gertrude Jekyll, built garden pools which still inspire delight and emulation.

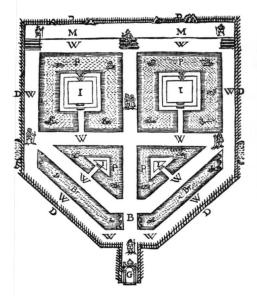

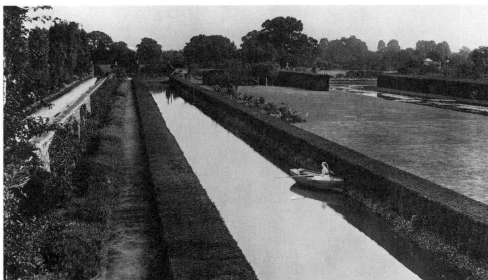

Jekyll's use of water, like her use of plant material, was designed with a painter's eye.

"The association of water and trees is always desirable; in the case of gardens where the trees are of full growth, the tank may be of more than ordinary pictorial value. The level surface fosters the sensation of repose and enhances the impressiveness of the tree masses. Even a feeling of awe may be inspired when the reflection of an unbroken dark mass of foliage creates an illusion of unknown depth. The actual fact of reflection is the source of numberless effects of the highest pictorial beauty—pictures that change from hour to hour, and change again with every altered point of view assumed by the spectator. Any garden ornament or piece of architecture mirrored in water receives an addition to its dignity by the repetition and continuation of upright line."

Many of Jekyll's pools were relatively modest in size. Most were geometric, though she found "room for an occasional burst of gaiety in outline, especially when the rest of the garden plan is of necessity treated in a severe fashion." The pools were seldom more than two feet deep and were often built with a three-foot-wide ledge around the perimeter, which was only one foot deep to provide a shallower planting area. This ledge was not only a convenience for planting but a safety measure as well, for Jekyll was partial to pools bordered by a flat curbing laid flush with the surrounding lawn or pavement.

Such modest geometric pools are often found in modern American gardens, as are designs drawn from other traditional European sources. At Longue Vue in New Orleans the long reflecting pool with its arched jets recalls the Moorish gardens of Spain, as do the octagonal pools connected by a narrow channel. One of the most elaborate pools is the water parterre at Dunbarton Oaks. There a sheet of water only a few inches deep glistens over an intricate design laid in colored pebbles with an effect reminiscent of 17th-century broideries. See photograph below.

WATER, JAPANESE USES

Japanese Ponds The ponds in Japanese gardens are made to represent specific types of scenery, such as the open sea, ocean lagoons, marshes, lakes, or rivers. The banks, islands, bridges, and planting all conform to the chosen mode. The shape of the pond is important. Some shapes are considered auspicious and others bad luck. A small fish pond in a garden of limited size is generally round, square, or crescent shaped, although the outline is never clearly evident but concealed by rocks and planting. Larger ponds are often made in the shape of the written cursive symbols for *heart* or *water* or in the *running water*

shape, which resembles a broad slow-moving river. The inlet and outlet of a pond should seem naturalistic in location but are usually hidden behind a hill or rocks so that an artificial source is not evident.

The ponds that represent lakes have islands connected to the shore by bridges. The banks are planted with grasses and are relatively free of rocks. Marsh-style ponds are surrounded by low dunelike hills and are planted with reeds and bamboo. Broad-river ponds are shallow, with exposed sandbanks, and are bordered with appropriate planting.

The banks of Japanese ponds may be treated in ways other than those mentioned

here; often they are lined with stakes, either of charred chestnut or, in modern ponds, of concrete cast to resemble logs. The stakes are driven into the ground like pilings and may be used to border the entire pond or only intermittently in combination with rocks. Horizontal wooden rails, held in place by posts and backed by an area of pebbles, are sometimes used. Modern ponds are usually lined with concrete, but it is always carefully concealed. The outer edges are formed into a step where half-submerged rocks can be set. Smaller stones, plantings, and turf cover any hint of concrete at the rim, and the bottom of the pool is covered with sand and pebbles.

In some gardens, where "dry" ponds are made, water is suggested by white sand that has been raked into wave patterns. Islands are indicated by groupings of rocks; shrubs may represent distant hills or mountains.

Japanese Streams Japanese garden streams are usually constructed on gentle slopes and are curved to follow natural formations. The stream beds are strewn with rocks to create ripples. The source is always hidden in undergrowth. If the source is an artificial one, it is made to issue from between rocks or from a deep pool as though from an underground spring. Where a stream changes course, a large "turning stone" is set so that it looks as if the water was forced to flow around it. The banks of streams are never completely lined with rocks. Low, mossy banks and small-scale planting hide portions of the stream to create a mood of woodsy mystery and cool freshness. Dry streams may be constructed in the same manner with white sand or pebbles representing water.

Japanese Waterfalls A Japanese garden in rarely without at least one waterfall. While it is an important feature, it is seldom placed in the forefront of the garden composition. Instead, it is seen first, or merely heard, from a distance. The 12th-century garden manual *Sakuteiki* laid out the conventions for the building of waterfalls and is still considered a valuable guide for this as well as almost every other facet of garden making. The *Sakuteiki* lists a number of different waterfall types as well as the stones used in their construction.

Josiah Conder, in *Landscape Gardening in Japan*, describes some of these traditional forms. "*Thread-falling*—a term used when the water pours over the rough surface of a rock in such a way as to fall in thread-like lines. *Right-and-left-falling*—applied to a Cascade dividing on two sides. *Side-falling*—to indicate water falling on one side only. *Folding-falling*—a Cascade bounding from rocks in several steps or falls. *Front-falling*—a Cascade pouring evenly

over a rock or cliff in full front view of the spectator. *Stepped-falling*—a Cascade which is broken into steps like a torrent. *Leaping-falling*—a Cascade shooting out with great force from its source. *Wide-falling*—descriptive of a Cascade of great width in proportion to its height. *Heaven-falling*—a Cascade of great elevation in which the water tumbles in layers. *Linen-falling*—to indicate a weak and wavy fall, suggestive of a sheet of linen in the wind."

The stones that make up a waterfall are very important and have specific functions and names. The stone at the lip of the falls over which the water flows is the *mirror*, or *cliff*, stone. The flanking stones on either side and slightly forward of the cliff stone are the *guardian*, or *tall vertical*, stone and the *low vertical*, or the *Fudo*, stone. Fudo is a Buddhist deity to whom waterfalls are dedicated. At the foot of the two flanking stones are two or more horizontal stones that embrace the basin. These are the *base* stones. In the center of the basin is a smaller stone, inclined toward the falls; it is called a *water-dividing* stone.

WATER, NATURAL USES
English Ponds and Streams

William Kent, one of the first of the great English landscape designers of the 18th century, studied painting in Italy as a young man. He was not a success as an artist, but he put his painter's eye to use in his subsequent profession. Walpole, writing of Kent's contribution to the revolution in garden design, said, "Of all the beauties he added to the face of this beautiful country, none surpassed his management of water. Adieu to canals, circular basons, and cascades tumbling down marble steps, that last absurd magnificence of Italian and French villas. The forced elevation of cataracts was no more. The gentle stream was taught to ser-

pentize seemingly at its pleasure. . . . A few trees scattered here and there on its edges sprinkled the tame bank that accompanied its meanders; and when it disappeared among the hills, shades descending from the heights leaned towards its progress; and framed the distant point of light under which it was lost, as it turned aside to either hand of the blue horizon."

What Kent had begun, Lancelot (Capability) Brown carried to its ultimate end. Brown would have nothing that was not "natural." His speciality was creating lakes by damming streams and letting them spread to fill along the natural contours of the land. He concealed his dams by hiding them behind clumps of

trees or hillocks. Landscaped lakes and streams continued to be popular in English gardens even after the revival of more formal styles in the early Victorian era. However, a connection was starting to be made between the presence of water and the incidence of malaria, though the role of the mosquito was not yet understood. J. C. Louden, in *The Villa Gardener*, warns that "the evaporation from clear water is simply injurious by increasing the quantity of moisture held in suspension by the atmosphere; but the evaporation from water containing a mixture of decaying vegetables from the park above it, contains, in addition to water, those deleterious gases known as malaria."

French Ponds and Streams

The English landscape garden soon became the rage in France. A taste for Chinese gardens had already been awakened by the Jesuit, Père Attiret, who had written an account of his visit to the gardens of the Chinese emperor near Peking. His description of these gardens accorded well with the landscape theories of England. "They consist of extensive grounds in which mountains to a height of 20 to 50 feet have been built up, which gives rise to a vast number of little vales. Canals with clear water irrigate these dales and flow together in several places to form ponds or lakes, on which one may journey to and fro in beautiful boats."

Rousseau's book *Julie, ou la Nouvelle Héloïse* added another voice to the chorus. In it he describes a completely natural garden where the hand of man was not apparent. This, too, caught the imagination of a society weary of the formality and grandeur of Versailles. The Marquis de Girardin, Rousseau's friend and patron, built Ermenonville garden in the new style, lacing it with streams and including a lake dotted with islands. Marie Antoinette's Hameau, Mereville, and Monceau all had their romantic lakes and winding streams and rushing cataracts.

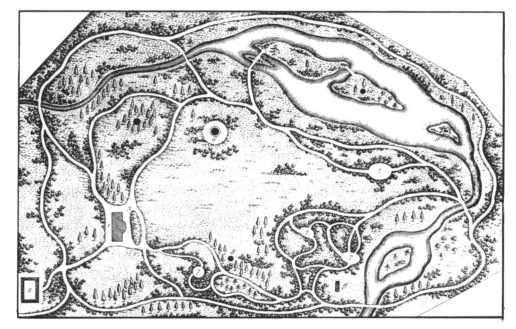

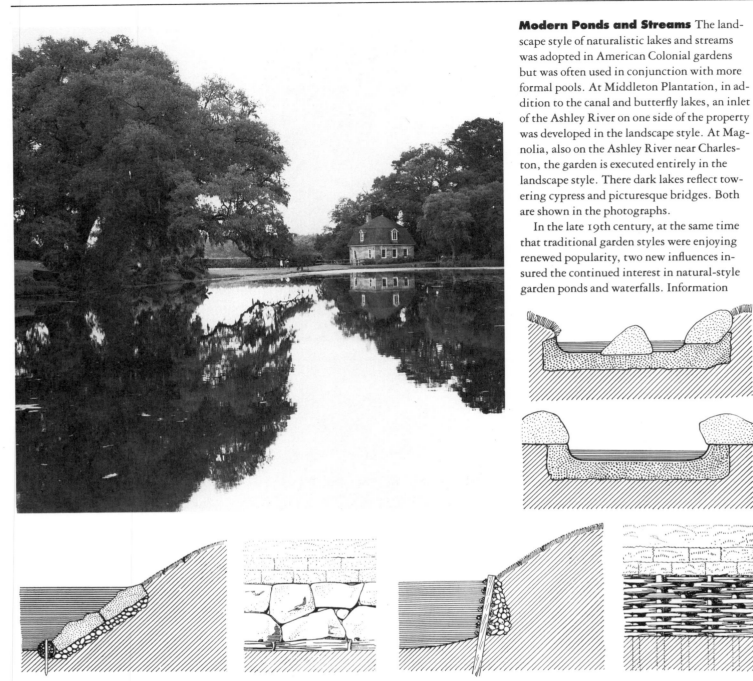

Modern Ponds and Streams The landscape style of naturalistic lakes and streams was adopted in American Colonial gardens but was often used in conjunction with more formal pools. At Middleton Plantation, in addition to the canal and butterfly lakes, an inlet of the Ashley River on one side of the property was developed in the landscape style. At Magnolia, also on the Ashley River near Charleston, the garden is executed entirely in the landscape style. There dark lakes reflect towering cypress and picturesque bridges. Both are shown in the photographs.

In the late 19th century, at the same time that traditional garden styles were enjoying renewed popularity, two new influences insured the continued interest in natural-style garden ponds and waterfalls. Information

about Japanese garden techniques was just beginning to find its way into Europe although the major impact of Japanese genius was not to be felt for another half-century. Of more immediate importance was the introduction of new alpine plants that created a vogue for rock gardens. The chapter on rock gardens contributed by Raymond E. Negus in Jekyll's book *Gardens for Small Country Houses* states, "Water properly employed forms a charming feature in any rock garden. Few things are more delightful than the reflection in still water of overhanging rocks clothed with masses of blossom. . . . Upon the margins contained within the actual boundaries of the pond Japanese irises, primulas, dodecatheons and other moisture-loving plants will flourish. Primula rosea grown in this way is a prod-

igy of vigour and abundant bloom." In *Wall, Water and Woodland Gardens* Jekyll gives directions for the construction of streams and waterfalls in the rock garden: "Where water is available, and especially where there is a natural supply and a good fall in the ground level, the delights of the rock-garden may be greatly increased. . . . It is sometimes advised, in books dealing with the construction of rock-gardens, that where water is used the whole substructure should be put together and bedded in cement. This may be advisable where water is a good deal limited in quantity, but if the necessity for economy of water is not urgent, and if the nature of the rock allows (as it does in the case of the slaty formations and some of the limestones) to have pieces with a flattish surface, that in building up can be set

slightly tilted and lapping over one another, the water can be conducted with very little waste. . . . The tiny rills will have little falls at intervals, and where these occur the water will be widened into a pool; then at the point of overflow the rill goes on again, making its way between the rocks till it falls at last into a larger pool below." Jekyll's waterfalls and streams were gentle, as befitted her controlled and quiet gardens.

At Longwood Gardens in Pennsylvania, we see another type of waterfall. That large and rushing cataract, more in the style of the romantic French gardens of the 18th century, empties into a wild stream bordered with huge boulders (see photograph).

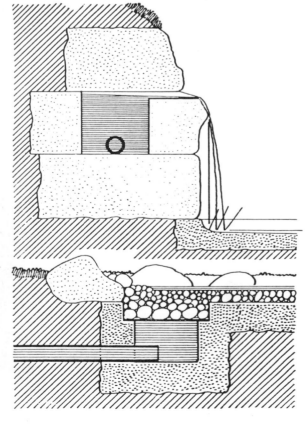

WATER SURPRISES

No Renaissance garden was complete without a full complement of water surprises and tricks. The object was to lure the unsuspecting visitor with some marvelous mechanical or musical whimsy and then drench him with water from hidden jets. No one was safe from attack, for being soaked was one of the expected hazards of a stroll in any garden.

What triggered the rage for these frivolities may have been the allegorical romance *Hypnerotomachia Poliphili*, written in 1467 by the Dominican monk, Francesco Colonna. In it he describes a particularly rude water surprise: A bath is supplied with cold water by the statue of a little boy urinating, and when a visitor approaches, a hidden trap makes the boy's penis lift and squirt water into the victim's face. Such jokes, crude and vulgar by today's standards, were not considered offensive in the 16th century. Even the great Leonardo da Vinci was said to have set his hand to creating such mechanisms.

Falda's engraving, reproduced at right, of the Villa d'Este shows some trick fountains in action; the two men peeking from behind a post seem to be enjoying the fruits of their treachery.

The idea of using water tricks quickly caught on in England. Paul Hentzner, in *Journey into England in the Year 1598*, tells of the fountains at Whitehall. "In a garden joining to this palace, there is a Jet d'eau, with a sundial, which while strangers are looking at, a quantity of water forced by a wheel . . . plentifully sprinkles those that are standing round."

WATER TOWERS *See Towers.*

WEATHERVANES AND WHIRLIGIGS

Weathervanes The earliest recorded weathervane was atop the Tower of the Winds in Athens, built by the astronomer Adronicus in the first century B.C. It was in the shape of Triton, a mythological being, half man, half fish, who called up the winds with his seashell horn.

Old weathervanes were usually symbolic. The cock was the device traditionally used for a church and it had two meanings; it was a reminder to the faithful of Peter's denial of Christ "before the cock crowed thrice," and it has been a symbol of watchfulness since pre-Christian times.

Early American weathervanes were copies of traditional European designs, with flag vanes and cocks predominating. Even the most famous vane in the United States, the great copper grasshopper atop Faneuil Hall in Boston, was a copy of the insect that graced the Royal Exchange in London since 1558.

Until the mid-19th century, weathervanes were handmade, one-of-a-kind products; each maker reinterpreting old and creating new designs. Each piece of the weathervane was of copper, hammered over a wooden "mold" then soldered together and burnished.

That technique continued to be used by the commercial vane makers who began mass producing weathervanes in the 1850s. Although the vanes were still mostly hand crafted, the same molds were used over and over, and hundreds of stock designs were sold by catalog.

Many of the best of these designs are still made either in copper or in cast aluminum.

Whirligigs Whirligigs are near relatives of weathervanes. The traditional form is a carved wooden figure, like a large toy soldier, with paddlelike arms that spin in the wind. They were sometimes used as weathervanes, for they turned into the wind and the "arm speed" gave an indication of wind velocity. Other whirligigs use a small windmill to power moving figures: a washerwoman at her tub or a man perpetually sawing wood. Occasionally these wind toys were used in the garden as scarecrows, but most often they were displayed simply for the fun of the action.

63

WELLS

Japanese Wells Japanese wellheads are rustic or refined, depending on the character of the garden. They may be made of either wood or stone. Rustic stone curbs are made of natural shapes or crudely cut stones. More formal stone wellheads are made of carefully fitted ashlar work.

Wooden wellheads in the rustic style may be made of several courses of heavy branches laid log-cabin-wise and tied at the crossings with coarse black or brown cord. Others are constructed of thick, rough boards or squared timbers that form an octagonal or square edging. In more refined gardens wellheads are made of fine finished wood and are meticulously crafted. Another interesting Japanese wellhead, though of a more utilitarian type and seldom used in a garden setting, resembles a large barrel. Long shaped and fitted staves are driven down to line the well as it is dug. The upper eighteen inches of the staves, forming the wellhead, are bound at the top with twisted bamboo strips.

The area around the well is provided with stepping stones and a sea of pebbles so that spilled water does not form puddles.

European Wells In medieval European gardens a central water supply, either a spring or a well, was generally treated in a decorative manner. Carved stone or marble wellheads were often dominant features in patio and cloister gardens. Spanish wellheads were usually made of brick or stone in circular, six- or eight-sided forms and were about three feet high. They were sometimes faced with colorful tiles and coped with a decorative majolica rim made in a single piece.

Medieval and Renaissance sculptors in Italy carved fine marble wellheads, often fitted with either pillared and pedimented overthrows or lacy wrought iron supports for the pulley mechanism. Typically, the opening in these wellheads was round, and the face was either six- or eight-sided and lavishly carved. Sometimes ancient Roman capitals were used for this purpose.

American Wellhouses American colonists developed a distinctive type of wellhead, many examples of which may be seen at Williamsburg and restored plantations throughout the southern states. These wells were often dug in close proximity to the house, and the structures covering them were more in the

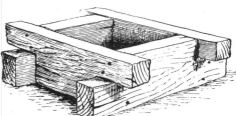

nature of outbuildings because they were completely roofed. In some, the wellhead itself formed the foundation for the uprights that carried the roof beams; in others, a completely independent building sheltered the wellhead. These wells were generally covered with wooden lids when not in use to keep out debris.

In the late 18th century pumps started to replace the bucket-and-pulley method for raising water. Short pumps might be used on raised wellheads, and taller ones on platforms placed directly over the mouth of the well. In garden settings the pump mechanism was often hidden by decorative housings of wood, masonry, or metal.

WINDMILLS *See Towers.*
ZIGGURATS *See Mounts.*

Glossary

Ashlar, or Ashler In masonry, often used as a term for any squared or dressed block of building stone or for work employing such stones. We have chosen to use it in a more restricted sense; that is, it applies only to masonry where the stones are cut and fitted so precisely as to allow joints between them of only one-eighth inch or less, regardless of the finish of the face of the stones.

Atrium The central room in a Roman house, originally containing the hearth and therefore provided with an opening in the roof to allow smoke to escape. The atrium later developed into a formal reception room, where a small decorative pool, or impluvium, was placed under the opening to catch rain water.

Barbican A projecting tower with gun ports or arrow slits placed so as to aid in the defense of a gate.

Batter The slope of the face of a wall from top to bottom.

Bond Any of the many patterns in which bricks are arranged in a wall to afford strength and stability.

Bosquet, or Bosco A dense grove of trees, either in a natural planting or arranged in formal rows and clipped straight along the tops and sides.

Cabinets de verdure Roomlike clearings in bosquets, usually bordered with clipped hedges and latticework fences or with more elaborate treillage and used as settings for fountains and statuary. Typical of French gardens of the late 17th century.

Carpenter work Wooden latticework on which vines and shrubs are trained to form topiary or galleries.

Casino In Italy, a small country house or a garden house.

Chinoiserie In Western art and architecture, a style reflecting the influence of Chinese design motifs.

Colonnade A row of regularly spaced columns.

Commodity A privy.

Coping A protective cap on the top of a wall, usually projecting slightly to direct rain water away from the face of the wall.

Espalier A tree or shrub trained to grow flat against a wall or trellis, usually in a symmetrical pattern.

Ferme ornée Literally an ornamental farm, it was a short-lived experiment in the 18th century where working farms were disguised behind exotic architectural facades. Fields were bordered with flowering plants and hedges, and farm ponds were transformed into romantic lakes and serpentine rivers.

Festoon Ornamental garland strung from one point to another forming suspended loops, as in vines trained to grow along chains hung from the tops of a series of posts or trees.

Finial A decorative terminal piece on a roof peak, gate post, or such.

Forecourt A courtyard, usually walled or fenced, in front of a building.

Giardino segreto From the Italian, a small enclosed garden placed near the house and reserved for the use of the family. A common feature in Renaissance gardens.

Glorieta Originating in Persia and subsequently used in Moorish-style gardens in Spain, a structure at the intersection of paths or water channels. It may consist of masonry piers arched over with metal supports on which roses or flowering vines are grown. More typical are those formed entirely of cypresses trained and clipped into a radiating circle of arches.

Kiosk Similar to a gazebo but usually smaller and often reflecting a flavor of the East with a mosquelike roof or with Moorish arches.

Lambrequin A decorative panel running from one pillar to the next just under a connecting stringer or under the eaves of a roof. Seen in the covered walkways of Chinese gardens.

Loggia A roofed arcade open on one side along the front or side wall of a building, sometimes on an upper level overlooking a courtyard.

Nymphaeum In ancient Greece, an area dedicated to the nymphs, usually including a grove of trees, a grotto, an altar, and water, either in a spring or a waterfall. Nymphaea were incorporated into Roman gardens in the form of small temples or artificial grottoes with fountains and pools.

Ogee, or Reverse Curve A plane curve composed of two connected arcs with centers on opposite sides that takes on the shape of an elongated S.

Overthrow Ornamental ironwork spanning the space between two gate piers above the gate itself. Also a similar structure, over a wellhead, supporting the pulley mechanism.

Pale A picket or a vertical board or stake in a fence.

Palladian In architecture, any structure in the style typical of the Renaissance architect Andrea Palladio, characterized by classical symmetry, elegance, and serenity. This style strongly influenced the English architecture of the 18th century.

Patte d'oie A number of tree-lined avenues radiating fanwise from a semicircular central area and in form somewhat resembling a goose foot.

Pediment In classical architecture, the gable end of a roof, also any similarly shaped architectural feature.

Peristyle In Greek and Roman houses, a large courtyard, usually surrounded on several or all sides by a colonnaded walkway and planted as a garden. A peristyle that included a pool was called a viridarium.

Plinth board A baseboard along the bottom of a fence.

Portcullis A grille of wood or iron, suspended over a fortified gateway, which can be lowered when needed for defense.

Portico A roofed porch at the entrance to a building, supported by a series of columns or piers.

Riad In northern Africa, an enclosed garden bordered on one or more sides by colonnaded walks, corresponding to the Roman peristyle.

Schist A kind of rock composed of many layers of micaceous minerals that can be easily split into thin slabs.

Serpentine Having the shape of a serpent or of a series of connected arcs with their centers on alternate sides.

Shingle Beach pebbles that have been rounded and polished by wave action.

Stringer A long, horizontal beam used to connect upright building members and often supporting shorter crossbeams, as in a roof.

Spandrel The triangular space between two contiguous archways or the space between the outside curve of a single archway and a rectangular frame.

Term A bust of Terminus, the Roman god of boundaries, rising from a square, tapering pillar, often used to mark boundaries. Generally used for any statue of this form.

Tufa A rough pumice stone used to decorate the walls of grottoes or other surfaces where a rustic effect is desired.

Trompe l'oeil A French term meaning literally "to fool the eye," it is used to describe the effect created by painting a solid wall so as to create the illusion of distant scenery seen beyond an open doorway. It can also refer to flat treillage screens built to suggest niches or long receding galleries.

Wicket A small auxiliary door or gate next to or built into a larger one.

Ziggurat A type of stepped pyramid first built by the Sumerians around 3000 B.C., consisting of from three to seven broad terraces and topped with a temple.

List of Suppliers

The numbers that appear with certain of the drawings and photographs in the text of this book refer to suppliers who may be identified by the corresponding number in the list that follows.

1 *Adirondack Designs, 350 Cypress Street, Fort Bragg, CA 95437. TEL 800-222-0343.* Adirondack Designs makes sturdy, nicely detailed redwood furniture, such as swings, tables, planters, benches, and picnic tables, as well as traditional Adirondack-style chairs and love seats. The catalog is free.

2 *Adjusta-Post Manufacturing Company, P.O. Box 71, Norton, OH 44203. TEL 261-745-1692, FAX 216-745-9742.* Adjusta-Post carries a complete line of outdoor lighting fixtures, including hidden landscape lighting systems and traditional and contemporary wall-mounted and freestanding fixtures. Write for the name of a local representative or dealer.

3 *Alpine Millworks Company, 1231 West Lehigh Place, Englewood, CO 80110. TEL 303-761-6334.* Alpine Millworks makes quality garden furniture and planters in teak and mahogany. Its line includes both Adirondack-style and simple English garden chairs, love seats, dining tables, planters, and benches. Send for a free brochure.

4 *Amdega Ltd., P.O. Box 713, Glenview, IL 60025. TEL 800-922-0110, FAX 708-729-7214.* Amdega makes cedar conservatories in modular units that may be arranged in many combinations to form freestanding or attached structures. A variety of sash designs and decorative details are available to blend with the architectural style of the house. Write for a free brochure or send $5.00 for a catalog.

5 *Amish Country Gazebos, 11151 Hunting Horn Drive, North Tustin, CA 92705. TEL 714-838-0910.* Handcrafted by the Amish in Lancaster County, PA, gazebos come in a variety of sizes and designs in kit form, which the company will install or you can put together yourself. Amish Country Gazebos makes wishing wells and 8- to 20-foot-long bridges. Send for a free brochure.

6 *Arroyo Craftsman Lighting, Inc., 4509 Little John Street, Baldwin Park, CA 91706. TEL 818-960-9411, FAX 818-960-9521.* Arroyo Craftsman makes elegant outdoor lighting fixtures, some inspired by the Arts and Crafts Movement, others by Greene and Greene, Frank Lloyd Wright, and the Prairie School Movement. Its lanterns, which come in post-mounted, hanging, and wall-mounted versions, are made of solid brass with a verdigris patina. Write for the name of a dealer in your area.

7 *Ascot Designs, Ltd., 334 Boyleston Street, Boston, MA 02116. TEL 617-536-9083, FAX 617-536-8934.* Ascot Designs imports cast-stone garden ornaments from England. Available in two finishes, Doulting stone (cream) and Portland stone (greyish white), the line includes statuary, vases, fountains, finials, sundials, birdbaths, and seats, as well as balustrading and paving blocks. The catalog is free.

8 *Asian Artifacts, P.O. Box 2494, Oceanside, CA 92051. TEL 619-723-3039.* Asian Artifacts imports carved granite lanterns, water basins, pagodas, bridges, and figures for Asian-style gardens. It also carries a line of antiqued brass statuary depicting antelope, deer, and cranes. Send $2.00 for a brochure.

9 *Austin Garden Sculpture, 815 Grundy Avenue, Holbrook, NY 11741. TEL 800-645-7303, FAX 516-467-8823.* This company offers a selection of hollow-cast garden sculptures, including many small-scale pieces in both contemporary and classic designs. Send $10.00 for a catalog.

10 *Bamboo and Rattan Works, Inc., 470 Oberlin Avenue South, Lakewood, NJ 08701. TEL 908-370-0220, FAX 908-905-8386.* This company sells both raw materials and manufactured items. It carries bamboo poles in numerous lengths and diameters in lots ranging from two hundred pieces to one piece, depending on size. Preassembled reed and bamboo fencing strung on galvanized wire is sold by the square foot. Rain capes in 42-inch squares or rounds up to 12 feet in diameter are available as an inexpensive substitute for a thatched roof on a cabana or gazebo. If you want to build your own Japanese bamboo fence, it has all the makings. Send for a current price list.

11 *Bamboo Fencer, 31 Germania Street, Jamaica Plain, MA 02130. TEL 617-524-6137, FAX 617-524-3596.* Bamboo Fencer designs, manufactures, and installs (or ships) fences, sleeve fences, gates, arbors, gutters, and other garden accessories of bamboo. Normally, designs are worked out using plot plans, drawings, photos, site visits, or sketches and, if local, installed by Bamboo Fencer. If products are crated and shipped to the site, detailed installation specifications are provided for contractors or do-it-yourself builders. In addition to virtually hundreds of types of traditional Japanese-style fences and gates, Bamboo Fencer makes custom-designed containers, bamboo foundations, deer scarers, and dippers. The catalog costs $2.00, refundable with a purchase.

12 *Barlow Tyrie, Inc., 1263/230 Glen Avenue, Moorestown, NJ 08057. TEL 609-273-7878, FAX 609-273-9199.* Barlow Tyrie produces a handsome collection of garden furniture designed and made in England of plantation-grown Javanese teak. Its extensive line includes a fine reproduction of the Sir Edwin Lutyens Sissinghurst seat; tables, benches, and lounges in a variety of other designs; a round tree seat; a tea cart; umbrellas and planters. It has a small catalog that is free and a large catalog for $2.00.

13 *Bauer Casting Design, 118 Main Street, P.O. Box 385, Lexington, GA 30648. TEL 404-743-3268, FAX 404-353-2336.* This company makes historic reproductions of Victorian garden curbs in colored cast stone. It now produces curbs in three patterns: a scalloped-top design stamped with a diamond within a sunburst, a quatrefoil, and a rope border with a ball finial end piece. Six more patterns are planned for future production. Send for a free brochure.

14 *Boston Turning Works, 42 Plympton Stret, Boston, MA 02118. TEL 617-482-9085, FAX 617-482-0415.* This company produces turned architectural elements such as finials, columns, column bases and caps, balusters, and porch and newel posts of kiln-dried laminated pine or mahogany. It will also do custom turnings in sizes up to 15 inches in diameter. It caters to landscape architects and contractors only.

15 *Bow House, Inc., 92 Randall Road, P.O. Box 900, Bolton, MA 01740. TEL 508-779-6464, FAX 508-779-2272.* Bow House manufactures a variety of delightful garden structures in kit form to be assembled on site. They range from arbors and open gazebos to enclosed garden houses so well constructed that they can be heated or air-conditioned. Bow House also makes arched garden bridges in a variety of styles, in any length up to 80 feet, and as wide as 8 feet, which can be shipped assembled or in kit form. The catalog costs $3.00.

16 *Bowmanite Corporation, P.O. Box 599, Madera, CA 93639-0599. TEL 800-854-2094, FAX 209-673-8246.* Bowmanite is concrete that is colored and imprinted with a pattern and/or texture to very closely resemble genuine and more costly decorative paving products, such as slate, granite, cobblestone, tile, brick, stone, and block. It is typically about half the price of the real thing. Free pattern brochures are available from local Bowmanite contractors. Call the 800 number for contractor locations.

17 *British-American, 718 Pickering Way, Lionville, PA 19353. TEL 800-344-0259, FAX 215-363-0433.* British American makes beautifully crafted teak furniture in traditional English garden styles. It also makes a well-designed contemporary line suitable for both indoor and outdoor use. Write for a free catalog.

18 *Brown Jordan, 9860 Gidley Street, El Monte, CA 91734. TEL 818-443-8971, FAX 818-575-0126.* Brown Jordan manufactures fine-quality indoor and outdoor garden furniture made of aluminum, wrought iron, teak, wicker, and rattan in a wide range of styles from traditional to contemporary. Write for a free brochure and the name of a dealer in your area.

19 *Cape Cod Cupola Commpany, Inc., 78 State Road, Route 6, North Dartmouth, MA 02747. TEL 508-994-2119.* Cape Cod Cupola Company, in addition to a variety of sizes and styles of preassembled cupolas, makes copper and aluminum weathervanes. Full-bodied copper weathervanes made in traditional antique molds depict everything from farm animals to sailing ships. Send $2.00 for a catalog.

20 *The Carolina Gardener, 11746 Route 108, Clarksville, MD 21029. TEL 410-531-3035, FAX 410-531-5650.* The Carolina Gardener makes cedar garden boxes, railing cachepots, and hose stakes in a variety of attractive designs, many of them decorated with sandblasted flora and fauna motifs. Send $2.00 for a brochure.

21 *Cassidy Brothers Forge, U.S. Route 1, Rowley, MA 01969-1796. TEL 508-948-7303.* Cassidy Brothers Forge designs, manufactures and restores fine wrought ironwork, specializing in hand-forged fences and gates. Most of its work is done with architects and general contractors for large projects requiring custom metalwork.

22 *Charleston Battery Bench, Inc., 191 King Street, Charleston, SC 29401. TEL 803-722-3842, FAX 803-722-3846.* This company makes authentic reproductions of the famous Charleston Battery Bench. The benches are made with heavy cast-iron sides and durable South Carolina cypress slats and may be ordered in custom sizes. The brochure is free.

23 *Classic and Country Crafts, 5100-1B Clayton Road, Suite 291, Concord, CA 94521. TEL 510-672-4337.* This company makes an attractive copper-and-bronze landscape light in the form of a flower. The fixtures are 23 inches tall and are wired for low-voltage (12v) use. Write for a free brochure.

24 *Classic Casuals, Inc., Main & Trunk, P.O. Box 154, Crandall, TX 75114. TEL 800-874-8618.* Classic Casuals makes reproductions of traditional lampposts, urns, furniture, and mailboxes in cast aluminum. Send for a free brochure.

25 *Cliff Finch's Zoo, 16923 North Friant Road, P.O. Box 54, Friant, CA 93626. TEL 209-822-2315.* Cliff Finch makes topiary frames in a marvelous variety of animal shapes. He will also custom design frames to your specifications. You may purchase the frames bare or he will plant and train them for you. Send a stamped, self-addressed envelope for a brochure.

26 *Continental Bridge, Route 5, Box 178, Alexandria, MN 56308. TEL 800-328-2047, FAX 612-852-7067.* Continental Bridge manufactures attractive, utilitarian, heavy-duty bridges custom engineered and fabricated to meet your specifications and delivered to the job site ready for installation. Send for a free brochure.

27 *Country Casual, 17317 Germantown Road, Germantown, MD 20874-2999. TEL 800-872-8325, FAX 301-540-7364.* Country Casual manufactures and imports a large selection of classic English garden furniture made of plantation-grown Javanese teak. It also carries a line of modular architectural trelliswork. This trellis system, with 2- and 4-foot-wide base panels, interchangeable top panels, and a choice of post caps or ball finials, allows maximum flexibility of design. Send $5.00 for a 39-page color catalog.

28 *Creative Playthings, 33 Loring Drive, Framingham, MA 01701-8768. TEL 800-444-0901, FAX 508-872-3120.* Creative Playthings makes rugged, attractively designed backyard swing sets with many options, including slides, towers, climbing ropes and ladders, and sandboxes. Write for the name of a dealer in your area.

29 *Cross Industries, Inc., 3174 Marjan Drive, Atlanta, GA 30340. TEL 800-521-9878, FAX 404-457-5125.* Cross Industries makes reinforced polyvinyl lattices with welded joints. The lattice panels are made in three weights and two patterns. Cross will also make custom patterns. The lattices come in white and nine other colors. Since the color pigments are added to the strip material during the extrusion process, the lattice has the appearance of finely finished wood and will never require painting. With a variety of accessory moldings, framing channels, and caps, Cross Vinylattice offers strong, maintenance-free, latticework for exterior and interior uses. The brochure is free.

30 *Cumberland Woodcraft Company, Inc., 10 Stover Drive, P.O. Drawer 609, Carlisle, PA 17013. TEL 717-243-0063, FAX 717-243-6502.* This company specializes in reproductions of Victorian millwork for both interior and exterior use. Exterior pieces suitable for embellishing garden houses and gazebos include such items as fancy sawed and turned balusters, gable decorations, spandrels combining fretwork and spindles, and a large selection of gingerbread brackets and corbels. It can also provide decorative cedar shingles and authentically styled Victorian screen doors. Send $4.75 for a 56-page color catalog.

31 *Custom Cascades, P.O. Box 2008, La Habra, CA 90632. TEL 800-621-8610, FAX 714-744-3295.* Custom Cascades designs and manufactures a line of prefabricated waterfall manifolds that can produce effects from a soft glasslike sheet to a raging wall of water. Its brochure is free.

32 *Custom Ironwork, Inc., 10619 Big Bone Road, P.O. Box 180, Union, KY 41091. TEL 606-384-4122, FAX 606-384-4848.* Custom Ironwork is a manufacturer of ornamental iron, specializing in reproductions of antique fences and gates. All fences and gates are handmade to order. Send $1.00 for a catalog.

33 *Dalton Pavilions, Inc., 7260-68 Oakley St., Philadelphia, PA 19111. TEL 215-342-9804.* Dalton manufactures prefabricated cedar gazebos in five different traditional designs (including a charming Chinese-Victorian model) and in five sizes. The buildings can be purchased with flooring or with hardware to secure them to an existing paved surface. All styles are suitable for screening. Send $3.00 for a color brochure.

34 *De Santana Fountains, 3111 East McDowell, Phoenix, AZ 85008. TEL 602-231-0971, FAX 602-225-9890.* De Santana makes custom hand-carved stone fountains, columns, architectural moldings, and sculptures in a variety of natural stone colors. It also produces handsome adoquin stone pavers, in either smooth, saw-cut or rough, hand-chiseled finishes. The brochure is free.

35 *Doner Design, Inc., 2175 Beaver Valley Pike, New Providence, PA 17560. TEL 717-786-8891.* This company makes forged-copper landscape lights in five versions. One is a simple, traditional shaded post; the others are in the shapes of single-, double- and triple-stemmed mushrooms. The brochure is free.

36 *Dura Art Stone, 11010 Live Oak, Fontana, CA 92335. TEL 800-821-1120, FAX 714-350-9632.* Dura Art Stone manufactures architectural ornaments and landscape furnishings in cast stone. Its products include a wide variety of large-scale planters, bollards, tree grates, picnic tables and benches, urns and pedestals, columns and piers, balustrading, pool curbing, and fountains. The catalog is free.

37 *Eurocobble, 4265 Lemp Avenue, Studio City, CA 91604-2811. TEL 213-877-5012, FAX 818-766-6363.* Eurocobble imports authentic European cobblestone preassembled in modules for ease of installation. The modules are available in several patterns and in grey or red stone. Write for a free brochure.

38 *Fairchild Associates, 4736 North 44th Street, Phoenix, AZ 85018. TEL 602-952-9292, FAX 602-840-5970.* Fairchild Associates imports Guatemalan Indian ceramics. Each of these large-scale pots is handmade without the aid of a potter's wheel and features local pigments and motifs. If desired, Fairchild Associates will refire these handsome jugs and bowls for durability against the elements, moving, or planting. To the trade only.

39 *Five O Seven Antiques, 507 King Street East, Toronto, Ontario M5A 1M3, Canada. TEL 416-891-1273, FAX 416-359-0502.* Five O Seven Antiques carries a large inventory of antique garden ornaments in cast iron,

lead, stone, and terra cotta, Victorian and Georgian urns, benches, and fountains. Send $5.00 for a catalog (to the trade only), refundable with any purchase.

40 *Florentine Craftsmen, 46-24 28th Street, Long Island City, NY 11101. TEL 800-876-3567, FAX 718-937-9858.* This company offers a large selection of garden furnishings, including fountains, statuary, ornaments, and furniture. It will also do custom work to your specifications. The catalog costs $5.00.

41 *Fortune's Inc., 150 Chestnut Street, San Francisco, CA 94111-1004. TEL 800-331-2300, FAX 415-398-7588.* Fortune's Inc. puts out two catalogs, Fortune's Almanac and The Home Book. Both show furnishings and accessories for the garden. This company offers several types of outdoor furniture, the Deauville group, a reproduction in steel of a 19th-century French garden set, a classic Adirondack-style chair and ottoman, and an attractive oversized rustic chair and ottoman. Call or write for free catalogs.

42 *Garden Concepts, P.O. Box 241233, Memphis, TN 38124-1233. TEL 901-756-1649, FAX 901-755-4564.* Garden Concepts makes an extensive line of handsome, handcrafted garden furniture in a large choice of woods and finishes. Designs range from traditional Lutyens pieces to Biedermeier to Chippendale. It also makes a number of trelliage items, such as urns, obelisks, fences, gates, and arches. This extensive collection includes planter boxes, wooden gates, a variety of garden arches, and a selection of charming Chinoiserie bird structures. Send $5.00 for a catalog.

43 *Gardener's Eden, P.O. Box 7307, San Francisco, CA 94120-7307. TEL 800-822-9600, FAX 415-421-5153.* Gardener's Eden puts out a mail-order catalog devoted entirely to garden furniture and accessories. It features molded resin chairs and tables, charming reproductions of French cafe furniture, a line of traditional folding canvas and beechwood deck chairs, and teak and wicker furnishings. Accessories include planters, trelliswork and arches, tableware, tools, and birdbaths. Call or write for a free catalog.

44 *The Garden Gate, P.O. Box 1117, Cedar Ridge, CA 95924. TEL 916-272-8109, FAX 916-346-6756.* This small company builds garden gates in several sizes and heights and in a number of attractive designs. They are constructed of 1¾-inch redwood and shipped unfinished, ready to paint or stain. The brochure is free.

45 *Garden Iron, 116 North Clifton Avenue, Louisville, KY 40206.* Garden Iron makes steel topiary forms in three stock shapes: a 24-inch-high flame, a 30-inch-high cone, and a 21-inch-diameter sphere. All are fitted with bottom rings to fit into a 14-inch-diameter container. Write for a free brochure.

46 *Gazebos Ltd., 48973 West Road, Wixom, MI 48393. TEL 313-347-1239, FAX 313-347-0953.* Gazebos Ltd. makes ready-to-assemble kits for several

designs of simple, attractive cedar gazebos. It also makes a roofed sandbox. Send for a free brochure.

47 *Haddonstone (USA) Ltd., 201 Heller Place, Interstate Business Park, Bellmawr, NJ 08031. TEL 609-931-7011, FAX 609-931-0040.* Haddonstone makes a wide range of architectural elements and garden furnishings, many of them reproductions of pieces from England's great historic homes. Restoration work is one of its specialties. The large line of stock pieces, besides columns, pediments, balustrades, and other architectural elements, includes sun dials, urns, obelisks, finials, fountains, statues, decorative curbing, paving, and fur-

niture. The material used in these pieces is, according to the catalog, "a special form of reconstituted limestone with a surface texture resembling that of natural Portland stone. It mellows and develops character rapidly." Send $5.00 for a handsome 75-page catalog.

48 *Handy Home Products, 2000 Easy Street, P.O. Box 548, Walled Lake, MI 48390. TEL 800-221-1849, FAX 313-624-1082.* Handy Home Products manufactures ready-to-assemble wooden kits for a variety of small garden structures. It offers an attractive barnlike storage shed in four sizes, and three styles of smaller storage sheds that can be used as lean-to or freestanding buildings. For the younger set, it makes a playhouse and a roofed sandbox. This company also offers round and square gazebos in several sizes, a weekend cottage large enough to sleep six adults, and a dog house. The catalog is free.

49 *The Hatteras Group, P.O. Box 1602, Greenville, NC 27834. TEL 800-334-1078, FAX 919-758-0375.* The Hatteras Group makes hammocks, hammock stands, hammock chairs, and swings. The hammocks come in several colorful stripes as well as in the more traditional woven rope style. Write for the name of a dealer in your area.

50 *Heath Manufacturing Company, P.O. Box 105, Coopersville, MI 49404-1239. TEL 800-678-8183, FAX 616-837-9491.* This company carries a large variety of redwood, aluminum, and clear plastic bird feeders and houses. It also stocks several types of squirrel feeders. The brochure is free.

51 *Hinkley Lighting, 12600 Berea Road, Cleveland, OH 44111-1632. TEL 216-671-3300, FAX 216-671-4537.* Hinkley Lighting manufactures an extensive line of traditional-style, wall- and post-mounted lanterns. Write for the name of a dealer in your area.

52 *Hughes & Wentworth, Main Street, P.O. Box 35, Francestown, NH 03043. TEL 603-547-3633.* Hughes & Wentworth makes a number of attractive wooden birdhouses, including a delightful reproduction of an English dovecote suitable for purple martins or small songbirds. The brochure costs $1.00.

53 *Idaho Wood, P.O. Box 488, Sandpoint, ID 83864. TEL 800-635-1100, FAX 208-263-3102.* Idaho Wood makes a line of simple, well-designed cedar wall, post, and bollard lights. The brochure is free.

54 *Irving & Jones, Village Center, Colebrook, CT. 06021. TEL 203-379-9219.* Irving & Jones makes elegant reproductions of classic wrought-iron furniture based on English Regency (1800–1830) designs. It also produces a charming Gothic rose arch. The brochure costs $2.00.

55 *Janco, 9390 Davis Avenue, Laurel, MD 20707. TEL 800-323-6933, FAX 301-497-9751.* Janco manufactures an extensive line of residential greenhouses in both freestanding and lean-to models. Write for a free brochure or send $5.00 for the complete catalog.

56 *Kingsley-Bate, P.O. Box 6797, Arlington, VA 22206. TEL 703-931-9200, FAX 703-931-6124.* Kingsley-Bate manufactures teak and mahogany furniture in traditional and contemporary designs. Many of the chairs and settees are decorated with handcarved motifs. The brochure costs $2.00 (free to the trade).

57 *Lamplighter Corner, Inc., P.O. Box 235, Pease's Point Way, Edgartown, MA 02539. TEL 508-627-4656.* Lamplighter Corner is a small, family-owned business on the island of Martha's Vineyard. It handcrafts solid brass and copper lanterns in a number of traditional designs. The lanterns are not lacquered or chemically treated in any way so that the copper turns verdigris with age; the brass, a very pleasing leather brown. Write for a free brochure.

58 *Lilypons Water Gardens, P.O. Box 10, Buckeystown, MD 21717-0010. TEL 301-874-5133, FAX 301-874-*

2959. Lilypons sells everything needed to build, plant, and maintain a water garden—from liners and fiberglass pool shapes, pumps, and filters to an enticing selection of aquatic plants and the planters to hold them. Send $5.00 for a 98-page color catalog.

59 *Lister by Geebro, 1900 The Exchange, Suite 655, Atlanta, GA 30339. TEL 404-952-4272, FAX 404-952-4489.* Lister imports from England plantation-grown teak garden furniture in a number of pleasing traditional designs. The catalog is free to the trade.

60 *Litchfield Industries, Inc., 4 Industrial Drive, P.O. Box 317, Litchfield, MI 49252. TEL 800-542-5282, FAX 517-542-3939.* Litchfield Industries offers a large line of garden and park shelters, including gazebos, roofed seats, and picnic tables as well as larger park structures, benches, and planters. Send for a free catalog.

61 *Lloyd/Flanders Industries, Inc., 3010 Tenth Street, P.O. Box 550, Menominee, MI 49858-0550. TEL 906-863-4491, FAX 906-863-6700.* This company produces a line of simple 1920s-style wicker furniture complete with a castered tea cart, an etagere, and a porch swing. The brochure is free.

62 *Lumiere Design and Manufacturing, Inc., 31360 Via Colinas #101, Westlake Village, CA 91362. TEL 818-991-2211, FAX 818-991-7005.* Lumiere specializes in simple, unobtrusive low-voltage outdoor lighting. The brochure is free to the trade.

63 *Kenneth Lynch & Sons, 84 Danbury Road, P.O. Box 488, Wilton, CT 06897-0488. TEL 203-762-8363, FAX 203-762-2999.* Kenneth Lynch & Sons can make almost anything you can think of in the way of garden furnishings from a large collection of molds and patterns. To give you an idea of the extent of its line, the general catalog, *The Book of Garden Ornament*, is a 400-page hardcover volume, and it has several specialized catalogs showing additonal pieces. The above-mentioned catalog is available for $9.50.

64 *Madera Woodworks, P.O. Box 640, Marstons Mills, MA 02648. TEL 800-437-8778.* Madera Woodworks imports a small line of reasonably priced outdoor furniture and planters made of Caribbean cedar, rosita, and Honduras mahogany. Send for a free brochure.

65 *Mee Industries, Inc., 4443 North Rowland Avenue, El Monte, CA 91731. TEL 800-732-5364, FAX 818-350-4196.* The Mee Fog System creates clouds of water vapor, indoors or out, to achieve misty tropical effects and produce microclimates with cooling up to 20° F. These systems are used primarily in large installations at zoos, arboretums, parks, and greenhouses. The brochure is free.

66 *Meridiana Design, P.O. Box 2122, Prince Frederick, MD 20678. TEL 301-855-1001.* Meridiana Designs makes astronomically accurate sundials. Each dial is individually oriented to the owner's specific location and cast in bronze by Equestrian Forge of Leesburg, VA. Meridiana makes horizontal, vertical, equinoctial, and polar dials as well as armillary spheres. Write for a free brochure.

67 *Monumental Iron Works, a Division of Anchor Fence, Inc.*, 6500 Eastern Avenue, Baltimore, MD 21224. TEL 301-633-6500, FAX 301-633-6506. Monumental Iron Works manufactures decorative iron picket fences and gates in a variety of simple, attractive designs. Write for a brochure and the name of a dealer in your area.

68 *Moultrie Manufacturing Company*, P.O. Drawer 1179, Moultrie, GA 31776-1179. TEL 800-841-8674. This company manufactures aluminum replicas of Victorian cast-iron furniture as well as some contemporary designs. It also makes accessories, such as urns, planters, fountains, and birdbaths. Moultrie makes cast-aluminum fencing and gates and offers a planning kit to help determine your needs. Send $3.00 each for the furniture and fencing catalogs.

69 *New England Garden Ornaments*, 38 East Brookfield Road, North Brookfield, MA 01535. TEL 508-867-4474. New England Garden Ornaments is a remarkable resource for all manner of fine and unusual garden furnishings, including English cast-lead statuary, urns, cisterns, planters, fountains, and birdbaths as well as architectural dry-cast stonework, such as temples, balustrades, columns, pedestals, obelisks, pools, etc. This company also carries a line of metal arches, bowers, screens, pergolas, and gazebos in a variety of traditional designs as well as a selection of garden antiques, fine wood trelliswork, and furniture. Send $7.00 for the catalog.

70 *Nightscaping, Loran, Inc.*, 1705 East Colton Avenue, Redlands, CA 92374. TEL 714-794-2121, FAX 714-794-7292. Nightscaping manufactures a system of 12-volt outdoor lighting with a versatile group of fixtures that can be used alone or in combination to achieve uplighting, downlighting, and backlighting. Send $3.00 for a handbook for outdoor lighting.

71 *W. F. Norman Corporation*, 214 North Cedar, P.O. Box 323, Nevada, MO 64772-0323. TEL 800-641-4038. W. F. Norman Corporation makes a fabulous variety of metal architectural ornamentation, including balusters, urns, capitals, finials, weathervanes, downspout conductor heads, caryatids, and gargoyles as well as pressed metal roofing and siding materials. Send $3.00 for the catalog, *Architectural Sheet Metal Ornaments*.

72 *Pompeian Studios*, 90 Rockledge Road, Bronxville, NY 10708. TEL 800-457-5595, FAX 914-337-5661. Pompeian Studios designs and produces original sculptures, mosaics, fountains, garden temples, and other features in marble and bronze here and at its studios in Carrara, Italy. Send $10.00 for a 72-page catalog. tension. Send for a free illustrated brochure.

73 *Popovitch Associates, Inc.*, 346 Ashland Avenue, Pittsburgh, PA 15228. TEL 412-344-6097. Popovitch Associates makes graceful garden lamps in plant forms, the stems and leaves in copper and the flower petal shades of handcrafted ceramics. Send for a color brochure.

74 *Rain Jet Fountains*, 27671 La Paz Road, Laguna Niguel, CA 92656. TEL 800-444-2734, FAX 714-831-0637. Rain Jet manufactures fountains of four different types. It has a line of fountain-heads suitable for the individual who wished to design a pool or incorporate a fountain in an existing pool. A second type consists of a catch basin, fountainhead, pump, and lights in a completely self-contained unit that needs only water and an electrical connection. The third type is the Aquavator aeration system, which can be floated on any pond, anchored in a place, and connected to an electrical cable. This can be equipped with a choice of eight different fountain nozzles, lights, and time controls. Its fourth line is designed for large architectural fountain displays in pools from 15 to 300 feet in diameter. Write for the name of a distributor in your area.

75 *Rare Art Motif*, 1179 Simpson Street, P.O. Box 677, Kingsburg, CA 93631. TEL 209-896-8828, FAX 209-897-2423. Rare Art Motif imports hand-sculptured natural stone fountains, columns, copings, balustrades, moldings, and pavers from Mexico. Write for further information and the name of a showroom in your area.

76 *Reed Brothers*, Turner Station, Sebastopol, CA 95472. TEL 707-795-6261, FAX 707-829-8620. This company makes an extensive group of well-designed outdoor furniture, planters, bird feeders, and other decorative accessories. The pieces are handcrafted and handcarved in redwood and finished in weathered white, natural, or a silvery weathered stain. "Left outdoors the furniture is durable, requires no maintenance, and weathers beautifully." The carved motifs include plant forms, birds, animals, and shells. Write for the name of a showroom in your area. Send $10.00 for a catalog.

77 *The Renovator's Supply, Inc.*, Miller's Falls, MA 01349-1097. TEL 413-659-2211, FAX 413-659-3113. This firm is primarily a source for reproduction interior and exterior hardware, but it also carries copper weathervanes and cast-urethane architectural details. For $5.00 you get a two-year subscription (12 issues) to its catalog.

78 *Robinson Iron*, Robinson Road, P.O. Box 1119, Alexander City, AL 35010. TEL 205-329-8486, FAX 205-329-8960. Robinson Iron manufactures a large line of cast-iron reproductions of pre-Civil War garden furnishings, including furniture, statuary, vases and urns, fountains, and hitching-, fence-, and lampposts. It also does custom castings for restoration work. The furniture is made of extremely heavy castings and is electrically welded rather than assembled with bolts or screws. Send $5.00 for a catalog.

79 *Sculpture Source International Sculpture Center*, 1050 Potomac Street NW, Washington, DC 20007. TEL 202-

965-6066, FAX 202-965-7318. Sculpture Source is an advanced, computerized slide registry allowing for simultaneous text and slide viewing with over 125 criteria from which to choose. Sculpture Source has more than 1,975 artists registered, representing sculptors in over 25 countries. Write or call for more specific information.

80 *Shanti Bithi*, 3047 High Ridge Road, North Stamford, CT 06903. TEL 203-329-0768, FAX 203-329-8872. Shanti Bithi has been importing bonsai since 1974 and today has what is probably the largest collection in North America. It will ship plants anywhere in the United States. Shanti Bithi also imports stone lanterns and natural stone water basins from Japan and T'ai-hu and bamboo stones from China. Send $3.00 for a catalog.

81 *Christine Sibley, Architectural & Garden Ornaments*, 15 Waddell Street NE, Atlanta, GA 30307. TEL 404-688-3329, FAX 404-688-0665. Christine Sibley creates a variety of decorative elements for the garden, including wall plaques, planters, fountains, and bird baths with a marked flavor of the Arts and Crafts style. In addition to her original works, she carries a line of compatible reproductions. Write to her for the name of a representative in your area.

82 *Smith and Hawken*, 25 Corte Madera, Mill Valley, CA 94941. TEL 415-383-2000, FAX 415-383-7030. Smith and Hawken carries a wide selection of choice wood and metal garden furniture as well as planters, trellises, umbrellas, decorative accessories, books, tools, and even a large variety of clothing to wear while gardening. Write for a free catalog.

83 *Special Places*, P.O. Box 9711, New Haven, CT 06536. TEL 203-777-3387. Special Places sells blueprints and plans for a delightful collection of gazebos, gateways, fences, pergolas, and even complete cottages that could be used for garden hideaways. Send $5.95 for a 16-page color brochure.

84 *Steptoe & Wife Antiques, Ltd.*, 322 Geary Avenue, Toronto, Ontario, Canada M6H 2C7. TEL 416-530-4200, FAX 416-530-4666. This company specializes in quality restoration products. It makes several designs of reproduction Victorian and Georgian cast-iron stairways in spiral and straight flights. Send $2.00 for the brochure.

85 *Stewart Iron Works Company*, P.O. Box 2612, 20 West 18th Street, Covington, KY 41012-2612. TEL 606-431-1985. This company has been in business since 1886 handcrafting fences and gates in Victorian and Edwardian styles using 19-century forge and anvil techniques. In addition to its stock designs, Stewart Iron Works Company will do restoration and custom work. Send $2.00 for a catalog.

86 *Stickney's Garden Houses and Follies*, One Thompson Square, P.O. Box 34, Boston, MA 02129. TEL 617-242-1711. Stickney's produces a line of classic garden houses, covered seats, and temples. It also makes a delightful wooden tent with a carved swag entry. These small follies are shipped primed and ready to assemble, roofing finish to be provided by buyer. Send $3.00 for a color brochure or $10.00 for a video, refundable with a purchase.

87 *Stone Forest, P.O. Box 2840, Santa Fe, NM 87504.* TEL 505-986-8883, FAX 505-982-2712. Stone Forest creates handcarved granite garden ornaments with a unique combination of traditional Japanese and Western design elements. The line includes water basins, lanterns, sundial plinths, birdbaths and feeders, and granite spheres. Send $2.00 for a catalog.

88 *Sturdi-built Greenhouse Manufacturing Company, 11304 Southwest, Boones Ferry Road, Portland, OR 97219.* TEL 800-334-4115. Sturdi-built manufactures prefabricated redwood greenhouses that are factory preassembled and shipped in large sections for easy installation. The company makes an attractive glazed octagonal flower gazebo as well as the more traditional lean-to and freestanding home greenhouses. The catalog is free.

89 *Summit Furniture, Inc., P.O. Box S, Carmel, CA 93921.* TEL 408-375-7811, FAX 408-375-0940. Summit Furniture makes elegant, contemporary-style teak garden furniture. This line is available through designer showrooms only. Write on your letterhead for a free catalog (to the trade only).

90 *Sun Designs, P.O. Box 6, Oconomowoc, WI 53066.* TEL 414-567-4255. Sun Designs publishes a series of study plan-books of garden structures and sells detailed construction plans for each structure for do-it-yourself builders. The books are worth having for their artwork, historical notes, and humor alone. The book *Bridges and Cupolas* sells for $8.95 and includes designs for twenty-two footbridges, eight covered bridges, and thirty-six cupolas. Four construction plans are included in this 104-page book. *Gazebos and Other Garden Structures,* $9.95, contains ideas for fifty-five gazebos of various styles and sizes, thirteen strombrellas (a small structure shading a bench or activity area), seven arbors, fourteen bird feeders, and four bird houses. *Backyard Structures* at $8.95 contains designs for domestic animal shelters, storage and tool sheds, cabanas, studios, barns, vegetable stands, lemonade stands, a small guest house, and a chapel. *Privy,* $7.95, shows twenty-five designs for privies and the possibilities for converting them to other uses, such as playhouses, saunas, or bus shelters. Add $2.95 for postage and handling for first book, $.50 for each additional book. Send $.50 for a brochure describing the books in more detail.

91 *Terralight, Hanover Lantern, Hoffman Products, Inc., 470 High Street, Hanover, PA 17331.* TEL 717-632-6464, FAX 717-632-5039. The Terralight line of landscape lighting fills a wide range of outdoor lighting needs. In addition to a selection of utilitarian spotlights, it carries an attractive variety of high and low lighting fixtures in clean modern, traditional, and oriental designs. All fixtures, with the exception of the spotlights, can be converted from 120 volt to 12 volt for safer and more economical operation. Send for a free brochure.

92 *Topiaries Unlimited, RD 2 Box 40C, Pownal, VT 05261.* TEL 802-823-5536. This company makes topiary frames in a variety of geometric and animal shapes and sizes. It will also do custom work. Send for a free catalog.

93 *Veneman, a Div. of Tropitone Furniture Company, 5 Marconi, Irvine, CA 92718.* TEL 714-951-2010, FAX 714-951-0716. Veneman manufactures an attractive line of metal garden furniture in designs that range from delicate-looking simulated bamboo to sleek modern to ornate Belle Epoque styles. Write for a free catalog and the name of a dealer in your area.

94 *Walpole Woodworkers, 767 East Street, Route 27, Walpole, MA 02081.* TEL 800-343-6948, FAX 508-668-7301. Walpole makes small garden buildings in prefabricated sections, ready to be bolted together on site. They are shipped with doors, windows, and shutters in place and in working order, all painting and staining done. Buildings include gazebos, playhouses, poolside cabanas, and one- or two-box stall stables. This company also makes a line of sturdy cedar furniture, rustic swings, picnic tables, fencing, and trellises. Send $2.00 for the furniture catalog and $2.00 for the building catalog.

95 *Warren Imports, Far East Fine Arts, 1910 South Coast Highway, P.O. Box 1138, Laguna Beach, CA 92652.* TEL 714-494-6505; also 73-199 El Paseo Avenue, Suite L, Palm Desert, CA 92260. TEL 619-340-9410. This company imports fine oriental antique and contemporary stone garden lanterns, water basins, white marble sculptures, and garden stools. Write for a free brochure.

96 *Weatherend Estate Furniture, P.O. Box 648, 374 Main Street, Rockland, ME 04841.* TEL 207-596-6483, FAX 207-594-4968. Weatherend makes a line of simple, elegant outdoor furniture based on designs originated for a turn-of-the century Maine estate. The furniture is fashioned of mahogany and teak, using time-honored boatbuilding techniques for beauty and durability. Send for a free catalog.

97 *Whitehall Products Ltd., 8786 Water Street, Montague, MI 49437-1204.* TEL 800-624-8643, FAX 616-894-6318. Whitehall makes hand-cast aluminum sun dials, weathervanes, birdbaths, house signs and numbers, full-bodied sea gulls and flagpole eagles, and other metal ornaments. The catalog is free.

98 *The Wicker Garden, 1318 Madison Avenue, New York, NY 10128.* This company specializes in antique American wicker furniture dating from the 1870s to the 1930s, with emphasis on unusual and fancy Victorian pieces. Write for information about current stock.

99 *Wild Bird Company, 617 Hungerford Drive, Rockville, MD 20850.* TEL 301-279-0079, FAX 301-424-3938. Wild Bird Company specializes in products to house, feed, and generally encourage wild birds, squirrels, bats, and owls. It can help you with your backyard wildlife problems and advise you on how to attract desirable birds and beasts. Send a self-addressed, stamped envelope and specify your interests for the appropriate brochure or catalog.

100 *Wind & Weather, P.O. Box 2320, Mendocino, CA 95460.* TEL 707-937-0323. Wind and Weather carries all sorts of intriguing weather instruments a as well as a delightful collection of aluminum and full-bodied copper weathervanes. It also stocks an interesting selection of armillary, pedestal, and wall-mounted sundials. The 35-page catalog is free.

101 *Windsor Designs, Ltd., 37 Great Valley Parkway, Malvern, PA 19355.* TEL 215-640-1212, FAX 215-640-5896. Windsor Designs carries a selection of traditional English garden furniture in teak or shorea (a type of mahogany). It also has cast-aluminum furniture in a variety of attractive designs as well as planters, a reproduction of an antique mailbox, and a five-bulb street lamp. Write for a free brochure.

102 *Winterthur Museum and Garden Catalogue, 100 Enterprise Place, Dover, DE 19901.* TEL 800-767-0500. The Winterthur catalog offers a choice collection of unusual garden ornaments, gifts, and rare plants propagated at the Winterthur Garden. The catalog is free.

103 *Woodbrook Furniture Manufacturers, Inc., P.O. Box 175, Trussville, AL 35173.* TEL 800-828-3607. Woodbrook makes cypress garden furniture in a number of classic English designs and in a variety of stains and painted finishes. It also builds custom furniture to the customer's specifications. Send for a free catalog.

104 *Wood Classics, P.O. Box 291, Osprey Lane, Gardiner, NY 12525.* TEL 914-255-7871, FAX 914-255-7881. Wood Classics makes easy-to-assemble teak and mahogany outdoor furniture and preassembled market umbrellas. The furniture can be delivered assembled at a slightly higher cost in the Northeastern states. The designs are simple, sturdy, and attractive. One features handcarved decorations. The catalog is free.

105 *Woodplay, P.O. Box 27904, Raleigh, NC 27611-7904.* TEL 800-982-1822. This company makes sturdy, well-designed play equipment in redwood, including swings, climbers, slides, lookout towers, seesaws, balance beams, and sandboxes. Send for a free catalog.

106 *Yanzum, Art for Gardens and Civilized Jungles, P.O. Box 8573, Atlanta, GA 30306-0573.* TEL 404-874-8063. This company makes a select line of cast-concrete planters, statuary, finials, corbels, brackets, etc., in four colors. It also stocks imported Mexican pottery, birdhouses and feeders, lanterns, and other garden art. Send for a free brochure.

CANADIAN DISTRIBUTORS

Berghem Importing, 2861 Walker, Windsor, ON N8W 3R2. TEL 519-972-4999. Importers of marble pots, Italian marble statues, fountains, benches, and lampposts. Call for more information.

Bricks and Blocks, 1371 McKeen Avenue, North Vancouver, BC V7P 3H9. TEL 604-984-3008. Provides patio slabs, imported pots and planters, lawn and garden furniture, pagodas, tables, outdoor lighting, and cedar planters. Call for more information.

Gardens Antique, 3518 Main Street, Vancouver, BC V5V 3N3. TEL 604-876-2311. Offers antique garden accessories including furniture, ornaments, and sculptures. Call for more information.

Nastri Interiors & Gifts, 609 Mt. Pleasant Road, Toronto ON M4S 2M5. TEL 416-484-1647. Provides classic ornamental urns, planters, stone statuary, and sundials. Call for more information.

Rubaiyat, 722-17th Avenue SW, Calgary, AB T2M 0N7. TEL 403-939-2770. Manufactures rattan and twig furniture, ceramic planters, wooden and stone garden sculptures, and cast-iron tables and benches. Call for more information.

Selected Bibliography

Adams, William Howard. *The French Garden, 1500–1800*. New York, 1979.

Akisato, Rito. *Tsukiyama Teizoden*. 1823.

Amherst, The Hon. Alicia. *A History of Gardening in England*. London, 1896.

André, Edouard. *L'Art des Jardins*. Paris, 1879.

Bacon, Francis. "Of Gardens," *Essays*. 1625.

Baumann, Albert. *Neues Planen und Gestalten*. Munsingen, 1953.

Berrall, Julia S. *The Garden*. New York, 1966.

Bicknell, A. J. *Details, Cottage, and Constructive Architecture*. New York, 1873.

————. *Bicknell's Cottage and Villa Architecture*. New York, 1881.

Blomfield, Sir Reginald Theodore. *The Formal Garden in England*. London, 1892.

Blondel, Jacques François. *De la Distribution des Maisons de Plaisance, et de la décoration des edifices en général*. Paris, 1737–1738.

Bockler, Georg Andreas. *Architectura Curiosa Nova*. Nuremberg, 1664.

Boerschmann, Ernst. *Chinesische Architektur*. Berlin, 1925.

Boitard, Pierre. *Traité de la Composition et de l'Ornament des Jardins*. Paris, 1825.

————. *L'Art de Composer et Décorer les Jardins*. Paris, 1847.

Bona, Théodore. *Tracé et Ornementation des Jardins d'Agrément*. Paris, 1859.

Bottomley, William Lawrence. *Spanish Details*. New York, 1924.

Boussard, Jacques. *Construction et Décorations pour Jardins; Kiosques-Orangeries-Volières-Abris Divers*. Paris, 1881.

Bring, Michell, and Wayembergh, Josse. *Japanese Gardens*. New York, 1981.

Browne, Sir Thomas. *Sir Thomas Browne's Hydriotaphia and the Garden of Cyrus*. Edited by W. A. Greenhill. London, New York, 1896.

Byne, Arthur, and Byne, Mildred Stapley. *Spanish Gardens and Patios*. New York, Philadelphia, London, 1924.

Calkins, Carroll C. *Great Gardens of America*. New York, 1969.

Cane, Percy S. *Garden Design of Today*. London, 1934.

Cause, Henri. *De Koninglycke Hovenier*. Amsterdam, 1676.

Caus, Isaac de. *Le Jardin de Wilton*. London, 1644.

Caus, Salomon de. *Les Raisons des Forces Mouvantes*. Frankfort, 1615.

Chi Ch'eng. *Yüan Yeh*. 1634. Reprint. Peking, 1932.

Church, Thomas. *Your Private World*. San Francisco, 1969.

Coats, Peter. *Great Gardens of the Western World*. London, 1968.

————. *House and Garden Book of Garden Decorations*. New York, 1970.

Colonna, Fra Francisco. *Hypnerotomachia di Poliphili*. Venice, 1499.

Conder, Josiah. *Landscape Gardening in Japan*. Yokohama, 1893.

Consten, Eleanor Von Erdberg. *Chinese Influence on European Garden Structures*. Cambridge, Mass., 1936.

Cooke, Arthur O. *A Book of Dovecotes*. London, 1920.

Crescenzi, Pietro. *Opus Ruralium Commodorum*. 1471.

Crisp, Frank. *Medieval Gardens*. London, 1924.

d'Argenville, A. J. Dézallier. *The Theory and Practice of Gardening*. Translated by John James. London, 1712.

Decker, Paulus. *Gothic Architecture Decorated*. London, 1759.

————. *Chinese Architecture, Civil and Ornamental*. London, 1759.

Dell'arte de giardini inglesi. Based on Hirschfield's *Theorie der Gartenkunst*. Milano, 1813.

Dollman, Francis Thomas. *An Analysis of Ancient Domestic Architecture in Great Britain*. London, 1861–1864.

Downing, Andrew Jackson. *A Treatise on the Theory and Practice of Landscape Gardening*. New York, London, Boston, 1841.

Du Cerceau, Androuet. *Les plus excellents bastiments de France*. 1576. Reprint, Paris, 1865.

Dutton, Ralph. *The English Garden*. London, 1937.

Dye, Daniel Sheets. *A Grammar of Chinese Lattice*. Cambridge, Mass., 1949.

Eberline, Harold D., and Hubbard, Cortland Van Dyke. *The Practical Book of Garden Structure and Design*. Philadelphia, London, New York, 1937.

Edwards, Paul. *English Garden Ornaments*. London, 1965.

Elyard, S. John. *Some Old Wiltshire Homes*. London, 1894.

Evelyn, John. *The Diary of John Evelyn*. Edited by E. S. Beer. London, 1959.

Falda, Giovanni Battista. *Le Fontane di Roma nelle Piazze*. Rome, 1675.

Farrer, Reginald John. *My Rock Garden*. London, 1908.

Fiennes, Celia. *Through England on a Side Saddle, in the Time of William and Mary*. London, 1888.

Fitzgerald, Ken. *Weathervanes and Whirligigs*. New York, 1967.

Forestier, J. C. N. *Gardens, a Notebook of Plans and Sketches*. New York, 1924.

Fox, Helen Morgenthau. *Patio Gardens*. New York, 1929.

Gallotti, Jean. *Moorish Houses and Gardens of Morocco*. New York, 1925.

Garrick, David, and Colman, George. *The Clandestine Marriage from English Plays, 1660–1820*. Edited by E. E. Morgan. London, 1935.

Gell, Sir William, and Gandy, J. P. *Vues des Ruins de Pompeii*. Paris, 1827.

Gille, Philippe. *Versailles et les Deux Trianons*. Tours, 1899–1900.

Gothein, Marie Luise. *A History of Garden Art*. Translated by Mrs. Archer-Hind. New York, 1928.

Gotze, Karl. *Album für Teppichgärtenerei und Gruppenbepflanzung*. Erfurt, 1897.

Grohmann, Johann Gottfried. *Recueil de dessins d'une Execution peu Dispendieuse*. Venice, 1805.

Guernieri, Giovanni Francesco. *Disegno del Monte Situato Presso la Citta Metropolitana di Cassel*. Rome, 1706.

Halfpenny, William. *Twelve Beautiful Designs for Farm-houses with Their Proper Offices*. London, 1759.

Henderson, Peter. *Gardening for Pleasure*. New York, 1907.

Henslow, T. Geoffrey. *Garden Architecture*. London, 1926.

Hibberd, Shirley. *Rustic Adornments for Homes of Taste*. London, 1870.

Hill, Thomas. *The Gardener's Labyrinth*. London, 1651–1652.

Hirschfield, Christian Cajus Lorenz. *Theorie der Gartenkunst*. Leipzig, 1779–1785.

Holme, Charles. *Old English Country Cottages*. London, 1906.

Hooghe, Romein de (Hogue). *Platte Grond en Opgelighte, Bouw, Plant, en Sheer-werken van Het Onweergadelijke Lust-park van Enguien*. Leyden, 1670.

Hottes, Alfred C. *A Little Book of Climbing Plants*. New York, 1933.

Hubbard, Henry Vincent, and Kimball, Theodora. *An Introduction to the Study of Landscape Design*. New York, 1917.

Hughes, John Arthur. *Garden Architecture and Landscape Gardening*. London, 1866.

Humphreys, Phebe Westcott. *The Practical Book of Garden Architecture*. Philadelphia, London, 1914.

Hyams, Edward. *A History of Gardens and Gardening*. New York, Washington, 1971.

Inn, Henry. *Chinese Houses and Gardens*. Honolulu, 1940.

Jager, Hermann. *Gartenkunst und Garten sonst und jetzt*. Berlin, 1888.

James, T. *The Carthusian*. 1839.

Jekyll, Gertrude. *Children and Gardens*. London, 1908.

————. *Colour in the Flower Garden*. London, 1908.

————. *Garden Ornament*. London, 1918.

————. *Wall, Water, and Woodland Gardens*. London, New York, 1933.

Jekyll, Gertrude, and Weaver, Sir Lawrence. *Gardens for Small Country Houses*. London, New York, 1912.

Jellicoe, Geoffrey, and Jellicoe, Susan. *The Landscape of Man*. London, 1975.

Jones, Barbara. *Follies and Grottos*. London, 1953.

Karl, Jean Frederic. *Vue et Prospect des Différentes Parties du Park Près du Château de Freundenhain*. Passau, 18–.

Kemp, Edward. *How to Lay Out a Garden*. London, 1864.

Keswick, Maggie. *The Chinese Garden*. New York, 1978.

King, Ronald. *The Quest for Paradise*. New York, 1979.

Kip, Johannes. *Nouveau Théâtre de la Grande Bretagne*. London, 1708.

Kitamura, Enkin. *Tzukiyama Teizo-den*. 1735. Reprint. Kyoto, 1918.

Knight, Richard Payne. *The Landscape, A Didactic Poem*. London, 1795.

————. *Analytical Inquiry into the Principles of Taste*. London, 1805.

Knoop, Johann Hermann. *Beschouwende en Werkdadige Hovenier-konst*. Leeuwarden, 1753.

Krafft, Johann Carl. *Maisons de Campagne*. Paris, 1849.

————. *Plans des Plus Beaux Jardins Pittoresques de France*. Paris, 1809–1810.

Krutch, Joseph Wood. *The Gardener's World*. New York, 1959.

Kuck, Loraine E. *The World of the Japanese Garden*. New York, 1968.

Laborde, Alexander. *Déscriptions des Nouveaux Jardins de la France*. Paris, 1808–1815.

Labyrinthe de Versailles. Amsterdam, 1682.

Langley, Batty. *The City and Country Builder's and Workman's Treasury of Designs*. London, 1740.

————. *New Principles of Gardening*. London, 1728.

Lawrence, John. *The Clergy-man's Recreation*. London, 1717.

Lawson, William. *New Orchard and Garden*.

Leighton, Ann. *American Gardens in the 18th Century, for Use and Delight*. New York, 1976.

Leonardi, Domenico Felice. *Le Delizie della Villa de Castelazzo*. Milano, 1743.

Lethaby, W. R. *Leadwork, Old and Ornamental and for the Most Part English*. London, New York, 1893.

Liu Tun-chen. *Suchou Gardens (Suchou Ku Tien Yüan Lin)*. Peking, 1978.

Lloyd, Nathaniel. *Garden Craftsmanship in Yew and Box*. London, 1925.

Long, Elias A. *Ornamental Gardening for Americans*. New York, 1902.

Loudon, John Claudius. *An Encyclopaedia of Gardening*. London, 1825.

————. *The Villa Gardener*. London, 1850.

McDougal, D. *Two Royal Domains of France*. London, 1931.

M'Intosh, Charles. *Book of the Garden*. Edinburgh, London, 1853–1855.

Mangin, Arthur. *Les Jardins*. Tours, 1867.

Markham, Gervase. *The English Husbandman*. London, 1613.

————. *Maison Rustique (The Countrey Farme)*. London, 1616.

Martin, George A. *Fences, Gates and Bridges*. New York, 1892.

Matthews, W. H. *Mazes and Labyrinths*. London, 1922.

Mawson, Thomas H. *The Art and Craft of Garden Making*. London, New York, 1912.

Messent, Claude J. W. *The Weathervanes of Norfolk and Norwich*. Norwich, 1937.

Meyer, Franz Sales, and Ries, Frederich. *Die Gartenkunst in Wort und Bild*. Leipzig, 1904.

Middleton, Charles D. *Decorations for Parks and Gardens*. London, 1818.

Montaigne, Michel de. *The Journal of Montaigne's Travels in Italy by way of Switzerland and Germany in 1580 and 1581*. Translated by W. G. Waters. London, 1903.

Morse, Edward S. *Japanese Homes*. Boston, 1888.

Mothes, Oscar. *Geschichte der Baukunst und Bildhauerei Venedigs*. Leipzig, 1859–1860.

Mott Ironworks Catalog. *Illustrated Catalog of Statuary, Fountains, Vases, Settees*. New York, 1875.

Moynihan, Elizabeth B. *Paradise as a Garden: In Persia and Mughal India*. New York, 1979.

Nakajima, S. *Tsukiyama toi-zo-ho*. Tokyo, 1896.

Newcomb, Rexford. *Architectural Monographs on Tiles and Tilework, No. 1–7*. Beaver Falls, Pa., 1924–1929.

Nichols, Rose Standish. *English Pleasure Gardens*. New York, London, 1902.

————. *Spanish and Portuguese Gardens*. New York, 1924.

Over, Charles. *Ornamental Architecture in the Gothic, Chinese and Modern Taste*. London, 1758.

Overton, Thomas Collins. *Original Designs of Temples and Other Ornamental Buildings for Parks and Gardens*. London, 1766.

Percier, Charles, and Fontaine, Pierre François Léonard. *Romische Villen und Parkenlagen*. Berlin, 1898.

Perelle, Gabriel. *Veues des Belles Maisons de France*. Paris, 168–.

————. *Recueilles des plus Belles Veues des Maisons Royale de France*. Paris, 168–.

Perrot, Georges, and Chipiez, Charles. *A History of Art in Ancient Egypt*. London, 1883.

Pliny the Younger. *Letter to Apollinaris*. Translated by William Melmoth. London, 1810.

Pontanus, Jovianus. *De Hortis Hesperidum*. 1500.

Pope, Alexander. *The Guardian, No. 173*. London, 1713.

Rademaker, A. *L'Arcadie Hollandoise*. Amsterdam, 1730.

Repton, Humphrey. *Fragments, or the Theory and Practice of Landscape Gardening*. London, 1816.

Robinson, Peter Frederick. *Rural Architecture*. London, 1823.

Rogers, William Snow. *Garden Planning*. London, 1910.

Roubo, André Jacob. *L'Art du Menuisier*. Paris, 1775.

Royer, Johann. *Beschreibung des Ganzen Furstl*. Braunschweig, 1651.

Saita, Heijiro. *Chasitsu kojo*. Tokyo, 1905.

Saito, Katsuo. *Japanese Gardening Hints*. Tokyo, 1969.

Schmidlin, Eduard. *Schmidlin's Gartenbuch*. Berlin, 1905.

Scott, Frank Jesup. *The Art of Beautifying Suburban Home Grounds*. New York, 1873.

Sgrilli, Bernardo Sansone. *Descrizione della Regia Villa, Fontane, e Fabriche di Pratolino*. Florence, 1742.

Sieveking, Albert Forbes. *Gardens Ancient and Modern*. London, 1899.

Siren, Osvald. *Gardens of China*. New York, 1949.

Stein, Henri. *Les Jardins de France*. Paris, 1913.

Stephenson, Sue Honaker. *Rustic Furniture*. New York, 1979.

Stewart Iron Works Company. *Catalog No. 50A*. Cincinnati, Ohio, 1917.

Stopendaal, Daniel (Stoopendaal). *La Triumphante Riviere de Vecht*. Amsterdam, 1729(?).

Street, George Edmund. *Brick and Marble in the Middle Ages*. London, 1874.

Taylor, A. D. *Landscape Construction Notes*. Cleveland, Ohio, 1922–1931.

Thacker, Christopher. *The History of Gardens*. Berkeley, Calif., 1979.

Thomas, Graham Stuart. *Great Gardens of Britain*. New York, 1979.

Thonger, Charles. *The Book of Garden Furniture*. London, New York, 1903.

Tijou, Jean. *A New Booke of Drawings Invented and Designed by John Tijou*. London, 1896.

Triggs, Harry Inigo. *The Art of Garden Design in Italy*. London, 1906.

——. *Formal Gardens in England and Scotland*. London, 1902.

——. *Garden Craft in Europe*. London, 1913.

——. *Some Architectural Works of Inigo Jones*. London, 1901.

Van Damme, J. *Cieraad der Lusthoven*. Leyden, 1730.

Van der Groen, Jan. *Den Niederlandische Gartner (Den Nederlandtsen Hovenier)*. Amsterdam, 1669.

Van Nidek, Mattaeus Brouerius. *Het Zegenpraland Kennemerland*. Amsterdam, 1729.

Varro, Marcus Terentius. *De Rustica*. First century B.C.

Villiers-Stuart, Constance Mary. *Spanish Gardens*. London, 1929.

Wang Shin-fu. *Hsiu hsiang tseng chu ti liu ts-'ai tzu shu shih chich*. 1295–1307. Reprint. Shanghai, 1887.

Warwick, Francis Evelyn, Countess of. *An Old English Garden*. London, 1898.

Weaver, Lawrence. *English Leadwork, Its Art and History*. London, New York, 1910.

White, John P. *Garden Furniture and Ornament*. Bedford, England, 1890–1910(?).

White Pine Series of Architectural Monographs. *The Monograph Series, Records of Early American Architecture*. New York, 1915–1940.

Wilber, Donald N. *Persian Gardens and Garden Pavilions*. Rutland, Vt., 1962.

Wolseley, Frances Garnet, Viscountess of. *Gardens, Their Form and Design*. London, 1919.

Woolridge, John (Worlidge). *Systema Horticulturae, the Mystery of Husbandry Discovered*. London, 1677.